The DAMA Dictionary of Data Management

2nd Edition 2011

Susan Earley, Editor

Technics Publications, LLC
New Jersey

The DAMA Dictionary of Data Management is a collection of over 2000 terms, defining a common data management vocabulary for IT professionals, data stewards and business leaders.

The Dictionary was developed by members of DAMA International and the larger international data management community. For content inquiries, please contact Deborah Henderson at VP_Education@dama.org.

Under the support and control of DAMA International, the DAMA International Foundation is a 501(c)(3) not-for-profit entity, whose mission is to foster the advancement of the data management profession through education, research, and the construction of standards and best practices. The Dictionary is one example of the effort to set standards and distribute best practices.

The Dictionary is also of the Foundation's fundraising vehicles. By purchasing this electronic document, you are supporting further research and development in the field of data management. For further information about how you can support DAMA International, the DAMA Foundation, and the future of data management and data management professionalism, please contact info@dama.org.

ISBN: 9781935504122
First Printing 2011
Printed in the United States of America
Library of Congress Control Number: 2011924676

Published by:
Technics Publications, LLC
Post Office Box 161
Bradley Beach, NJ 07720 U.S.A.
www.technicspub.com

Contents

Preface to the Second Edition

The DAMA International Foundation is pleased to publish the Second edition of the DAMA Dictionary of Data Management. The DAMA-DMBOK Guide is a "definitive introduction" to data management, summarizing data management goals, principles, processes, deliverables, roles, technology, practices, and organizational/cultural issues.

The First Edition was originally drafted as the Glossary Appendix for the DAMA Guide to the Data Management Body of Knowledge (DAMA-DMBOK Guide®, a trademark of the DAMA International Foundation). Development of the DAMA-DMBOK Guide began in 2006, and DAMA Foundation Board quickly realized the value of the Glossary in its own right, and urged for the early completion and publishing of the Glossary as the DAMA Dictionary of Data Management, which was done in 2008.

We offer the Second Edition of the DAMA Dictionary of Data Management, a compendium of over 2,000 terms, to an industry in great need of clarity in its terminology and semantics. While experts may never reach 100% agreement, we believe there is general consensus agreement with these definitions across the data management profession. We hope this Dictionary will be as successful as the First edition, and continue to be taken up as a useful reference tool for data management professionals, managers and business data stewards.

The Dictionary also continues to be an important integration tool guiding collaborative development of the DAMA-DMBOK Guide. This Second Edition refers back to the DAMA-DMBOK and completes an alignment with it.

DAMA International and The DAMA International Foundation wish to thank Susan Earley of DAMA Chicago who has taken the baton on this second version as editor, and has steered this fine follow-on and expanded version that you find here. Her volunteer efforts to produce this document on behalf of DAMA are most appreciated. We also wish to thank Mark Mosley, the first edition editor for setting the benchmark for this important contribution to our profession. Mark is a senior data management thinker also living and working in Chicago.

The DAMA International Foundation was established in 2005 as the education and research affiliate organization of DAMA International, the world's premiere professional organization for data management professionals. The mission of the DAMA International Foundation is to lead the data management profession to maturity through funding education initiatives and sponsored research.

There will continue to be productive and valuable discussions over the meaning and use of data management terms. This Second Edition provides a new foundation for these discussions. As the definitions are continually refined and clarified, DAMA intends to update and publish regularly scheduled revisions. Your comments, concerns, and contributions are welcomed. Please contact the editor at DMBOKeditorinchief@dama.org to offer your suggestions for improvement.

Deborah Henderson
President, DAMA International Foundation,
Toronto, Ontario
March 2011

Acknowledgments

As is consistent with all DAMA International Foundation products, this is a collaborative work of many professional contributors, who volunteered their time, expertise, and knowledge to this document. I was merely the wrangler, wrestling the contents into a workable format, and then managing the incoming flows of contributions and commentary, a human integration engine managing data from start to finish.

The following individuals volunteered to review the dictionary, and have our thanks:

Francine Adams
John Biderman
Bill Brink
Susan Burk
Larry Burns
John Cheffy
Powers Dale
Norman Daoust
Olena Dikina
Lee Edwards
Michael Fitch
Lowell Fryman
Patricia Gilson
Kathy Hadzibajric
Steve Hoberman
Mike Jennings
Sanjay Kapoor
Ron Klein
Gina LaRosa
Sivan Mahadevan
Shahidul Mannan
Michael Mattmiller
Bob McBride
Diane McElhiney
Patrick McMullen
Brian Metras
Pat Morley
Thomas Mueller
Janet Nickel
Kim Olson
Mehmet Orun
Amy Oshita
Salih Oztop
Annette Pence
Marcel Saleh
Ashok Sivanandi
Eva Smith
Sutherland Tom
Elize van der Linde
Sukhvir Virk
James Viveralli
Dan Weller
Joel Wittenmyer
Missy Wittmann
Teresa Wylie
Kavuda Yugandhar Raj

These individuals not only signed up to review, but added terms and/or quite useful comments.

Robert J. Abate
Mike Brackett
Peter Cooper
Pat Cupoli
Trudy Curtis
Christine Denney
Gordon Everett
Cynthia Hauer
Art Heine
Deborah Henderson
Ben Hu
Ingrid Hunt
Rod MacPherson
Peter Marotta
Dennis Miller
Doug Needham
Gina Perezella
Sivasubramaniam Ravishankar
Jane Roberts
Oliver Smith
Connie Taylor
Rik van der Schalie
GEIA

I would like to specially mention Gordon Everest, who contributed not only over a hundred terms and definitions before the review process, but also painstakingly reviewed each and every item within the review website. Over 200 comments from the review period were from him alone.

I would like to thank Michael Brackett for his assistance and support in protocols for publishing. His example during the DAMA-DMBOK editing process and as a major contributor of almost three hundred terms and definitions, and over 400 comments, are greatly appreciated.

I also wish to thank Eva Smith for her extraordinary transformation of a spreadsheet into a multi-page review site on Google Docs in short order. Having that website up with all terms, and having the ability to comment on and suggest new terms was crucial to the success of the review process.

Finally, I personally wish to thank Deborah Henderson, DAMA International Foundation President, for her trust and encouragement (and over 100 comments). I am honored to have been assigned this project. I learned quite a great deal, which is always my goal, and I hope I have added some improvement to this profession.

Susan Earley
dictionary.editorinchief@dama.org
Chicago, IL
March 2011

Document Construction Process

This document was constructed starting with the contents from the first edition, almost 1000 terms. In order to group similar terms alphabetically, some terms were reformatted. Some terms that were actually different forms of the same term were combined.

A review of the question and answer sets in the ICCP specialty exams that are part of the CDMP program (Data Management Core, Data Development, Data Warehousing, Business Intelligence & Analytics, Data & Information Quality, Data Operations, and Zachman Enterprise Architecture Framework[2] exams) was performed in order to keep the definitions and terms in synch with the exam contents. This resulted in 300 new terms and 25 updated terms. A thorough search through the DAMA-DMBOK was conducted, resulting in 40 new terms and 30 updated terms, including some citations. A search of relevant websites provided by Kewal Dhariwal, ICCP Executive Director, was also completed. References within the dictionary to definitions in the DAMA-DMBOK were also added. Several people suggested or sent in lists of terms and definitions to add to the Dictionary. Lastly, an internet search was conducted to find related terms in order to complete the dictionary. Each definition that has no citation was worded to accurately represent the term's meaning, while avoiding copyright issues. The result is a list of terms, more than double the original size.

Once this process was complete, the dictionary contents were put on a website using Google docs in order to conduct a peer review. Each entry was on a separate page allowing for edits and comments to be recorded on the term's definitions, as well as allowing suggestions of more entries. Sixty-seven people were added as reviewers, from an international distribution including the US, Canada, Australia, Turkey, South Africa, and the Netherlands.

Several terms were proposed that were not included, such as names of programming languages, and terms more specific to other specialized practices, such as project management. It is not within the scope of this dictionary to define specific terms outside of data management.

During the review period, over 450 comments were generated. This process resulted in more than 1000 changes and 350 new terms. Then the manuscript was prepared and hyperlinked before being turned over to the publisher for final review and processing.

The result of all this collaborative work is what you see before you now.

Document Organization

The first section is a complete list of acronyms, with hyperlinks to the proper terms and definitions.

The actual dictionary is in alphabetical order, although many modified terms have been grouped for clarity. The common form of the term will have a hyperlink reference to the grouped term.

All terms are nouns unless otherwise marked.

Each term may have an acronym and alternate forms, followed by the definitions. There may be hyperlinks within the definitions to other related or referenced terms.

There are also SEE references from a synonym or alternate form pointing to the preferred form of the term where it is defined only once.

Dictionary of Data Management

Acronyms

0..1:0..M	zero-or-one-to-zero-or-Many
0..1:1	zero-or-one-to-one
0..1:1..M	zero-or-one-to-one-or-Many
1:0..M	one-to-zero-or-Many
1:1	one-to-one
1:1..M	one-to-one-or-Many
1NF	first Normal Form
2NF	second Normal Form
3GL	Third Generation Language
3NF	third Normal Form
4GL	Fourth Generation Language
4NF	fourth Normal Form
5NF	fifth Normal Form
6NF	sixth Normal Form
ACID	Atomicity, Consistency, Isolation, and Durability
ACM	Association for Computing Machinery
ACS	American Community Survey
AI	Artificial Intelligence
ANSI	American National Standards Institute
API	Application Programming Interface
ARPANET	Advanced Research Projects Agency Network
ASCII	American Standard Code for Information Interchange
ASP	Application Service Provider
b	byte
B2B	Business-to-Business
B2C	Business-to-Consumer
B2G	Business-to-Government
BABOK	Business Analysis Body of Knowledge
BAM	Business Activity Monitoring
BATOG	Business, Applications, Technology, Organization, and Governance
BCNF	Boyce/Codd Normal Form
BI	Business Intelligence
BIMM	Business Image Management and Multimedia
BISP	Business Intelligence Service Provider
BIT	BInary digiT
BOI	Bill of Information
BOK	Body of Knowledge
BPEL	Business Process Execution Language
BPEL4WS	Business Process Execution Language for Web Services
BPM	Business Performance Management
BPM	Business Performance Measurement
BPM	Business Performance Modeling
BPM	Business Process Management
BPM	Business Process Model
BPM CBOK®	Business Process Management Common Body of Knowledge
BPMM	Business Process Maturity Model
BPMN	Business Process Modeling Notation
BPO	Business Process Outsourcing
BPR	Business Process Re-engineering
BPS	Bits Per Second
BSC	Balanced ScoreCard
BSP	Business Systems Planning

CART	Classification And Regression Tree
CASE	Computer Aided Software Engineering
CBA	Cost Benefit Analysis
CBIP	Certified Business Intelligence Professional
CBK	Common Body of Knowledge
CCA	Clinger-Cohen Act
CCMS	Component Content Management System
CDI	Citizen Data Integration
CDI	Common Data Architecture
CDI	Customer Data Integration
CDM	Conceptual Data Model
CDMP	Certified Data Management Professional
CDO	Chief Data Officer
CEP	Complex Event Processing
CGI	Common Gateway Interface
CGI	Computer-Generated Imagery
CI	Confidence Interval
CIF	Corporate Information Factory
CIO	Chief Information Officer
CITBOK	Canadian Information Technology Body of Knowledge
CKO	Chief Knowledge Officer
CMM	Capability Maturity Model
CMMI	Capability Maturity Model Integration
COBIT	Control OBjectives for Information and related Technology
COE	Center Of Excellence
COM	Common Object Model
CORBA	Common Object Request Broker Architecture
COTS	Commercial Off The Shelf
CPM	Critical Path Method
CPU	Central Processing Unit
CRM	Citizen Relationship Management
CRM	Customer Relationship Management
CRUD	Create-Read-Update-Delete
CSF	Critical Success Factor
CSS	Cascading Style Sheet
CTO	Chief Technology Officer

DA	Data Administration
DA	Data Administrator
DA	Data Architect
DAAS	Data As A Service
DAMA-DMBOK	Data Management Body of Knowledge
DARPA	Defense Advanced Research Projects Agency
DAS	Direct Attached Storage
DASD	Direct Access Storage Device
DBA	DataBase Administrator
DBMS	DataBase Management System
DCL	Data Control Language
DCMI	Dublin Core Metadata Initiative
DDE	Dynamic Data Exchange
DDL	Data Definition Language
DEM	Digital Elevation Model
DES	Data Encryption Standard
DFD	Data Flow Diagram
DGC	Data Governance Council
DGO	Data Governance Office
DKNF	Domain/Key Normal Form
DM	Data Management
DM	Data Mart
DMA	Direct Marketing Association
DMADV	Define, Measure, Analyze, Design, and Verify
DMAIC	Define, Measure, Analyze, Improve and Control
DML	Data Manipulation Language

DMS	Data Management Services
DMS	Document Management System
DNS	Domain Name System
DODAF	Department of Defense Architecture Framework
DOLAP	Desktop OnLine Analytical Processing
DOM	Document Object Model
DRDA	Distributed Relational Database Architecture
DSC	Data Stewardship Committee
DSN	Data Source Name
DSS	Decision Support System
DTD	Document Type Definition
DW	Data Warehouse
DW	Data Warehousing
EAI	Enterprise Application Integration
EAR	Entity Attribute Relationship
Eb	Exabyte
EBCDIC	Extended Binary Code Decimal Interchange Code
EDA	Exploratory Data Analysis
EDF	Enterprise Data Fabric
EDI	Electronic Data Interchange
EDIFACT	Electronic Data Interchange for Administration, Commerce, and Transport
EDM	Enterprise Data Model
EDM	Enterprise Data Management
EDMS	Electronic Document Management System
EDW	Enterprise Data Warehouse
EER	Extended Entity Relationship
EHR	Electronic Health Record
EII	Enterprise Information Integration
EIM	Enterprise Information Management
EIS	Executive Information System
EJB	Enterprise JavaBeans
EKNF	Elementary Key Normal Form
EPC	Event-driven Process Chain
EPM	Enterprise Performance Management
ER	Entity Relationship
ERA	Electronics Record Archive
ERD	Entity Relationship Diagram
ERM	Enterprise Risk Management
ERP	Enterprise Resource Planning
ESB	Enterprise Service Bus
ETL	Extract-Transform-Load
EVA	Economic Value Added
FAQ	Frequently-Asked Questions
FASB	Financial Accounting Standards Board
FAT	File Allocation Table
FIFO	First In, First Out
FIPS	Federal Information Processing Standard
FK	Foreign Key
FOAF	Friend Of A Friend
FOM	Fact Oriented Modeling
FTP	File Transfer Program
FTP	File Transfer Protocol
GA	Generally Acceptable release
GAAP	Generally Accepted Accounting Principles
GADMP	Generally Accepted Data Management Principles
Gb	Gigabyte
GIS	Geographic Information System
GMA	General Morphological Analysis
GML	Geography markup language
GPS	Global Positioning System

GQM	Goal-Question-Metric method
GSDN	Global Data Synchronization Network
GUI	Graphical User Interface
GUID	Globally Unique Identifier
HIPAA	Health Insurance Portability and Accountability Act
HOLAP	Hybrid OnLine Analytical Processing
HQL	Hierarchical Query Language
HTML	Hypertext Markup Language
HTTP	HyperText Transfer Protocol
IAM	Information Asset Management
IAO	Information Awareness Office
IASB	International Accounting Standards Board
ICCP	Institute for Certification of Computing Professionals
ICT	Information and Communication Technology
ID	IDentifier
IDE	Integrated Development Environment
IDE	Integrated Drive Electronics
IDEF	Integrated DEFinition
IDEF0	IDEF0 function modeling notation
IDEF1X	IDEF1X data modeling notation
IDEF2	IDEF2 simulation modeling notation
IDL	Interface Definition Language
IE	Information Engineering data modeling notation
IE	Information Engineering
IEEE	Institute for Electric and Electronic Engineers
ILM	Information Lifecycle Management
IM	Information Management
IP	Intellectual Property
IP	Internet Protocol
IQ	Information Quality
IS	Information System
ISAM	Indexed Sequential Access Method
ISBN	International Standard Book Number
ISC	Information Supply Chain
ISO	International Organization for Standardization
ISP	Information Systems Planning
IT	Information Technology
ITABOK	IT Architect Body of Knowledge
ITIL	Information Technology Infrastructure Library
ITU	International Telecommunications Union
J2EE	Java2 Platform Enterprise Edition
JAD	Joint Application Design
JDBC	Java Database Connectivity
JMS	Java Messaging Service
JOLAP	Java OnLine Analytical Processing
JPEG	Joint Photographic Experts Group
JSP	Java Server Page
Kb	Kilobyte
KIF	Knowledge Interchange Format
KM	Knowledge Management
KPI	Key Performance Indicator
LAN	Local Area Network
LDM	Logical Data Model

LTV	lifetime value
M:1	Many-to-one
M:N	Many-to-Many
MARC	Machine-Readable Cataloging
Mb	Megabyte
MDD	Model-Driven Development
MDDB	Multi-Dimensional DataBase
MDDBMS	Multi-Dimensional DataBase Management System
MDM	Master Data Management
MDX	Multi-Dimensional eXtensions to SQL
MeSH	Medical Subject Heading
MIPS	Million Instructions Per Second
MIS	Management Information System
MM	Meta-data Management
MME	Managed Meta-data Environment
MOLAP	Multi-dimensional OnLine Analytical Processing
MOM	Message Oriented Middleware
MPP	Massively Parallel Processing
MQ	Magic Quadrant
MQL	Multi-dimensional Query Language
MRM	Marketing Resource Management
MTBF	Mean Time Between Failures
MTF	Mean Time Between Failures
MTR	Mean Time To Recover
MTTR	Mean Time To Recover
MVC	Model-View-Controller
NAICS	North American Industrial Classification System
NAS	Network-Attached Storage
NDA	Non-Disclosure Agreement
NDL	Network Definition Language
NFS	Network File Share
NIAM	Nijssens Information Analysis Method
NIST	National Institute for Standards and Technology
NoSQL	Not Only SQL
NPV	Net Present Value
OASIS	Organization for the Advancement of Structured Information
OCR	Optical Character Recognition
OCW	OpenCourseWare
ODBC	Open Database Connectivity
ODBMS	Object-Oriented DataBase Management System
ODS	Operational Data Store
OER	Open Educational Resource
OGC	Open Geospatial Consortium
OHLC	Open-High-Low-Close
OID	Object Identifier
OIL	Ontology Inference Layer
OLAP	OnLine Analytical Processing
OLTP	OnLine Transaction Processing
OMG	Object Management Group
OMR	Optical Mark Recognition
OO	Object-Oriented
OODB	Object-Oriented DataBase
OODBMS	Object-Oriented DataBase Management System
OOPS	Object-Oriented Programming System
ORDBMS	Object Relational DataBase Management System
ORM	Object Role Model
OSF	Open Software Foundation
OSINT	Open Source Intelligence
OWL	Web Ontology Language

PAAS	Platform As A Service
Pb	Petabyte
PCI DSS	Payment Card Industry Data Security Standard
PDI	Product Data Integration
PDM	Physical Data Model
PERT	Program Evaluation and Review Technique
PGP	Pretty Good Privacy
PHI	Personal Health Information
PII	Personal Identifying Information
PIM	Product Information Management
PK	Primary Key
PKI	Public Key Infrastructure
PMBOK®	Guide to the Project Management Body of Knowledge
PMI	Project Management Institute
POC	Proof-Of-Concept
POFN	Principle of Full Normalization
POOD	Principle of Orthogonal Design
POV	Point of View
PSPBOK	Personal Software Process Body of Knowledge
QA	Quality Assessment
QA	Quality Assurance
QC	Quality Control
QFD	Quality Function Deployment
QFH	Query From Hell
QUEL	QUEry Language
RACI matrix	Responsible Accountable Consulted Informed matrix
RAD	Rapid Application Development
RAID	Redundant Array of Independent Disks
RAM	Random Access Memory
RDBMS	Relational DataBase Management System
RDF	Resource Description Framework
RDM	Reference Data Management
RFID	Radio Frequency IDentification
RM	Records Management
RMI	Remote Method Invocation
ROI	Return On Investment
ROLAP	Relational OnLine Analytical Processing
ROM	Read-Only Memory
RPC	Remote Procedure Call
RPO	Recovery Point Objective
RSA	RSA encryption
RTO	Recovery Time Objective
RTOLAP	Real Time OnLine Analytical Processing
SAAS	Software as a Service
SAM	Sequential Access Method
SAN	Storage Area Network
SAX	Simple API for XML
SCM	Software Configuration Management
SCM	Source Code Management
SCM	Supply Chain Management
SCSI	Small Computer Storage Interface
SDK	Software Development Kit
SDLC	Systems Development LifeCycle
SDM	Semantic Data Model
SDMX	Statistical Data and Metadata eXchange
SEI	Software Engineering Institute
SET	Secure Electronic Transactions

SGML	Standard Generalized Markup Language
SHOE	Simple HTML Ontology Extension
SI	Sales Intelligence
SIC	Standard Industrial Code
SIG	Special Interest Group
SIMM	Service Integration Maturity Model
SKU	Stock-Keeping Unit
SLA	Service Level Agreement
SME	Subject Matter Expert
SMP	Symmetrical Multi-Processing
SMS	Short Message Service
SNIA	Storage Networking Industry Association
SOA	Service-Oriented Architecture
SOAP	Simple Object Access Protocol
SOI	Service-Oriented Integration
SOLAP	Spatial OnLine Analytical Processing
SOM	Self-Organizing Map
SOX	Sarbanes-Oxley Act
SPARQL	SPARQL Protocol and RDF Query Language
SQC	Statistical Quality Control
SQL	Structured Query Language
SSD	Solid State Drive
SSL	Secure Sockets Layer
STD	State Transition Diagram
SVG	Scaled Vector Graphics
SVM	Support Vector Machine
SWEBOK®	Software Engineering Body of Knowledge
SWOT	Strengths, Weaknesses, Opportunities, and Threats
SysML	Systems Modeling Language
Tb	Terabyte
TCO	Total Cost of Ownership
TCP/IP	Transmission Control Protocol (TCP) and the Internet Protocol (IP)
TDWI	The Data Warehouse Institute
TIFF	Tagged Image File Format
TOGAF	The Open Group Architecture Framework
TQM	Total Quality Management
UAT	User Acceptance Test
UCS	Universal Character Set
UDDI	Universal Description, Discovery, and Integration
UML	Unified Modeling Language
UNSPSC	Universal Standard Products and Services Classification
UPC	Universal Product Code
UPU	Universal Postal Union
URI	Uniform Resource Identifier
URL	Uniform Resource Locator
USPS	United States Postal Service
VLDB	Very Large DataBases
VLSI	Very Large Scale Integration
VRML	Virtual Reality Markup Language
VSAM	Virtual Storage Access Method
W3C	World Wide Web Consortium
WAN	Wide Area Network
WCM	Web Content Management
WFS	Web Feature Service
WMS	Web Map Service
WOLAP	Web-based OnLine Analytical Processing
WOM	Word of Mouth
WORM	Write Once, Read Many
WSDL	Web Services Description Language

WS-I	Web Services Interoperability Organization
WSRP	Web Services for Remote Portlets
WWW	World Wide Web
WYSIWYG	What-You-See-Is-What-You-Get
XBRL	eXtensible Business Reporting Language
XFML	eXchangeable Faceted Metadata Language
XIE	eXtended Intelligent Enterprise Architecture
XMI	eXtensible Markup Interface
XMI	XML Meta-data Interchange
XML	eXtensible Markup Language
XML/A	XML for Analysis
XP	eXtreme Programming
XSL	eXtensible Stylesheet Language
Y2K	Year 2000

Terms and Definitions

.net **Alternate form: "dot net"**

Microsoft's XML-based framework.

abort

Verb. To terminate a processing activity.

abstract

Adjective. Less specific in representation, or without a relation to a specific instance. Does not mean 'more generalized.' SEE ALSO generalization.

abstraction

1. Generally, a form of representation showing classification (member of), aggregation (part of), or generalization (is-a). (Smith and Smith, TODS, 1977)
2. In data modeling, the redefinition of data entities, attributes, and relationships by removing details to broaden the applicability of data structures to a wider class of situations, often by implementing supertypes rather than subtypes. (DAMA-DMBOK Guide, 1st edition, pg. 97.)
3. In data services, the process of layering virtualization between data and its source. It re-defines the data attributes or relationships by hiding details of the location, entities, and/or relationships of the information to broaden the applicability of data structures to a wider class of situations (i.e.: implementing supertypes rather than subtypes, data access objects, data services, etc.).

abstraction, horizontal

The process of partitioning a model into smaller subparts for presentation. Used in data modeling to show related areas in a more readable scale.

abstraction, vertical

The presentation of all or part of a model detail. Used in data modeling to show higher levels of entities and relationships to illustrate the basic subject area contents.

access

1. Generally, the ability to obtain or make use of something.
2. In data management, the operation of reading or writing information.
3. *Verb.* To obtain or retrieve.

accessibility

The ability to readily obtain data when needed.

accumulating snapshot fact

SEE fact table, accumulating snapshot.

accuracy

Freedom from mistakes or error, conformity to truth or to a standard, exactness, the degree of conformity of a measure to a standard or true value. (Brackett 2011)

accurate

1. *Adjective.* Complying with a standard, model, or rule.
2. *Adjective.* Free from defect or error.

active data warehousing

SEE data warehouse, active.

activity

1. A contribution to the performance of a function or process. An activity is a lower level process than a function or process, but higher level than a task or step. Inputs, activities, and outputs combine to form a process.
2. One of the DAMA Functional Framework Environmental Elements. Each function is composed of lower level activities, which may be grouped into sub-activities, and then further decomposed into tasks and steps. (DAMA-DMBOK Guide, 1st edition, pg. 13.)

activity group

In the DAMA-DMBOK Functional Framework, one of four types of activities – either a Planning Activity, Control Activity, Development Activity or Operational Activity. SEE ALSO activity.

acyclic

1. In general, not cyclic, or not composed of regular cycles.
2. A characteristic of a graph where there exists at most one path between any two nodes. SEE ALSO connected.

ad hoc query **Alternate form: ad-hoc query**

A query constructed and executed to answer an immediate and unanticipated question or need, in contrast to a planned query. For example, a dynamic SQL SELECT statement against a relational database, constructed by a knowledge worker using an English-like or point-and-click interface of a desktop-resident Business Intelligence tool. The data returned may drive further analysis and reporting.

adequate

Adjective. Sufficient for a specific requirement; sufficient or satisfactory; or lawfully and legally sufficient. (Brackett 2011)

adjective

A type of word that modifies or adds characteristics to a noun.

administrative meta-data

SEE meta-data, administrative.

Advanced Research Projects Agency Network (ARPANET)

The world's first operational packet switching network, developed by the U.S. Department of Defense. It became the precursor to the internet, which evolved into the World Wide Web.

affinity analysis

An analysis technique that relates occurrences of activities by individuals or groups. Market basket analysis is a type of affinity analysis.

affinity diagram

SEE chart, affinity diagram.

age

The length of time that an entity has existed, or in the case of an organic entity, lived.

aggregate data

Data resulting from processes that combine and summarize atomic data.

aggregation

1. Generally, the process of gathering into a whole from parts.
2. In data management, a process that transforms atomic data into aggregate-level information by using an aggregation function such as count, sum, average, standard deviation, etc.

agile software development

A group of software development methodologies based on iterative and incremental development, where requirements and solutions evolve through collaboration between self-organizing, cross-functional teams.

alert

The notification of an event, usually exceeding a pre-defined threshold.

algorithm

A set of rules or steps that will result in a defined end from a defined start.

alias

1. Generally, an alternative reference to a standard name or term.
2. In RDBMS, a database object that indirectly references another database object, for example, an abbreviated table reference within an SQL query.
3. In a distributed environment, an object that refers to another object to avoid having to use the full location qualifier of the other object. This alias is not dropped if the object referred to is dropped.

alpha release

The first version of something released to a formal testing team.

alternate key

SEE key, alternate.

alternate primary key

A primary key that is valid and acceptable, but is not the preferred primary key. (Brackett 2011)

ambiguity

Uncertainty in meaning or reference, depending on the context or usage. An ambiguous reference may have multiple meanings in the absence of context or usage specifications.

American Community Survey (ACS)

In the U.S., a large continuous demographic survey that is sent to residents on a monthly basis, rather than decennially. It contains more demographic questions than the old census long form, and provides more up-to-date information than was previously collected.

American National Standards Institute (ANSI)

A private not-for-profit organization that coordinates the development and use of voluntary consensus standards in the United States and represents the needs of U.S. stakeholders in worldwide standardization forums. Formerly, the American Standards Association from which we get the American Standard Code for Information Interchange. (www.ansi.org)

American Standard Code for Information Interchange (ASCII)

A common code used in transmitting information over networks, using seven or 8 data bits, a parity bit, and a stop bit. SEE ALSO EBCDIC.

amount

A class word, abbreviated usually to amt.

analog signal

A signal that is represented by an oscillating wave rather than digital pulses.

analysis

Separation of the whole into its parts; an examination of a complex, its individual parts, and their relations; the separation of the ingredients of a substance; a statement of the constituents of a mixture. (Brackett 2011) SEE ALSO synthesis.

analyst

A person who performs analysis or is skilled in analysis. SEE ALSO business analyst; business systems analyst; data analyst; systems analyst.

analytic application

Software that packages Business Intelligence technology to support a specific knowledge-driven business process.

analytical data

SEE data, analytical.

analytical framework

The system of criteria and standards within which data are analyzed.

analytics

Business Intelligence procedures and techniques for exploration and analysis of data to discover and identify meaningful information and trends.

anamorphic map

SEE chart, area cartogram.

ANSI SQL

The standard form of SQL concurrently defined by ANSI and ISO and first released in 1986. Most recent version of the standard (SQL:2008) dates from 2008.

applet

A small Java program that can be embedded in an HTML page. Applets cannot access certain resources on local computers, such as files and serial devices. Applets are also prohibited from communication with most other computers across a network.

applicability

1. Relevant to the current subject.
2. Ability to be put to specific use.

application

In computing, software functions and services implemented together to support one or more related business processes.

application architecture

1. SEE architecture, application portfolio.
2. SEE architecture, application component.
3. SEE architecture, system.

application component architecture

SEE architecture, application component.

application DBA

SEE DataBase Administrator, application.

application development

1. The process of building and maintaining software applications.
2. Commonly, the IT organization responsible for application development. Synonymous with Software Development or Software Engineering.

application portfolio architecture

SEE architecture, application portfolio.

Application Programming Interface (API)

A published standard format for communicating with applications.

application server

In a three-tier application architecture, the middle tier of software (and possibly hardware) where business logic is performed.

Application Service Provider (ASP)

A company offering network access to application programs and services for other parties. ASPs typically provide the applications, infrastructure, and technical support for a monthly service charge.

approach of no coupling

A programming technique where each module is independent: has no dependency on, is unrelated to, and does not communicate with, all other modules.

appropriate

Adjective. Especially suitable or compatible; fitting. (Brackett 2011)

arc

1. In graph theory, a connection between two nodes in a graph. Also known as an edge.
2. In trigonometry, a curved line.

architect

1. Generally, a person trained in the planning, design, and oversight of the construction of something, usually buildings.
2. In information technology, an experienced and skilled designer responsible for architecture supporting a broad scope of requirements over time beyond the scope of a single project. The term implies a higher level of professional experience and expertise than an analyst, designer, modeler, or developer.

Architects as Designers

Zachman Framework row name, matches System Logic.

architectural framework

A way of thinking about and understanding architecture and the structures or systems requiring architecture.

architecture

1. Generally, the design of any complex object or system, including the implied architecture of abstract things such as music or mathematics, the apparent architecture of natural things such as geological formations or living things, or explicitly planned architecture of human-made things such as buildings, machines, organizations, processes, software and databases.
2. In data management, the organized arrangement of components to optimize the function, performance, feasibility, cost, and/or aesthetics of an overall structure.
3. In common use, the art and discipline of designing buildings and structures, from the macro-level of urban planning to the micro-level of creating furniture and machine parts.

architecture, application component

A set of standard programming structures, design patterns, formats and protocols for how software applications should operate and communicate with each other.

architecture, application portfolio

A master blueprint for an organization's existing and planned portfolio of software applications, how they support the organization's processes, and how interface with each other and with the organization's databases.

architecture, business

The portion of an enterprise architecture that describes organizational goals, roles, reporting structures and locations, but excluding the enterprise data architecture, process architecture, technology architecture and application architecture. The business architecture includes those artifacts identified in rows 1 and 2 of the Zachman Framework, but limited to columns 4, 5 and 6.

architecture, Business Intelligence

The overall design and implementation of components of the Business Intelligence environment, including:

1. the Data Warehouse, data marts and staging area databases,
2. the flow of data from operational sources and these databases,
3. the selection and configuration of Database Management Systems and database administration tools used for Business Intelligence,
4. the selection and configuration of data integration products used to extract, cleanse, transform, and load data,
5. the design patterns and standards for data integration programs,
6. the selection and configuration of BI software products that enable access, reporting, and analysis,
7. the data schemas presented to business professionals for ad hoc query and analysis,
8. the user interfaces for query, analysis and reporting, and
9. the administrative controls put in place to safeguard the data.

architecture, business process

The future state business process models of an enterprise, used in conjunction with a business data architecture to perform information value chain analysis. Part of an enterprise architecture.

architecture, client/server

A distributed technology approach where application software processing is divided by function. Servers perform shared functions such as processing business rules, managing communications, managing databases, or providing print services. Clients performs individual user functions -- providing customized interfaces, performing screen to screen navigation, offering help functions, etc. Client and server software may reside on the same hardware platform, but each component is designed to be distributed across a networked environment for efficiency.

architecture, closed

An architecture where only the original manufacturer can make add-ons and peripherals.

architecture, data

1. In common usage, the physical technology infrastructure supporting data management, including database servers, data replication tools, and middleware.
2. The method of design and construction of an integrated data resource that is business driven, based on real-world subjects as perceived by the organization, and implemented into appropriate operating environments. It consists of components that provide a consistent foundation across organizational boundaries to provide easily identifiable, readily available, high-quality data to support the current and future business information demand. (Brackett 2011)

architecture, enterprise

1. Generally, an integrated collection of models and design approaches used to align information, processes, projects, and technology with the goals of the enterprise. These high-level design artifacts typically describe target views of the enterprise. Enterprise architecture may include:
   a) an enterprise data model,
   b) related data integration architecture,
   c) a business process model,
   d) an application portfolio architecture,
   e) an application component architecture,
   f) an IT infrastructure technology architecture,
   g) an organizational business architecture, and
   h) the enterprise information value chain analysis that identifies the linkage and alignment across these perspectives, and to enterprise goals.
2. Other models and other forms of architecture may also be included within the enterprise architecture.
3. In the Zachman Framework, the enterprise architecture generally includes design artifacts identified in Rows 1 and 2 (conceptual views of data, process, locations, events, roles and goals), the value chain analysis describing the linkages between these perspectives, and high-level decisions about how to implement technology supporting these concepts in an integrated manner.
4. An initiative to describe comprehensively the architectures in an organization. It describes the terminology, composition, and relationships within each architecture, the relationships between architectures, and the relationships with external organizations. It includes business goals, business processes, hardware, software, data, and information systems. (Brackett 2011)

architecture, information

The analysis and design of the data stored by information systems, concentrating on entities, their attributes, and their relationships.

architecture, information systems

The integrated set of design artifacts defining how data (including the logical data model), applications (including the application portfolio architecture and data integration architecture), and technology (including portfolios of technology products and standards) will integrate to support the business architecture.

architecture, in-memory

An architecture that uses flash memory rather than conventional disk storage.

architecture, meta-data

The design for integration of meta-data across data dictionaries, directories, and repositories.

architecture, multi-tier **Alternate form: n-tier architecture**

A form of architecture where the user interface layers, the application processing layers, and the data management layers are all logically separate parts which communicate through services. SEE ALSO architecture, three-tier.

architecture, open

The published specifications for a computer by a vendor, allowing other companies to create add-ons to enhance and customize the machine, and to make peripheral devices that work properly with it. In practice, has been difficult to engage on a corporate basis due to the risk involved in a source that has multiple editors and has little to no assurance of quality when in use. Outsourcing the risk to a second party who then use the open source and accept the liability for the code is then the way to engage with open source code.

architecture, process

1. The structural design of process systems, such as computers, businesses, or other complex systems.
2. The first two rows of the "function" column of the Zachman Framework for Enterprise Architecture:
   Row 1: Objectives/Scope (contextual) – Planner View: a list of processes important to the business (may be a hierarchical list outlining a functional decomposition of processes)
   Row 2: Enterprise Model (conceptual) – Owner View: a business process model (process flow diagrams, sometimes called data flow diagrams, showing the flow of data and other business resources between processes as inputs and outputs).
   a) Enterprise process architecture typically includes
   b) a functional decomposition,
   c) process flow diagrams, and
   d) value chain analysis linking processes to data (subject areas or entities), organizations, roles, goals, applications, and/or projects.
3. Includes functions, activities, workflows, events, cycles, products, and procedures. DAMA-DMBOK 1st edition, pg. 66.

architecture, product

Part of a technology architecture, identifying selected vendor-specific software tools and services. Although not implied in the name, it may also include industry-wide standards and protocols.

architecture, system

Includes applications, software components, interfaces, and projects. DAMA-DMBOK 1st edition, pg. 66.

architecture, technology

The master plan for the IT technical infrastructure depicted in diagrams and specifications of hardware and system software products, locations, configurations, standards and adopted protocols, along with linkages of computing platforms and/or servers to existing and planned applications and databases. Includes diagrams and specifications of the kinds described in Column 3 ("Network") of the Zachman Framework.

architecture, three-tier

A structure for a database environment consisting of a presentation tier, an application tier, and a data tier. The presentation tier is the one seen and used by the programmers and other users of a DBMS, also called the user schema, or the external schema. Presentation tiers can overlap. The application tier is the combination of all the defined structures in the presentation tier for a given database, also called the logical tier, data access tier, or middle tier. There may be additional data in the application tier that is not in any presentation tier. The data tier is the database administrator's view of the database, also called the internal schema. The data tier is the definition of the physical storage structure of a database.

archival database

SEE database, archival.

archive

1. A copy of a database or documents preserved in a secondary, lower cost storage location, for infrequent historical reference and/or recovery.
2. *Verb.* To move stored data (structured or unstructured) to a secondary, less readily accessed location, at lower storage costs, for historical reference and/or recovery.

area cartogram

SEE chart, area cartogram.

area chart

SEE chart, area.

argument

SEE parameter.

argument slide

SEE chart, argument slide.

arity

In object role modeling, the number of objects t a role in a predicate, or relationship. SEE predicate. SEE ALSO n-ary.

array

A grouping of similar items of the same storage type in a sequential pattern, and referenced by a sequential index value. SEE ALSO matrix.

artifact

An object made or modified by a human.

Artificial Intelligence (AI)

Software that performs a function previously ascribed only to human beings, such as natural language processing.

asset

1. Generally, something that has value or produces benefit.
2. In accounting, something of value on a balance sheet.

asset condition

Asset condition describes how an asset or a service will perform in objective and measurable terms. The measurement is sometimes as simple as assigning a number. An example would be a range of 1 to 5, where one = poor and five = excellent.

asset, intangible

Non-physical assets, such as accounts receivable.

asset, tangible

Physical assets, such as equipment.

associate

Verb. To determine relationships between entities, including characteristics of the relationship: dependent or not (optional, orphan), exclusive (at most one) or not (multiple). SEE ALSO relationship.

association

1. SEE relationship.
2. In statistics, any relationship between measured quantities that shows a statistic dependency.
3. In object-oriented programming, a relationship between object classes which enables an object instance to perform an action on another's behalf.

Association for Computing Machinery (ACM)

The largest and oldest international scientific and educational computer society.

association rule analysis

SEE relationship rule analysis.

associative entity

SEE data entity, associative.

asynchronous

Adjective. Describes a style of communication in which the initiator does not wait for a reply. Opposite of synchronous.

asynchronous replication

Data replication where the target database is updated as soon as possible after updates occur to the source database, but not as part of a single integrated transaction. Failure to update the target has no impact on the source database. Sometimes referred to as "near real time" replication.

atomic data

1. Data at the lowest chosen level of detail (granularity). The level of detail chosen depends on the information requirements of the enterprise. For example, address could be one atomic item, or address could be split into further composite items such as house identifier and city. Opposite of aggregate data.
2. Non-aggregated observations, or measurements of characteristics of individual units, which cannot be further decomposed and retain any useful meaning.

Atomicity-Consistency-Isolation-Durability (ACID)

Standard properties of relational databases.

attribute

An inherent characteristic, an accidental quality, an object closely associated with or belonging to a specific person, place, or office; a word ascribing a quality. (Brackett 2011)

attribute class

SEE class, attribute.

attribute generalization

SEE generalization, attribute.

attributed relationship

SEE relationship, attributed.

attributive entity

SEE data entity, dependent.

audit

A formal and official verification of validity, accuracy, and conformance to requirements, regulations, standards, and/or guidelines.

audit trail

Data maintained to trace activity, such as a transaction log, for purposes of recovery or audit.

augmentation

1. The process of adding to something to make it more or greater than the original.
2. In logic, a relationship where if X leads to Y, then XZ will lead to YZ.

authentication

1. In data security, the process of verifying whether a person or software agent requesting a resource has the authority or permission to access that resource.
2. In data quality, the process of verifying data as complying with what the data represents.

authoritative source

A source of data or information that is recognized by members of a Community of Interest to be valid or trusted because its provenance is considered highly reliable or accurate. During the life cycle process, the authoritative source (or system of use in which it is housed) can evolve according to use. Subject Matter Experts validate that the data is authoritative, and Data Management assures that data from the authoritative source is provided to users, and that it is current.

authorization

In data security, the granting of authority allowing a person, group, or software agent to access a resource.

authorization request

In data security, a request to grant authority to a person, group, or software agent to access data for which the data consumer does not presently have access privileges.

authorization rule

SEE rule, authorization.

automation

The act of replacing control of a manual process with computer or electronic controls.

availability

1. The percentage of time a system or data resource is accessible compared to the time it is expected to be accessible.
2. The percentage of time a system or database can be used for productive work. DAMA-DMBOK Guide, 1st edition, pg. 134.

B

Bachman diagram

Named after Charles Bachman, shows data using network or relational models. Also called a data structure diagram.

backup

1. *Verb.* To take a snapshot copy of a system to ensure its continued availability in the event of a hardware or software failure requiring recovery of the database to restore the data.
2. The copy of the system information and data used for recoverability.

backup, cold

A backup snapshot taken while the system is offline.

backup, hot

A backup snapshot taken while the system is online.

backward recovery

SEE recovery, backward.

backwards compatible

1. *Adjective.* Able to accept input from older or earlier versions of a device or software.
2. *Adjective.* Operational on older technology, even if limited in functionality.

Balanced ScoreCard (BSC)

A strategic performance management tool consisting of a semi-standard structured report supported by proven design methods and automation tools that can be used by managers to keep track of the execution of activities by staff within their control, and monitor the consequences arising from these actions. It provides a comprehensive, top-down view of organizational performance measurements with a strong focus on vision and strategy, based on concepts developed by Robert Kaplan and David Norton.

Baldrige Criteria for Performance Excellence

Criteria used to evaluate the qualification of companies for the Malcolm Baldrige National Quality Award; leading management practices used to measure organizational performance in seven categories: Leadership, Strategic Planning, Customer & Market Focus, Human Resource Focus, Process Management, "Measurement and Analysis and Knowledge Management", and Results.

bandwidth

The rate of transfer of data over a specific channel. SEE ALSO capacity.

bar chart

SEE chart, bar.

Barker data modeling notation

SEE data modeling notation, Barker.

base table

1. In Data Warehousing, the normalized data structures maintained in a Data Warehouse, in contrast to the de-normalized dependent data mart tables sourced from the base tables.
2. Outside of Data Warehousing, a table for an entity that is not dependent on any other entity in the database.

base unit

The unit used as the basis of an index number, or to which a constant series refers, examples; base period, base weight, base currency

Basel Accords

International banking supervision standards designed to ensure the liquidity of financial institutions doing business in European Union countries. Developed by the Basel Committee on Banking Supervision, and implemented in 2006 as Basel II New Accords. Basel III is currently under development.

behavior

What something does at any point in time. The execution or carrying out of a process constitutes behavior. Behavior is something that happens, as opposed to something that is. Opposite of state.

believability

Confidence in inherent truthfulness.

bell curve

A statistical frequency distribution pattern that is shaped like a bell (narrow at ends, wide in the middle of the range). SEE ALSO normal distribution.

benchmark

A point of reference for measurement, comparison, and evaluation. A benchmark can be a standard of excellence or a point-in-time snapshot measurement for comparison with other benchmarks. A benchmark may be an internal or external measurement.

benchmarking

Verb. To analyze and compare an organization's processes (an internal benchmark) against the performance to those of another organization or against an industry standard (an external benchmark).

best practice

A technique, method, process, discipline, incentive, or reward generally considered more effective at delivering a particular outcome than by other means.

beta release

A release of software to a limited population under controlled conditions, to test for functionality completeness and execution correctness.

beta test **Alternate form: beta-test**

SEE test, beta.

bias

1. Generally, a distortion of something to support a particular view.
2. In data analysis, a distortion of data or information that affects the interpretation, or a distortion of interpretation that supports a particular view.

bias, collection-based

A distortion of fact interpretation based on sole use of data provided by or pre-selected by the sponsor of the research, which may be skewed toward a certain result, rather than being completely objective.

bias, sampling

A distortion of fact interpretation due to non-random selection of sample contents.

bias, search-based

A distortion of fact interpretation based on sole use of data that supports the desired outcome, rather than a complete data set.

bias, use-based

A distortion of fact interpretation by only using the results that support the desired outcome, and ignoring or not displaying the other results.

bi-directionally named

Adjective. Using a naming convention for binary relationships where the relationship is described twice, in sentences, once with one entity named as the subject paired with the other entity as the object of a sentence, and the other in reverse order.

big data

Data volumes that are exceptionally large, normally greater than 100 Terabyte and more commonly refer to the Petabyte and Exabyte range. Big data has begun to be used when discussing Data Warehousing and analytic solutions where the volume of data poses specific challenges that are unique to very large volumes of data including: data loading, modeling, cleansing, and analytics, and are often solved using massively parallel processing, or parallel processing and distributed data solutions.

bilateral exchange

1. Generally, an exchange of something between a sending organization and a receiving organization where all aspects of the exchange process are agreed between counterparties.
2. In data management, an exchange of data and/or meta-data between a sending organization and a receiving organization where all aspects of the exchange process are agreed between counterparties, including the mechanism for exchange of data and meta-data, the formats, the frequency or schedule, and the mode used for communications regarding the exchange.

Bill of Information (BOI)

The information and relationships that document the entire life cycle of a product; includes the associated product information (administrative, programmatic, technical, and financial) and its location.

bill-of-material

A list of raw materials down to the atomic level necessary to create a final item.

binary

1. *Adjective.* Consisting of two components or values.
2. The format of a compiled and linked program that is ready to execute on a specified system.

BInary digiT (BIT)

A unit of measurement for data based on the binary number system using zero and one.

binary relationship

SEE relationship, binary.

bioinformatics **Alternate form: bio-informatics**

The application of information technology to molecular biology.

bitmap index

SEE index, bitmap.

Bits Per Second (BPS)

The amount of bits transferred per second over a conduit or connection.

block index

SEE index, block.

blocking

The situation where one process locks a resource that another resource needs. The second resource is 'blocked'.

blog

A type of website containing regular entries of commentary, notes on events, or links to graphics or video. Short for 'web log'.

Body of Knowledge (BOK)

The sum of all professional knowledge in a given field, or what is generally accepted to be true.

Body of Knowledge, Business Analysis (BABOK)

A body of knowledge document available from the International Institute for Business Analysis. (DAMA-DMBOK Guide, 1st edition, pg. 11.)

Body of Knowledge, Business Process Management Common (BPM CBOK®)

A body of knowledge document created by the Association of Business Process Management Professionals.

Body of Knowledge, Canadian Information Technology (CITBOK)

A project undertaking by the Canadian Information Processing Society to outline the knowledge required of a Canadian Information Technology Professional. (DAMA-DMBOK Guide, 1st edition, pg. 11.)

Body of Knowledge, Common (CBK)

Published by the International Information Systems Security Certification Consortium. contains the information tested to achieve the Certified Information Systems Security Professional designation. (DAMA-DMBOK Guide, 1st edition, pg. 11.)

Body of Knowledge, Data Management (DAMA-DMBOK)

A guide to knowledge about data management, or at least that which is commonly accepted as true about data management. SEE DAMA-DMBOK Guide.

Body of Knowledge, Guide to the Project Management (PMBOK®)

An acronym and registered trademark for the Guide to the Project Management Body of Knowledge, a publication by the non-profit Project Management Institute (PMI) and an internationally recognized standard (IEEE Std 1490-2003) defining the fundamental vocabulary of project management and identifying generally accepted project management practices. First published in 1987, the current third edition was released and copyrighted in 2004. The PMBOK® Guide is the ANSI standard for project management (ISO 9906 and PRINCE2 are related project management standards).

Body of Knowledge, IT Architect (ITABOK)

A body of knowledge document created by the International Association of Software Architects.

Body of Knowledge, Personal Software Process (PSPBOK)

Developed by Carnegie Mellon University, a body of knowledge on Personal Software Process and Team Software Process.

Body of Knowledge, Software Engineering (SWEBOK®)

The Guide to the Software Engineering Body of Knowledge, a book published by the IEEE. (DAMA-DMBOK Guide, 1st edition, pg. 11.)

bookmark

A marker used to save a place in a book, a data set, or an Internet address.

Boolean

Adjective. Relating to or of an algorithm or calculation that results in only a True or False result. Named for George Boole.

Boolean operator

Logical operators that combine propositions to evaluate to only a True or False result. Includes AND, OR, IF THEN, EXCEPT, and NOT.

Boolean search

A search method using Boolean operators (AND, OR, NOT) to focus the search.

Boston Consulting Group matrix (BCG) **Alternate forms: BCG matrix, Boston box**

SEE chart, portfolio.

box and whisker diagram

SEE chart, box plot.

box plot chart

SEE chart, box plot.

Boyce/Codd Normal Form (BCNF)

SEE normal form, Boyce/Codd.

braking mechanism

In databases, a software function that prevents users from querying a database once transaction loads reach a certain level.

brick

In architecture, a common term for technology architecture components. (DAMA-DMBOK Guide, 1st edition, pg. 140.)

bridge of negotiation chart

SEE chart, bridge of negotiation.

bridge table

SEE table, bridge.

b-tree index

SEE index, b-tree.

bubble chart

SEE chart, bubble.

bulk data transfer

A software mechanism to move large data files which uses compression, blocking and buffering to optimize transfer times.

bullet chart

SEE chart, bullet.

bus architecture

SEE data warehouse bus architecture.

bus matrix

In Data Warehousing, a tabular representation of the intersection of shared dimension tables with data subject areas, data processes, data facts, data marts, etc.

business

1. Generally, any purposeful activity.
2. Specifically, a commercial or industrial enterprise. Commercial activity engaged in as a means of livelihood.

business activity

A set of methods or procedures that may be executed in the form of transactions relative to a business. SEE ALSO activity; business process.

Business Activity Monitoring (BAM)

The ability to automatically monitor events in an executing business process through immediate notification thanks to a sophisticated technical infrastructure.

business analysis

1. The study of business processes, practices and business systems requirements.
2. The application of information to better understand business opportunities and challenges. SEE ALSO Business Intelligence.

Business Analysis Body of Knowledge (BABOK)

SEE Body of Knowledge, Business Analysis.

business analyst

1. Generally, a knowledge worker responsible for interpreting data, performing calculations, and distributing reports to other knowledge workers.
2. In data management, a professional responsible for understanding the business processes and the information needs of an organization, for serving as a liaison between IT and business units, and acting as a facilitator of organizational and cultural change. Also known as a business systems analyst or systems analyst.

business analytics

Meta-data that includes data definitions, report definitions, users, usage statistics, and performance statistics.

business architecture

SEE architecture, business.

business case

A structured format for organizing the reasons, benefits, and estimated costs for initiating a project or program.

Business Concepts

Zachman Framework row name, matches Executive Leaders as Owners.

business continuity

The degree of uninterrupted stability of an organization's systems and operations in spite of potentially disruptive events.

business data

Data about people, places, things, rules, events, or concepts used to operate and manage any enterprise (not just commercial enterprises). Used to identify data that is not considered to be meta-data.

business data steward

A knowledge worker, business leader, and recognized subject matter expert assigned accountability for the data specifications and data quality of specifically assigned business entities, subject areas or databases, but with less responsibility for data governance than a coordinating data steward or an executive data steward.

business driven data resource

A data resource where the design, development, and maintenance are driven by business needs, as defined by the business information demand. (Brackett 2011)

business entity

SEE entity, business.

business event

A happening in the real world, such as a sale, purchase, fire, flood, accident, and so on. (Brackett 2011)

business event happening

The actual happening of a business event, such as a specific sale, a purchase, a fire, a flood, an accident, and so on. (Brackett 2011)

business feature

A trait or characteristic of a business object or business event, such as a customer's name, a city population, a fire date, and so on. (Brackett 2011)

Business Image Management and Multimedia (BIMM)

A course studying design, import, and manipulation of text, graphics, audio, and video used in presentation management and publishing systems.

business information demand

An organization's continuously increasing, constantly changing need for current, accurate, integrated information, often on short notice or very short notice, to support its business activities. It is a very dynamic demand for information to support the business that constantly changes. (Brackett 2011)

Business Intelligence (BI)

A set of concepts, methods, and processes to improve business decision-making using any information from multiple sources that could affect the business, and applying experiences and assumptions to deliver accurate perspectives of business dynamics. (Brackett 2011)

Business Intelligence administrative data **Alternate form: BI administrative data**

The data that helps a Data Warehouse administrator manage a Data Warehouse, such as user profiles and data access history.

Business Intelligence analyst **Alternate form: BI analyst**

An IT professional specializing in assisting and supporting business professionals become more self-sufficient in the use of query, reporting and analysis procedures and tools. A BI analyst trains knowledge workers, assists them in solving more complex analytical and reporting problems, provides second level support for user problems with Business Intelligence data and tools, and may serve as the administrator for the BI environment.

Business Intelligence architect **Alternate form: BI architect**

An IT professional with overall responsibility for the Business Intelligence environment, its architecture, and the effectiveness of knowledge workers engaged in Business Intelligence. A lead BI analyst. May also be the Data Warehouse architect, or these responsibilities may be distinct.

Business Intelligence architecture **Alternate form: BI architecture**

SEE architecture, Business Intelligence.

Business Intelligence developer **Alternate form: BI developer**

An IT professional software developer who specializes in report writing and/or the development of analytic applications.

Business Intelligence environment **Alternate form: BI environment**

The hardware, software and organizational support for Business Intelligence activity that enables knowledge workers to access, analyze and manipulate data. It generally includes the Business Intelligence software, user interfaces, associated infrastructure hardware and software, data mart databases and multi-dimensional data cubes. It may also include Data Warehouses and the data integration programs that provide data for Business Intelligence.

Business Intelligence platform **Alternate form: BI platform**

The infrastructure of selected enabling tools and technologies necessary for the development and deployment of Business Intelligence applications.

Business Intelligence Service Provider (BISP)

An Application Service Provider providing Data Warehousing and Business Intelligence capabilities as outsourced services hosted offsite. A BISP ties into source information systems and databases behind a corporation's firewall, providing traditional Data Warehouse and analytic application capabilities to internal knowledge workers and external customers. Often used to extend Business Intelligence functions into e-commerce.

Business Intelligence software **Alternate form: BI software**

Technology and products (tools) used by knowledge workers to access data, analyze and share information, understand business performance and improve decision-making. Includes query and reporting tools, OLAP technologies, statistical analysis tools, data mining tools, scenario modeling tools, planning and budgeting tools, advanced analytic applications, dashboards and scorecards for performance monitoring, and enterprise reporting tools. BI software is the current term for the current generation of decision support tools.

Business Intelligence support **Alternate form: BI support**

The training and assistance available to business professionals in use of Business Intelligence tools and techniques, and the valid interpretation of Business Intelligence data. Typically, a help desk provides Level 1 support, with BI analysts providing Level 2 support.

Business Intelligence Value Chain

A sequence of events where value is added from the data resource, through each step, to the support of business goals. (Brackett 2011)

Business Intelligence, mobile **Alternate form: Mobile BI**

The distribution of business data to mobile devices such as Smartphone and tablet computers.

Business Intelligence, social **Alternate form: Social BI**

The creation, publishing, and sharing of custom business analytics reports and dashboards by end users of "Cloud" technologies.

business key

SEE key, business.

business meta-data

SEE meta-data, business.

business model

A current or future state representation of some aspect of an enterprise, typically from a process, data, geographic, event, organizational or financial perspective.

business object

A person, place, thing, or concept in the real world, such as a customer, river, city, account, and so on. (Brackett 2011)

Business Performance Management (BPM)

An umbrella term for the methods, metrics, processes, and systems used to monitor and manage the performance of any enterprise.

Business Performance Measurement (BPM)

The use of techniques and tools to measure performance against specific key performance indicators, often coupled with comparative information from industry sources. Dashboards support business performance measurement. The Balanced Scorecard is a specialized form of business performance measurement.

Business Performance Modeling (BPM)

The use of techniques and tools to understand business the factors affecting business performance, and to explore "what if" scenarios to help consider the implications of alternative courses of action. SEE ALSO scenario modeling.

business process

A process that is intended to contribute to the overall value of an enterprise. The complex interactions between people, applications, and technologies designed to create customer value. A process is composed of activities.

business process architecture

SEE architecture, business process.

Business Process Execution Language (BPEL)

Standards for defining process flows using web services.

Business Process Execution Language for Web Services (BPEL4WS)

Standards for defining process flows controlled by web services.

Business Process Management (BPM)

The design, monitoring, and control of complex interactions between people, applications, and technologies designed to create customer value.

Business Process Management Common Body of Knowledge (BPM CBOK®)

SEE Body of Knowledge, Business Process Management Common.

Business Process Maturity Model (BPMM)

Developed by the Object Management Group, defines maturity levels for business processing from Initial through Managed, Standardized, and Predictable, to Innovating.

Business Process Model (BPM)

A model of the functions, activities, and procedures performed in any organization. A business process model may consist of:

1. A context diagram showing the relationship of the overall process to those outside the model's scope, along with the inputs to and outputs from the overall process,
2. One or more functional decomposition diagram showing how the overall process is made up of contributing processes at lower levels (a "vertical view"),
3. One or more process flow diagrams showing how the outputs of one process serve as the inputs to other process (a "horizontal view"). The process flow may be cross-functional or within a single function,
4. One or more business process model diagrams, each depicting the inputs, outputs, start and end events, component activities, roles, and metrics of a single process,
5. The business definition of each process, and
6. The value chain analysis of the process, identifying relationships to data, organizations, roles, and systems.

business process model diagram **Alternate form: BPM diagram**

A stylized approach to graphically documenting the definition, objectives, start and end events, inputs, outputs, component activities, roles and metrics of a single process. Sometimes referred to as a context diagram, but a BPM diagram includes more information than a traditional context diagram.

Business Process Modeling Notation (BPMN)

A standard for graphical representation of business processes maintained by the Object Management Group.

Business Process Outsourcing (BPO)

A form of outsourcing that involves transferring responsibilities for entire specific business functions or processes to a third party provider.

Business Process Re-engineering (BPR)

The process of analyzing and radically transforming existing business activities, eliminating or minimizing costs and maximizing value in order to achieve breakthrough levels of performance improvement.

business professional

A knowledge worker, manager, or executive.

business requirement

SEE requirement, business.

business rule

SEE rule, business.

business systems analyst

A professional responsible for understanding the business processes and the information needs of an organization, for serving as a liaison between IT and business units, and acting as a facilitator for organizational and cultural change. Also known as a systems analyst.

Business Systems Planning (BSP)

A method for defining an enterprise architecture and information systems architecture developed by IBM in the early 1980s.

business transaction

An event involving the exchange of products, money, and/or information.

Business, Applications, Technology, Organization, and Governance (BATOG)

An acronym for a list of core IT Architecture concerns, put forth by EDS in 2008 as a business foundation for technology planning.

Business-to-Business (B2B)

Commerce transactions between equivalent businesses, such as between a wholesaler and a retailer.

Business-to-Consumer (B2C)

Commerce transactions between a business and a consumer, such as in a retail sale.

Business-to-Government (B2G)

Commerce transactions between a business and a governmental body, such as between a business and an elected water commission.

byte (b)

1. A single character of data stored electronically in 16 binary bits. A datum.
2. The term originally coined by IBM with the announcement of the 360 series of computers in 1974. Originally consisted of 8 bits, and could be used to store a single character, digit, or two decimal digits ("packed decimal"), or in combination could be used to store numbers. ASCII and EBCDIC are the two dominant character coding schemes based on 8 bits.

C

C4.5 algorithm

Ross Quinlan's algorithm to generate decision trees for classification.

cache hit

A state when a data request can be supplied from data within a cache, rather than directly from disk storage.

cache hit ratio

A measurement of how often data in cache is used versus data accessed from disk.

call center

The part of an organization that handles inbound/outbound telephone or email communications with internal and/or external customers. An IT help desk is a call center for customers of the IT department.

campaign management

Detailed tracking, reporting, and analysis that provides precise measurements regarding current marketing campaign efforts, their performance, and the types of leads they attract.

Canadian Information Technology Body of Knowledge (CITBOK)

SEE Body of Knowledge, Canadian Information Technology.

candidate key

SEE key, candidate.

candidate primary key

A primary key that has been identified and considered as a primary key, but has not been verified. (Brackett 2011)

candlestick chart

SEE chart, candlestick.

canon

An accepted principle or role; a body of principles, rules, standards, or norms. (Brackett 2011)

canonical

Adjective. Conforming to a general rule or acceptable procedure reduced to the simplest and cleanest scheme possible. (Brackett 2011)

canonical model

A data model of the inherent structure of data without regard to applications, hardware, or software implementations. Built according to specific canons. Usually a result of canonical synthesis.

canonical synthesis

The concept that if everyone followed the canons (rules) for developing a data model, then those independent data models could be readily plugged together, just like a picture puzzle, to provide a single, comprehensive, organization-wide data architecture. (Brackett 2011)

Capability Maturity Model (CMM)

The common name for the Capability Maturity Model Integration and its more widely known predecessor, the Capability Maturity Model for Software, both published by the Software Engineering Institute of Carnegie-Mellon University. The CMM is a guide to improve an organization's software development process, featuring defined practices used to rank an organization at one of five process maturity levels.

Capability Maturity Model Integration (CMMI)

The most current system development process capability maturity model from the Software Engineering Institute at Carnegie-Mellon University. The CMMI replaces several older related maturity models, including the original Capability Maturity Model for Software (SW-CMM), the Systems Engineering Capability Model (SECM), and the Integrated Product Development Capability Maturity Model (IPD-CMM). The latest version of the CMMI, version 1.02, was released by the SEI in 2002.

capacity

The maximum amount that can be held, contained, or processed at one time.

cardinal number

A number measured on a scale with an arithmetically meaningful zero point. Generally used to measure quantities or volumes. Can be manipulated by all the binary operators: exponentiation, multiplication and division, addition and subtraction, comparison (e.g., less than), matching, and Boolean. SEE ALSO ordinal number; interval number; nominal number.

cardinality

The number of entities or members in a set.

Cartesian

Adjective. Related to the philosophy or mathematical method put forth by René Descartes.

Cartesian coordinates

The use of a set of points on a set of axes in order to show location or proximity.

Cartesian product **Alternate form: Cartesian join**

In data processing, given two or more populations, the Cartesian product is the set of all possible combinations, taking one value from each population. Usually a large and meaningless answer set for an incorrectly phrased query. SEE ALSO query from hell.

cartogram

SEE chart, cartogram.

cartography

The study and practice of making maps or globes. Maps function as visualization tools for spatial data. Most quality maps are now made with geographic information system (GIS) software and databases.

cascade chart

SEE chart, cascade.

cascade delete

The declaration made on a hierarchical (1:M) relationship between parent and child, that a request to delete a parent instance will also result in deleting the related child instances. Usually associated with a foreign key (which defines a hierarchical relationship), with the referring entity table (where the foreign key is stored) being the child and the referenced entity table is the parent.

Cascading Style Sheet (CSS)

A tag language that enables authors to associate formatting style (fonts, spacing and aural cues) to structured documents including HTML and XML applications.

case study

An evaluation of an instance of a process to determine what environmental or inherent attributes drove success or failure of the process.

catalog

1. Generally, a complete list of things, usually arranged systematically.
2. In databases, the component of a DataBase Management System where meta-data about DBMS objects is stored. Most relational DBMS products keep the catalog as relational tables. The majority of meta-data in a DBMS catalog is technical meta-data (names, types, lengths, occurrences, keys, etc.) collected automatically by the DBMS software, although business definitions can be added as comments. A catalog is an active data dictionary.

category

The generic term for items at any level within a classification.

category scheme

Scheme made up of a hierarchy of categories, which may include any type of useful classification for the organization of something.

causal loop diagram

SEE chart, causal loop diagram.

cause-effect chains

SEE chart, cause-and-effect diagram.

cell

1. Generally, any small compartment.
2. In multi-dimensional design, a data point defined by one member of each dimension of a multi-dimensional structure. Often cells in multi-dimensional structures are empty, leading to 'sparse' storage.

Center Of Excellence (COE)

A team of people that promote collaboration and using best practices around a specific focus area to drive business results.

Center of Excellence, Data Management

A centralized Data Management Services organization of data management professionals.

Central Processing Unit (CPU)

The part of a computer that reads, interprets, and performs instructions.

central-point cartogram

SEE chart, distance cartogram.

certificate

1. A token of authorization or authentication.
2. In data security, a computer data security object that includes identity information, validity specification, and a key.

certification

The process of reviewing something to verify it meets established standards.

Certified Business Intelligence Professional (CBIP)

A professional designation offered by The Data Warehouse Institute, using examinations developed and delivered by the Institute for Certification of Computing Professionals.

certified data

Passed data quality review, certifying it meets established standards.

Certified Data Management Professional (CDMP)

A professional certification program offered by DAMA International, using examinations developed by DAMA and the ICCP. Exam administration and delivery is handled by the ICCP.

chain of custody

The documentation of ownership of something, from capture, through possession, storage, and management, to disposition. This is especially important for compliance documentation. SEE ALSO data provenance.

chaining

1. *Verb.* To connect a series of commands or responses.
2. In cryptography, a method of encryption where each block defines or contributes to the encryption of the following blocks.

change control

The process of coordinating changes to a system, to minimize change-related errors and therefore improve data quality and system availability. Proposed changes need to be reviewed and evaluated for related impacts, grouped and scheduled, implemented and migrated through various test environments before being implemented into the production environment. Database change control disciplines are a very important responsibility of database administrators.

change data capture

The process of capturing changes made to a production data source. Change data capture is typically performed by reading the log file of the Database Management System of the source database. Change data capture consolidates units of work, ensures data is synchronized with the original source, and reduces data volume in a Data Warehousing environment.

characteristic

1. A distinguishing feature or quality. (dictionary.com based on Random House Dictionary)
2. *Adjective.* Pertaining to, constituting, or indicating the character or peculiar quality of a person or thing; typical; distinctive. (dictionary.com based on Random House Dictionary)
3. An abstraction of a property of an object or of a set of objects.

characteristic entity

SEE data entity, dependent.

chart

A visual representation of data, using shapes, colors, symbols, graphs, images, tables, diagrams, etc. to show patterns, relationships, or ideas, that makes it easier to understand, or gives context to create some form of information.

chart, affinity diagram

A form of visualization that shows patterns of ideas or data, by grouping them by topic or some attribute they share.

chart, area

A chart showing multiple lines from left to right, each which define the top line of an area within the chart. The areas are marked with colors, textures, and/or hatching. The areas may be overlapping or stacked.

chart, area cartogram

A chart that uses a geographic map of the world with the size of countries or their subdivisions distorted by the value of a property of that area such as population.

chart, argument slide

A diagram showing analysis of a claim in the form of a children's slide, where the premises and facts support the claim at the top of the slide, and consequences are represented by the actual slide, showing outcomes at the bottom of the slide.

chart, bar

A chart that shows bars to illustrate frequencies or values for individual categories.

chart, box plot

A chart that displays five values of a measurement where the median and quartile values are the center and edges of a box, and the lowest and highest values are the ends of lines extending from the box.

chart, bridge of negotiation

A diagram illustrating steps necessary for two disparate positions to come to a consensus in a middle area, crossing some gap between them, usually illustrated by a bridge over a river or chasm.

chart, bubble

A chart showing two dimensions on horizontal and vertical axes, and a third dimension in the size of the points.

chart, bullet

A variation of the bar chart, these feature a single, primary measure, compared to one or more other measures, such as a target or a quantitative scale, and displayed in qualitative ranges (poor, fair, good, etc.) by using variations of hue for a single color (which is helpful for colorblind eyes). These long narrow graphs can be grouped to save space, especially on web forms or dashboards.

chart, candlestick

A chart showing bars representing range of value change within a point's time interval.

chart, cartogram

A chart consisting of a geographic map modified to show some measurement of the map's area, contents, or qualities. Modifications can be to color or to proportional size. There are two types, area cartograms and distance cartograms.

chart, cascade

A chart with the X-axis showing a unit of measure and the Y-axis showing a rate per unit. Boxes show the result of X units x Y rate for a specific segment, such as customer. Tall thin boxes above the X-axis are desirable, long short boxes above the X-axis are less desirable, boxes below the X-axis are undesirable.

chart, causal loop diagram

A visual representation of a system's feedback loops, where positive loops cycle clockwise, and negative loops cycle counter-clockwise.

chart, cause-and-effect diagram

A chart that links an outcome to chains of possible contributing factors as tree structure working backwards from an event to determine possible root causes, drawn sideways so that it resembles the skeleton of a fish. Because the chart resembles the skeleton of a fish, it is often called a fishbone diagram. A quality improvement concept invented by the Japanese statistician Dr. Karu Ishakawa.

chart, class diagram

A type of diagram that shows a system's classes, contents, attributes, and relationships, including inheritance. UML is a common format for a class diagram.

chart, collaboration diagram

A representation of objects and their links to each other, sometimes including time and/or sequence of relationships. Numbers show the sequence of activities or messages.

chart, component diagram

A visual representation of the parts of a whole, usually a system, with sequences of dependencies between components shown.

chart, concentric circles

A form of visualization showing nested subsets of a set as circles within other circles, such as cities in states in countries in a total population, each level represented as the area of one of the circles.

chart, concept fan

A form of visualization where a concept is decomposed into components to the right, 'fanning' out levels.

chart, concept map

A form of visualization showing relationships among concepts as arrows between labeled boxes, usually in a downward branching hierarchy. SEE ALSO data model, conceptual.

chart, cone tree

A form of visualization that takes a tree diagram and turns it into a three-dimensional circle of attributes radiating from a parent.

chart, control

A graphical device for tracking process performance over time.

chart, coxcomb

SEE chart, polar area.

chart, Critical Path Method (CPM)

A form of visualization of the critical path for a set of interdependent activities, showing the longest discrete path through the tasks with the longest duration.

chart, cycle graph **Alternate form: cycle diagram**

A form of visualization showing cycles of a concept's stages, phases, or process steps in a clockwise path around a circle.

chart, data map

A form of visualization using a geographic map with overlaid data shapes using colors to illustrate ranges of values for each geographic block.

chart, decision tree

A graph of decisions and their possible consequences (including resource costs and risks) used to create a plan to reach a goal. Decision trees are constructed in order to help with making decisions. A decision tree is a special form of tree structure. Regression trees approximate real-valued functions (e.g., estimate the price of a house or a patient's length of stay in a hospital). Classification trees define the logic for categorization using Boolean variables such as gender (male or female) or game results (lose or win).

chart, distance cartogram

A chart consisting of a geographic map modified to show some relative travel times between points in a network.

chart, Edgeworth box

A form of visualization showing one pool of two fixed resources shared by two entities. Each point shows a possible division of resources between the entities. Curves can be drawn between points of equal value to both parties according to the value associated with each resource.

chart, event tree

A form of visualization that follows a process from a desired input through possible system events to final consequences. SEE ALSO chart, fault tree.

chart, fault tree **Alternate form: failure tree**

A form of visualization showing top-down, deductive analytical steps through Boolean logic gates to all possible failure states.

chart, force field diagram **Alternate form: forcefield diagram**

A form of visualization where a topic is in the center, and forces for and against the topic are listed on each side.

chart, functional decomposition

An outline or hierarchy diagram depicting the hierarchical decomposition of processes into their component processes. A functional decomposition can be depicted vertically as an outline or horizontally as a hierarchy chart.

chart, funnel

A form of visualization where inputs are drawn entering through the large end of a funnel, and outputs are drawn leaving the small end.

chart, Gantt

A horizontal bar chart used in project management; a graphical illustration of a schedule that helps to plan, coordinate, and track specific tasks in a project. Named for Henry Gantt.

chart, heat map

A chart where one set of values is represented by areas of rectangles, and other sets of values are represented by colors. invented by Professor Ben Shneiderman at the University of Maryland. Used to look at large, fast-changing sets of structured data. In this chart, the size of a rectangle reflects its importance, and color conveys the speed of change. Heat maps are often used in applications to monitor and analyze changes in stock market and portfolio data in financial services applications. SEE ALSO chart, tree map.

chart, heaven and hell

A graphic way to show positive and negative effects of some system or action, by illustrating the positive items at the top as 'heaven', and the negative at the bottom as 'hell', and neutral items in the center.

chart, house of quality

A form of visualization that resembles a house, showing interactions between 'whats' and 'hows', including 'hows vs. hows' as the triangular roof. Each comparison is a cell containing an evaluation as positive, neutral, or negative. Additional annexes on sides and bottom may include whys, how muches, etc.

chart, hype-cycle

A form of visualization that divides the process of adoption of something into five cycles: Trigger, Peak, Trough, Slope, and Plateau.

chart, hyperbolic tree **Alternate form: hypertree**

A form of visualization where a tree is displayed as a node-link diagram in a circular manner radiating out from the root rather than only descending.

chart, iceberg diagram

A form of visualization that has a medial line dividing attributes into two categories: visible, and invisible (or hidden). The visible attributes are listed above the line (the visible part of the iceberg); the invisible attributes are listed below the line.

chart, Kagi

A chart showing movement of a value regardless of time, based solely on some time-independent criteria.

chart, layer

Shows the decomposition of some object or system by exposing internal layers sequentially.

chart, lifecycle diagram

A form of visualization of a process or system over time compared to value at each point in time, grouped into four stages: R&D/initiation, ascent, maturity, and decline.

chart, line

A chart that shows ordered points connected by a line to show trends.

chart, Magic Quadrant (MQ)

A form of visualization that uses a quartered chart comparing companies selling similar products according to their completeness of vision and ability to execute on that vision. The quarters are Leaders (high on vision and execution), Challengers (high on execution, low on vision), Visionaries (high on vision, low on execution), and niche players (low on both vision and execution). Developed by Gartner, Inc. to evaluate vendors in specific market segments.

chart, marimekko **Alternate form: mekko chart, matrix chart, eikosogram**

A chart with the X-axis showing a list of values within a category (such as a list of business units) where the width is each bar's relative magnitude compared to the others and the Y-axis showing percentages or ratios. Each value is then a stacked area chart with each area shown as a percentage of the total for that X value.

chart, metro map

A form of visualization showing the progression of a topic, showing points of interest as subway or bus stops on a route to a current state.

chart, Open-High-Low-Close (OHLC)

A chart showing movements in a value over time at different points within each time grain, using both lines and bars. This chart shows values for high and low separate from those for start and end of each time period point on the chart.

chart, organization

A form of visualization showing the structure of an organization using trees and levels to show relative hierarchies of teams or individuals.

chart, parallel coordinates

A form of visualization showing a series of vertical parallel lines representing dimensions or axes, and horizontally oriented lines intersecting points on those exes. During development, the ordering of the vertical axes may need to be shifted to better show patterns in the coordinates.

chart, Pareto

A chart showing both bars and a line, where the line shows the cumulative total of the individual bars going left to right.

chart, performance charting

A form of visualization using a series of horizontal lines, each representing an evaluation range of a specific quality. A set of processes or performances are evaluated against the lines, and the points of the evaluations are connected into a line for each process or performance.

chart, perspectives

A form of visualization resembling looking down into a box, with the floor of the box being the main topic, the left and right sides representing positive and negative input or experiences, the lower side representing prior knowledge or experience, and the top side representing open questions or issues.

chart, petri net **Alternate form: place/transition net, P/T net**

A form of visualization for distributed systems, using bars and circles to represent events and conditions respectively. Directed arrows show the path between the events and conditions in the system.

chart, pie

A chart that shows percentages as sectors (slices) of a circle, resembling a pie.

chart, polar area

A chart showing a circle with sectors, using radius length of sectors to show relative differences. May have multiple sections to each sector to compare multiple values.

chart, Porter's five forces

A framework for evaluating strategic positions, suing five forces: threat from competitors, threat of substitute products or services, bargaining power of customers, bargaining power of suppliers, and barriers to entry. Named for Michael Porter.

chart, portfolio

A quartered plot chart used most frequently to determine priorities in business, using growth rate on one axis and market share as the other. Creates four categories: stars (high growth and market share), cash cows (low growth, high market share), dogs (low growth and market share), and question marks (high growth and low market share).

chart, process flow

A visual representation of how control moves between logical processes (how the end state of a process serves as the start state for other processes).

chart, radar

A chart representing three or more quantitative values represented on radial axes of a circle.

chart, rich picture

A form of visualization that represents complex or ill-defined topics by using diagrams, images, sketches, metaphors, icons, or other pictorial representations and linking them to each other and to short text descriptions to show understanding of a topic.

chart, scatter plot

A two-dimensional representation of values of a data set. Usually used to show dependency of one uncontrolled variable vs. another controlled variable.

chart, semantic network

A form of visualization consisting of vertices (concepts) and directed or undirected edges (relationships).

chart, sequence

A representation of the time sequence of objects participating in a process over time. Swim lane diagrams are a form of sequence diagram.

chart, snaky

A specific type of flow diagram in which the width of arrows is proportionate to the flow quantity or size.

chart, spark line

A chart showing trends and variations of multiple measurements over time in one chart.

chart, spectrogram

A form of visualization using time-varying image that shows the spectral density of a signal over time, using horizontal axis as time, vertical axis as frequency, and hue of the representation as amplitude.

chart, stakeholder map

A form of visualization where a project is in the center, and stakeholders are illustrated in terms of proximity of responsibility to the project. Internal stakeholders are above a central line through the project, external stakeholders below the line.

chart, stakeholder rating map

A form of visualization using a quartered chart to show stakeholders in terms of importance and influence.

chart, stock and flow

A visual representation of a system where quantities of something travel through the system from point to point over time.

chart, strategy map

A form of visualization used to document strategic goals from multiple perspectives.

chart, supply demand curve

A form of visualization which plots price vertically and quantity horizontally. The supply curve (usually trending upward left to right) shows the price per quantity offered by a supplier. The demand curve (usually trending downward left to right) shows the price per quantity desired by consumers. Equilibrium is the intersection of both curves.

chart, swim lane

A form of process flow diagram that shows involvement over time within the process for multiple equivalent actors, such as teams, departments, systems, etc.

chart, technology roadmap

A form of visualization that matches goals of different time horizons with the specific technologies necessary to meet or enable those goals.

chart, temple diagram

A form of visualization showing an image with a foundation, and two or more pillars supporting a roof, with or without a cloud of distantly related topics. The foundation contains fundamental elements, the pillars group supporting elements, and the roof includes overarching topics that cover all the pillars/groups.

chart, timeline

A chart showing a horizontal line or bar containing points labeled with dates and/or events.

chart, tree

A method of representing a hierarchical set of data in a graphical form, with fewer nodes at the either the top (i.e., descendent genealogy) or bottom (i.e., ancestor genealogy).

chart, tree map **Alternate form: treemap**

A chart where one set of values is represented by areas of rectangles, and other sets of values are represented by colors. invented by Professor Ben Shneiderman at the University of Maryland. Used to look at large, fast-changing sets of structured data. In this chart, the size of a rectangle reflects its importance, and color conveys urgency (blue shades for positive, red shades for negative). SEE ALSO chart, heat map.

chart, use case diagram

A form of visualization showing actors and roles when interacting with objects in defined scenarios. UML or flow charts are common formats for use case diagrams.

chart, vee diagram

A form of visualization that shows a problem, the steps to planning a solution, and then steps to evaluate the results afterwards. Shaped like a V, hence the name.

chart, Venn diagram

A form of visualization that shows all potential logical relationships between a finite set of objects. Used most often to illustrate the concepts of UNION, INTERSECTION, and EXCLUSIVE OR of sets.

chart, waterfall

A chart that shows cumulative effects of sequentially applied values.

check digit

An extra digit added to a computer code to check accuracy, calculated from the other digits in the code. SEE ALSO parity.

checkpoint

1. A synchronization step between a data system and an application where all changes to the data system are recorded to disk and noted as complete.
2. A copy of the state of a system at a point in time.

Chief Data Officer (CDO)

A corporate officer who is responsible for managing the enterprise's data assets.

chief data steward

An executive data steward who serves as the chair of the Data Governance Council and as the primary business champion of a data management program.

Chief Information Officer (CIO)

A job title for the head of the Information Technology group within an organization. They often report to Chief Executive Officer. The prominence of this position has risen greatly as information technology has become a more important part of organizations.

Chief Knowledge Officer (CKO)

An organizational leader responsible for ensuring that the organization maximizes the value it achieves through the organization's collective knowledge: their intellectual capital (including patents), the skills and experience of their people, the maturity of their processes, and their customer relationships. The CKO is responsible for managing these intangible assets through knowledge management, fostering innovation, sharing best practices, facilitating communication and avoiding knowledge loss after organizational restructuring.

Chief Risk Officer **Alternate form: Chief Risk Management Officer**

The executive accountable for discovery and governance of significant risks (strategic, reputational, operational, financial, or compliance-related) and related opportunities to an organization. Data Governance is a form of risk management, and may be part of this executive's organization.

Chief Technology Officer (CTO)

An executive position focused on technical issues in an enterprise. In technical industries, the CTO heads research and development. In other enterprises, the term is sometimes synonymous with Chief Information Officer, while sometimes the CTO is subordinate to the CIO (with responsibility for the IT infrastructure), and sometimes the CTO is the superior of multiple CIOs across the enterprise.

circle graph

SEE chart, pie.

citizen

A person recognized as a member of a public state, with associated obligations and rights. Not the same as customer.

citizen advocacy

The perception that a government does what is best for its citizens, not just what is best for its own bottom line.

Citizen Data Integration (CDI)

Solutions for capturing and maintaining accurate, up-to-date data about individual citizens and delivering information in an actionable form "just in time" at citizen touch points. A specialized form of Master Data Management, focusing on citizen master data.

Citizen Relationship Management (CRM)

Establishing relationships with individual citizens and then using that information to treat different citizens differently. Census profiles and taxpayer analysis are examples of decision support activities that can affect the success of citizen relationships. Effective CRM is dependent on high quality master data about individuals and organizations (citizen data integration).

clarity

A measurement that evaluates freedom from obscurity or extraneous data.

class — **Alternate form: classify**

1. A type or category of things with common attributes. Members of a class conform to the definition of the class. Type and category are synonyms for class. Classes are the basis for object-oriented analysis, design, and development, where a class is roughly equivalent to an entity with the addition of described functional behavior. SEE ALSO method.
2. A set of objects that share the same attributes, operations, methods, relationships, and semantics.

class diagram

SEE chart, class diagram.

class word

A word used in an attribute's name to show what type of data is contained therein, usually applied at the end. SEE ALSO prime word.

class, attribute

In .net framework, associates information with a target element.

class, process

In .net framework, associates information with local system processes.

class, role

Represents the security level that can be assigned to users.

classic data warehouse development

The traditional, top-down comprehensive approach to implementing Business Intelligence, including: building an enterprise data model, defining the Data Warehouse architecture, designing and constructing the physical database, designing and constructing and testing extract-transform-load programs, and populating the database using current sources and historical data conversions. Used in contrast to incremental Data Warehouse development.

classification

1. Generally, a set of discrete, exhaustive, and mutually exclusive observations that can be assigned to one or more variables to be measured in the collation and/or presentation of data.
2. In data modeling, the arrangement of entities into supertypes and subtypes.
3. In object-oriented design, the arrangement of objects into classes, and the assignment of objects to these categories.

classification and regression tree (CART)

SEE tree, classification and regression.

classification framework

Organizes the structure and views that encompass enterprise architecture. (DAMA-DMBOK Guide, 1st edition, pg. 67.)

classification system

Arrangement or division of objects into groups based on characteristics that the objects have in common.

client

1. Generally, an existing or prospective customer.
2. In client/server systems, a device (desktop, laptop, PDA, etc.) that communicates with a server.
3. In client/server programming, a software program used to contact and obtain data from a server software program on another computer. Each client program is designed to work with one or more specific kinds of server programs.

client/server architecture

SEE architecture, client/server.

Clinger-Cohen Act (CCA)

A more familiar name for the Information Technology Management Reform Act, a United States federal law co-authored in 1996 by Congressman William Clinger and Senator William Cohen, designed to improve the way the federal government acquires and manages information technology. It requires departments and programs to use performance-based management principles for acquiring IT, and it mandates the use of a formal enterprise architecture for all federal agencies.

closed architecture

SEE architecture, closed.

cloud computing

An architecture in which all access to shared resources is provided on-demand via self-service internet applications. Formerly known as distributed computing. Can be used as a delivery mechanism for Software-As-A-Service and Hardware-as-a-Service.

cloud services

Services that are made available in a distributed computing (cloud) environment.

clustered index

SEE index, clustered.

clustering

Verb. To output a smaller data set based on grouping criteria of common attributes.

code

1. Generally, a language-independent set of letters, numbers, or symbols that represent a concept whose meaning is described in a natural language.
2. In software, the program language lines of instruction that make up software.
3. In data modeling, a shorthand key value representing the domain value of an attribute. Code sets are intensional domain value sets.
4. *Verb.* To represent data in a form that can be accepted by a data entry program.

code management

1. The definition and maintenance of coded data values, descriptions, definitions, cross references, parent-child rollups, and other relationships for the valid instances of limited (intensional) domains. Code management is a specialized form of Master Data Management. It is a key responsibility of operational data stewards, because it has a very significant impact on overall data quality. Code management typically includes an approval process for all code value additions, changes, and retirements.
2. The definition and maintenance of program code for the purposes of controlling development on production systems.

code table

A relational database table containing rows for each valid value in a finite domain. Code tables contain some form of encoded data values. Code tables are reference data, maintained through code management.

coded data value

Any data value that has been encoded or shortened in some manner. (Brackett 2011)

coding

The process of converting verbal or textual information into codes representing classes within a classification system, to facilitate data processing, storage, or dissemination.

coding error

1. The assignment of an incorrect code to a data item
2. In software, an error in program lines of instruction that make up software or data transformation routines

cohesion

A close working relationship between parts, complete enough when together to enable some degree of autonomy without other extraneous parts.

cold backup

SEE backup, cold.

collaboration diagram

SEE chart, collaboration diagram.

collation

The assembly of documents or data entities or attributes into a standard order, such as alphabetical.

column

In data modeling, a data attribute as implemented in a relational database as a vertical component of a table, similar to a field in a flat file record.

columnar database

SEE database, columnar.

column-oriented database

SEE database, column-oriented.

combined key

SEE key, composite.

comment

In data modeling, supplementary descriptive text which can be attached to data or meta-data.

Commercial Off The Shelf (COTS)

Acronym to identify software that is used as-is, without any customization.

commit

The SQL statement that concludes a unit of work (database transaction).

Common Body of Knowledge (CBK)

SEE Body of Knowledge, Common.

Common Data Architecture (CDI)

A single, formal, comprehensive, organization-wide, data architecture that provides a common context within which all data are understood, documented, integrated, and managed. It transcends all data at the organization's disposal, includes primitive and derived data; atomic and combined data; fundamental and specific data; automated and non-automated (manual) data; current and historical data; data within and without the organization; high-level and low-level data; and disparate and similar data. It includes data in purchased software, custom-built application databases, programs, screens, reports, and documents. It includes all data used by traditional information systems, expert systems, executive information systems, geographic information systems, Data Warehouses, object oriented systems, and so on. It includes centralized and decentralized data regardless of where they reside, who uses them, or how they are used. (Brackett 2011)

common data architecture

A representative of an actual common data architecture built by an organization for their data resource, based on the concepts, principles, and techniques of the Common Data Architecture. The term Common Data Architecture (capitalized) represents the vision, construct, and the concepts, principles, and techniques for developing and managing an organization's data resource. (Brackett 2011)

Common Gateway Interface (CGI)

A standard protocol that defines web server delegation of webpage generation to console applications, known as CGI scripts.

Common Object Model (COM)

Microsoft's programming specification for object interoperability through sets of predefined routines called interfaces.

Common Object Request Broker Architecture (CORBA)

The Object Management Group vendor-independent architecture and infrastructure for object-based programming interoperability. SEE ALSO Common Object Model.

common word

A word that has consistent meaning whenever it is used in a data name. (Brackett 2011)

communication diagram

A form of UML diagram that shows the interactions between objects or parts in terms of sequenced messages. Each message is numbered regardless of its placement on the diagram, so that the reader can follow the path by following the numbers sequentially.

Community Of Interest (COI)

SEE Data Management Community of Interest.

comparability

The extent to which differences between statistics can be attributed to differences between the true values of the statistical characteristics.

Complex Event Processing (CEP)

An emerging technology for building and managing information systems. The goal of CEP is to enable the information contained in the events flowing through all of the layers of the enterprise IT infrastructure to be discovered, understood in terms of its impact on high-level management goals and business processes, and acted upon in real time. This includes events created by new technologies such as RFID.

complex fact data attribute

A data attribute that contains any combination of multiple values, multiple facts, and variable facts, and might be formatted in several different ways. (Brackett 2011)

compliance

1. The act of agreement to follow external government or industry regulations.
2. The process of conforming, completing, performing or adapting actions to meet the rules, demands, or wishes of another party.

component

1. A discrete object or entity that is a part of a larger system.
2. A modular part of a system that encapsulates its content, and whose manifestation is replaceable within its environment. (Object Management Group 2008, pg. 146.)

Component Assemblies

Zachman Framework row name, matches Technicians as Implementers.

Component Content Management System (CCMS)

A content management system that manages low-level objects (image, table, etc.) rather than higher-level documents.

component diagram

SEE chart, component diagram.

composite attribute

SEE data attribute, composite.

composite key

SEE key, composite.

composite model

A model that includes other models and the relationships between them.

composite partitioning

SEE partitioning, composite.

compound key

SEE key, composite.

compound primary key

A key that contains multiple home data attributes in their home data entity. (Brackett 2011)

comprehensive

Adjective. Covering completely or broadly. (Brackett 2011)

comprehensive data definition

A data definition that provides a complete, meaningful, easily read, readily understood definition that thoroughly explains the content and meaning of the data with respect to the business. (Brackett 2011)

Computer Aided Software Engineering (CASE)

Sometimes more broadly referred to as Computer Aided Systems Engineering. The use of software tools (CASE tools) to assist in the development and maintenance of software. All aspects of the software development lifecycle can be supported by software tools, so tools for project management, business and functional analysis, system design, code storage, compiler translation and testing can all be considered CASE tools. CASE tools are typically tools concerned with analysis and design. Sometimes planning and analysis tools are referred to as "upper CASE" tools, while lower level design, code generation, configuration management and testing tools are called "lower CASE" tools. The term CASE is used less frequently today, however, data modeling tools and UML object modeling tools today can still be considered CASE tools.

Computer Aided Software Engineering management **Alternate form: CASE management**

An old-fashioned term for the management of meta-data between the encyclopedias of multiple CASE tools, of the same type or different types.

Computer Aided Software Engineering tool **Alternate form: CASE tool**

Automated modeling tools for used model-driven systems planning, analysis, design, and development. "Upper CASE tools" are modeling tools used for planning, analysis, and high-level logical design. "Lower CASE tools" are used for program design, code generation, version control, and testing. Data modeling tools may be both upper and lower CASE tools. Object modeling tools using UML represent the latest generation of CASE tools.

Computer-Generated Imagery (CGI)

The application of computer graphics to video and printed media.

Computerized Patient Record (CPR)

SEE electronic health record.

concatenated key

SEE key, composite.

concentric circles

SEE chart, concentric circles.

concept

A unit of knowledge created by a unique combination of characteristics.

concept fan

SEE chart, concept fan.

concept map

SEE chart, concept map.

Conceptual Data Model (CDM)

SEE data model, conceptual.

conceptual model

SEE model, conceptual.

concise

Adjective. Including only necessary parts; not including unnecessary details or attributes.

concurrency

The simultaneous execution of processes against the database.

concurrency control

The control of process contention for resources within multi-process systems.

concurrency transparency

The ability of one process to see information about other processes that are executing at the same time.

conditional data structure rule

A data integrity rule that specifies the conditional data cardinality for a data relation between two data entities when conditions or exceptions apply. It specifies both the conditions and exceptions with respect to the business, not with respect to the Database Management System. (Brackett 2011)

cone tree chart

SEE chart, cone tree.

Confidence Interval (CI)

The space between an upper and lower limit of a range, where there is a high probability of the inclusion of a particular value.

confidence level

A measurement of certainty that a statistical prediction is accurate.

confidentiality

1. Ensuring that information is accessible only to those authorized to have access. ISO-17799.
2. In data security, a property of data indicating the extent to which their unauthorized disclosure could be prejudicial or harmful to the interest of the source or other relevant parties.

configuration management

A generic term that is often used to describe the whole of the activities concerned with the creation, maintenance, and control of databases and their environments.

conformance

Agreement to follow internal policies, standards, procedures, and architecture requirements.

conformed dimension

A dimension that means and represents the same thing when linked to different fact tables.

conformity

1. The state of being similar to accepted standards or to the attributes of peers.
2. The process of becoming similar to the attributes of peers or to a standard.

connected

The characteristic of a graph in which there exists at least one path from every node to every other node in the graph.

consensus

The agreement of a group to a decision, judgment or definition, when all stakeholders present can say, "I can live with it."

consistent

Adjective. Uniformity or agreement among things or parts of things. Having internal logical and numerical coherence; having no internal contradiction.

consolidation

The process of combining and aggregating data from different systems and possibly disparate formats to create a unified view of information.

constraint

1. Generally, a restriction on a business action and the resulting data. For example, "only wholesale customers may place wholesale orders."
2. In data management, a specification of what may be contained in a data or meta-data set in terms of the content or, for data only, in terms of the set of key combinations to which specific attributes (defined by the data structure) may be attached, and how. Examples of how include dependency (must have at least one), exclusivity (at most one; non-overlapping), subset, or equality.

constraint, domain

A type of constraint on an attribute that defines the values that may be assigned, through limits, lists, or ranges.

constraint, key

A type of constraint on a data set that restricts the combinations of attribute values according to certain rules (uniqueness, etc.)

content

1. The information contained within documents and web pages.
2. The name of a DCMI element set (Coverage, Description, Type, Relation, Source, Subject, Title). SEE ALSO Dublin Core Metadata Initiative.

content management

The processes, techniques, and technologies for organizing, categorizing, and structuring of information resources so that they can be stored, published, and reused in multiple ways. Content management is a critical data management discipline for data found in text, graphics, images, and video or audio recordings.

content management system

A system used to collect, manage, and publish information content, storing it as components or whole documents, while maintaining the links between components. It may also provide for content revision control.

content mashup

SEE mashup, content.

content neutrality **Alternate form: vendor neutral**

A DAMA policy stating its intention to avoid reference to specific technology vendor firms and their products.

context

1. Generally, facts or circumstances that relate to a situation or event.
2. In software design, the minimal set of data required for a task that allows interruption and resumption of the task without error.

contextual model

SEE model, contextual.

contextualization

The process of adding language to signal relevant aspects of an event or data attribute.

contingent relationship

SEE relationship, contingent.

continuous availability

A ready state of functionality that seeks to guarantee computing system operation despite any challenging event. Continuous availability requires seamless availability during any planned or unplanned event and seamless recovery of applications, data, and data transactions committed prior to the event.

continuum

Shows the transition of a topic from one extreme to the other, and all interesting points in between. Usually shown on a double-headed arrow, with each end being one extreme.

contributor

DCMI element in element set Intellectual Property: an entity that contributes to a resource. SEE Dublin Core Metadata Initiative.

control

The mechanism used to maintain acceptable performance of a process.

control activity

In the DAMA-DMBOK Functional Framework, a supervisory activity performed on an on-going basis. SEE ALSO activity group.

control chart

SEE chart, control.

control data

Data that guides a process, such as indicators, flags, counters, and parameters.

control limit, lower

The minimum or earliest acceptable value in a range of acceptable values.

control limit, upper

The maximum or latest acceptable value in a range of acceptable values.

Control OBjectives for Information and related Technology (COBIT)

Standards for IT governance, published by the IT Governance Institute, and available online at www.aisca.org/cobit. CobiT standards are organized into five subject areas, including Resource Management.

controlled vocabulary

A defined list of explicitly allowed terms and their definitions. The organization of a controlled vocabulary into a parent-child hierarchy is a taxonomy.

conversion

1. In systems, the migration from the use of one application to another.
2. In data management, the process of preparing, reengineering, cleansing and transforming data and loading it into a new target data structure. Typically, the term is used to describe a one-time event as part of a new database implementation. However, it is sometimes used to describe an ongoing operational procedure.

cookie

An identifier used by a web application to associate a present website visitor with their previous activity with that company.

cooperative processing

A style of application processing in which the presentation, business logic, and data management are split among two or more software services operating on one or more computers. In cooperative processing, individual software programs (services) perform specific functions that are invoked by means of parameterized messages exchanged between them.

coordinating data steward

A business data steward with additional responsibility for

a) leading Data Stewardship Teams, and
b) representing data stewardship issues and integrating team models and specifications on a Data Stewardship Committee.

copyright

The set of exclusive privileges granted to an author, creator, or owner of a work, allowing control of use of that work, including copying, distribution, and adaptation of the work.

Corporate Information Factory (CIF)

An architecture promoted by Bill Inmon that describes the complete data lifecycle within an organization through multiple layers and components of architecture in order to satisfy both operational and analytical needs.

corporate performance management

SEE business performance management.

correlation

A predictive relationship between two factors, such that when one factor changes, you can predict the nature, direction and/or amount of change in the other factor. Not necessarily a cause-and-effect relationship.

correlation database

SEE database, correlation.

correlation regression

A function that describes the correlation of the values of a data set to a line.

Cost Benefit Analysis (CBA)

Comparison of the estimated value of business benefits over time to the estimated cost of expenditures required to realize these benefits.

coverage

DCMI element in element set Content: the topic, jurisdiction, or spatial scope of a resource. SEE Dublin Core Metadata Initiative.

covering index

SEE index, covering.

Coxcomb chart

SEE chart, polar area.

Create-Read-Update-Delete (CRUD)

A list of the only functions of data in persistent storage, in a convenient acronym form.

Create-Read-Update-Delete matrix **Alternate form: CRUD matrix**

An information value chain analysis tool, documenting that a given organization, role, process or application "Creates", "Reads", "Updates", and/or "Deletes" data in a given subject area, entity or attribute. CRUD matrices are the vehicle for information value chain analysis. There are many different kinds of CRUD matrices. Each establishes the linkage between a data model and another model (data-to-process, data-to-organization, or data-to-application).

creation date

The date on which the record, data or meta-data item was created.

creator

DCMI element in element set Intellectual Property: an entity that is responsible for the first existence of a resource instance. SEE Dublin Core Metadata Initiative.

Critical Path Method (CPM)

SEE chart, Critical Path Method.

Critical Success Factor (CSF)

One of the few most important prerequisite conditions necessary for an enterprise to reach its goals.

cross-functional

Adjective. Interest in data or process by more than one organization in an enterprise.

cross-sell

The practice of suggesting the purchase of a related product to customers who are already making a purchase.

cross-tabulation

Cross-referencing of data from one or more sources for analysis or reporting.

cube

SEE data cube.

currency

1. A medium of exchange, usually a form of money.
2. Monetary denomination of the object being measured.

currentness

The degree to which data represents reality as of a point in time.

currentness date **Alternate form: currency date**

A date when the data is considered valid. Also known as the "as of" date.

customer

A person or organization whose needs are important to the enterprise or person, and whose satisfaction with the products and services provided by the enterprise determines its success, failure, and effectiveness. SEE ALSO citizen.

customer advocacy

The perception that an organization does what is best for its customers, not just what is best for its own bottom line.

Customer Data Integration (CDI)

Solutions for capturing and maintaining accurate, up-to-date data about individual customers and delivering information in an actionable form "just in time" at customer touch points. A specialized form of Master Data Management, focusing on customer master data. SEE ALSO Citizen Data Integration.

Customer Relationship Management (CRM)

Establishing relationships with individual customers and then using that information to treat different customers differently. Customer buying profiles and churn analysis are examples of decision support activities that can affect the success of customer relationships. Effective CRM is dependent on high quality master data about individuals and organizations (customer data integration). SEE ALSO Citizen Relationship Management.

cyber marketing

Any type of Internet-based promotion through web sites, targeted e-mail, Internet bulletin boards, e-commerce, and online social networking mechanisms.

cyberspace

A metaphoric abstraction for a virtual reality existing inside computers and on computer networks. The de facto term for the Internet during the 1990s, coined by science fiction writer William Gibson, who referred to it as "a consensual hallucination experienced daily by billions of legitimate operators in every nation". While cyberspace should not be confused with the real internet, a web site might be said to "exist in cyberspace." According to this interpretation, events taking place on the Internet are not therefore happening in the countries where the participants or the servers are physically located, but instead are happening "in cyberspace".

cycle graph

SEE chart, cycle graph.

cycle time

The time required to execute a process from start to finish.

D

DAMA Foundation, The

The Research and Education Affiliate of DAMA International with a mission to promote development of a formal, certified, recognized, and respected data management profession. Currently supporting this effort through publication of the DAMA Dictionary and DAMA-DMBOK.

DAMA International

An international not-for-profit association of data resource management professionals with chapters and members-at-large around the world, dedicated to advancing the concepts and practices of managing data, information and knowledge as enterprise assets. DAMA International is the leading data management professional organization worldwide.

DAMA-DMBOK Functional Framework

The organizing structure for the DAMA-DMBOK Guide, consisting of a functional decomposition of ten data management functions mapped against seven environmental elements (Goals & Principles, Activities, Deliverables, Roles & Responsibilities, Practices & Techniques, Technology, and Organization & Culture). (DAMA-DMBOK GUIDE 1st edition, pg. 12)

DAMA-DMBOK Guide

A document distributed by DAMA International, intended to be a "definitive introduction" to the Data Management Body of Knowledge.

dashboard

A Business Intelligence application that consolidates, aggregates, and graphically presents performance measurements compared to goals, arranged so that information can be monitored at a glance. Dashboards can be used to manage any scope of operations.

data

1. Facts represented as text, numbers, graphics, images, sound, or video. Data is the raw material used to represent information, or from which information can be derived. (Everest 2010)
2. The individual facts that are out of context, and have no meaning by themselves. They are often referred to as raw data, such as 123.45. Data have historically been defined as plural; datum is the singular form. (Brackett 2011)
3. "The digital shadow of haphazard events indifferently recorded." (Terry Hanold)

data acceptance

The formal, sometimes highly rigorous, process associated with acknowledging that data has been delivered or accepted for use in an acquiring system or organization.

data accuracy

The degree to which a data attribute value closely and correctly describes its business entity instance (the "real life" entities) as of a point in time.

data acquisition

1. The collection of processes of identification, selection, and mapping of source data to target data, including detection of source data changes, data extraction techniques, timing of data extracts, data transformation techniques, frequency of database loads and levels of data summary.
2. The activity performed to obtain data, or have access to it under either limited or unlimited rights for use.

Data Administration (DA)

The organization and management of data in multiple types of storage, including databases, spreadsheets, and image or content management systems.

Data Administrator (DA)

An individual or organization responsible for specifying, acquiring, and maintaining software for data management, and the security and validation of the contents, including the data dictionary and data models.

data analysis

The study and presentation of data to create information and knowledge.

data analyst

A business systems analyst who identifies data requirements, defines data, and develops and maintains data models.

data appliance

1. A combination of hardware, software, Database Management System, and storage, all under one umbrella; a "black box" that yields high performance in both speed and storage and makes data access simpler.
2. Servers built specifically for data transformation and distribution. These servers integrate with existing infrastructure either directly as a plug in, or peripherally as a network connection. (DAMA-DMBOK 1st edition pg. 35)

Data Architect (DA)

A master data analyst, responsible for the overall data requirements of an organization, its data architecture and data models, and the design of the databases and data integration solutions that support the organization.

data architecture

SEE architecture, data.

data architecture management

Defining the blueprint for managing data resources.

data architecture quality

The degree to which data models and database designs are stable, flexible, reusable, aligned with enterprise goals and supportive of data integrity.

data architecture, analysis, and design

The definition and modeling of the information needs of the enterprise and the designs to meet those needs. Includes information needs analysis, enterprise data modeling, definition of related data architecture, and project-related conceptual, logical and physical data modeling (physical database design is considered part of database management). Previous name of one of the ten data management functions identified in the DAMA-DMBOK Functional Framework.

data architecture, enterprise

1. A master set of data models and design approaches identifying the strategic data requirements and the components of data management solutions, usually at an enterprise level. Enterprise data architecture typically consists of
    a) an enterprise data model (contextual/subject area, conceptual or logical),
    b) state transition diagrams depicting the lifecycle of major entities,
    c) a robust information value chain analysis identifying data stakeholder roles, organizations, processes and applications, and
    d) data integration architecture identifying how data will flow between applications and databases.
2. The data integration architecture may divide into database architecture, Master Data Management architecture, Data Warehouse/Business Intelligence architecture, and meta-data architecture. Some enterprises also include
    a) lists of controlled domain values (code sets), and
    b) the responsibility assignments of data stewards to subject areas, entities, and code sets.
3. The enterprise data architecture is an important part of the larger enterprise architecture that includes business, process and technology architecture.
4. The "data" column of the Zachman Framework for Enterprise Architecture identifies six different classes of design artifacts, each representing a different level of abstraction:
    - Row 1: Objectives/Scope (contextual) – Planner View: a list of subject areas and/or entities important to the business (may be a class hierarchy identifying supertype/subtype inheritance between entities).
    - Row 2: Enterprise Model (conceptual) – Owner View: a conceptual data model showing the business relationships between entities.
    - Row 3: System Model (logical) – Designer View: a logical data model (a fully attributed and normalized logical data model).
    - Row 4: Technology Model (physical) – Builder View: a physical data model (tables, columns).
    - Row 5: Detailed Representations (out-of-context) – Sub-contractor View: data definitions (DDL).
    - Row 6: Functioning Enterprise: the actual data as stored in implemented databases.

data archival

The process that supports long-term storage of scientific data and methods used to read or interpret it. Data archival is a step along the path of data preservation, and can be phased for online, near online, or offline storage availability. The data archival process is an important part of data migration and data refresh.

Data As A Service (DAAS)

A model of delivering data where a provider licenses access via web based servers for on-demand use.

data assimilation

Most prevalently used in geosciences, this is the process of combining data samples having specific sample criteria with projected data from a model to create and improve a unified consistent physical system definition.

data attribute

1. An inherent fact, property, or characteristic describing an entity or object; the logical representation of a physical field or relational table column. A given attribute has the same format, interpretation, and domain for all occurrences of an entity. Attributes may contain adjective values (red, round, active, etc.).
2. A unit of data for which the definition, identification, representation, and permissible values are specified by means of a set of characteristics.
3. A representation of a data characteristic variation in the logical or physical data model. A data attribute may or may not be atomic. SEE ALSO attribute.

data attribute domain

The set of possible values for an attribute. The values must conform to the definition of the attribute (such as type or size), and may be expressed by enumeration, or by any combination of ranges and individual values, including values and ranges that are excluded from the set.

data attribute value

An instance of an attribute type or domain.

data attribute, composite

A composite attribute is one that is composed from the concatenation of other attributes.

data attribute, derived

An attribute created via calculation from some other attribute(s), either within the same object, or within a linked or referenced object. SEE ALSO data, derived.

data attribute, multi-valued

An attribute or data item which can have multiple values (instances) for an instance of the entity of which it is an attribute. Such an arrangement forms a many-to-many relationship between the entity type and the attribute type, unless each unique value of the attribute can only be associated with at most one instance of the entity, in which case it forms a hierarchical relationship (1:M). (Everest 2010)

data attribute, type 1

An attribute where history is not preserved - all changes overwrite the attribute at the time of the change.

data attribute, type 2

An attribute where all history is preserved by requiring new rows be written that include the new data. The row with the old data is untouched except to update an expiration date or current row indicator.

data attribute, type 3

An attribute where some history is preserved within the same record or row, in separate columns. When new data arrives, old data is moved to other columns within the same row, and the new data overwrites the old data in the column assigned to hold the current value.

data capture

The process by which collected data are put into a machine-readable form.

data cardinality

In relationships, the characteristic of a relationship that specifies the upper and lower bounds of how many instances of one entity or object type can be related to each instance of the same or some other entity or object type. Cardinality is separately specified at each end of the relationship. At each end the choices are 0, 1, or M. Combining the cardinality at both ends of a binary relationship, yields 3 x 9 - 1 = 8 possibilities (0:0 is not a valid option).

data certification

The process of verifying and stating that a data set's contents meets expected standards. SEE ALSO certification.

data chaos

A state where multiple redundant, inconsistent databases contain the same data attribute used for a similar purpose, rated by the maximum count of instances of a single data attribute.

data characteristic

An individual fact that describes or characterizes a data subject. It represents a business feature and contains a single fact, or related facts, about a data subject. (Brackett 2011)

data characteristic substitution

An indication that any data characteristic variation can be used for a data characteristic, such as "Date", can mean any form of a date. (Brackett 2011)

data checking

Activity through which the correctness conditions of the data are verified.

data cleansing

The process of correcting data errors to bring the level of data quality to an acceptable level for the information user needs.

data clustering

The process of partitioning the data attributes of an entity or table into subsets or clusters of similar attributes, based on subject matter or characteristic (domain).

data compilation

Operations performed on data to derive information according to a given set of rules.

data completeness

The degree to which data is captured.

data completeness, fact

Compares the attributes implemented in a database against all known requirements.

data completeness, value

A measure of the absence of null values for a database column.

data compression

1. Algorithms or techniques that change data to a smaller physical size that contains the same information.
2. The process of changing data to be stored in a smaller physical or logical space.

data consistency

The degree to which one set of attribute values match another attribute set within the same row or record (record-level consistency), within another attribute set in a different record (cross-record consistency), or within the same record at different points in time (temporal consistency). (DAMA-DMBOK GUIDE 1st edition, pg. 296.)

data consumer

A person or group that receives data (on a screen, in a report, or through a query) and uses the data to create information. SEE ALSO information consumer.

Data Control Language (DCL)

A subset of Structured Query Language used to define data security, user function permissions, and data access to data in relational tables.

data conversion

1. The process of changing data structure, format, or contents to comply with some rule or measurement requirement.
2. The process of changing data contents stored in one system so that it can be stored in another system, or used by an application.

data creator

A person who enters or updates data. Roughly equivalent to data producer. SEE ALSO Create-Read-Update-Delete.

data cube

A multi-dimensional data structure that contains an aggregate value at each point, i.e., the result of applying an aggregate function to an underlying relation. Data cubes are used to implement OLAP. SEE ALSO schema, star.

data currentness

A measure of how well the data values remain current with the business. (Brackett 2011)

data custodian

SEE data steward.

data definition

1. Statements that specify the business meaning associated with a conceptual, logical, or physical data entity or attribute.
2. The process of creating business meta-data, including names, meanings, integrity rules, and domain values.
3. In computer programming, the statements in a computer program that specify the physical attributes of the data to be processed, such as location and quantity of data.

Data Definition Language (DDL)

1. Generally, the subset of Structured Query Language commands used to define and implement structured database objects.
2. In Database Management Systems, the specific definitions to formally define and implement a database.

data definition quality

The degree to which data definitions are complete, accurate, current, correct, meaningful, thorough, and useful.

data denormalization

The process that adjusts the normalized data structure for optimum performance in a specific operating environment, without compromising the normalized data structure. (Brackett 2011)

data de-optimization

The technique that transforms the logical data structure into the deployment data structure for the data sites where the databases will be implemented. It deals with the specific data that will be maintained in different data sites. (Brackett 2011)

data description

The statements in a computer program that specify the physical attributes of the data to be processed, such as location and quantity of data.

data design artifact

A data model, an architecture model, or descriptive representation of any complex object.

data development

Analysis, design, implementation, testing, deployment, and maintenance of data. (DAMA-DMBOK Guide, 1st edition, pg. 6.)

data dictionary

Any place where business and/or technical terms and definitions are stored. Typically, data dictionaries are designed to store a limited set of available meta-data, concentrating on the names and definitions relating to the physical data and related objects of systems implemented or in development. SEE ALSO repository.

data dictionary, active

An active data dictionary interacts with its software environment to capture and update meta-data in real time.

data dictionary, integrated

An integrated data dictionary serves as a store for meta-data for multiple software tools. SEE ALSO repository.

data dictionary, passive

A passive data dictionary requires batch or user entry and update of meta-data.

data distribution

1. In data storage, the mathematical patterns of data values as they exist within a set.
2. In data networks, the patterns of storage of data within and through various systems and on various platforms or sites.
3. In data movement, transmission of data to one or more locations from a central point.

data domain

A set of allowable values for a data attribute. (Brackett 2011)

data dredging **Alternate form: data fishing, data snooping**

The use of data mining to uncover relationships in data that may be valid within a test set but are not valid within the wider population. Sometimes used to deliberately generate misleading conclusions.

data editing

Activity aimed at detecting and correcting errors, logical inconsistencies, and suspicious data. Data editing is the physical application of data integrity rules, which are developed logically and denormalized within the data to produce data edits, which are then applied to the data.

data element

SEE data attribute.

Data Encryption Standard (DES)

An encryption program. SEE ALSO encryption.

data entity

A classification of objects found in the real world described by the Noun part of speech -- persons, places, things, concepts, and events – of interest to the enterprise. Usually expressed in singular form.

data entity, associative

An entity or table that resolves a many-to-many relationship between two other related entities or tables.

data entity, dependent

In a relational model, a child entity of another parent entity that cannot exist on its own.

data entity-relation diagram

A diagram that shows the arrangement and relationships between data entities. It contains only data entities and the data relations between those data entities. It does not contain any of the data attributes in those data entities, nor does it contain any roles played by the data attributes. (Brackett 2011)

data error

A data value that provides incorrect or false knowledge about the business, or about business objects and events that are important to the business. (Brackett 2011)

data escrow

In Software-as-a-Service, the practice of keeping a set of data with an independent third party to prevent data loss.

data exchange

The process of sending and receiving data.

data exploration

The process of examining data in order to determine ranges and patterns within the data.

data export

1. The process of extracting information from a database into a file.
2. The result data set from the export process.

data extract

1. A snapshot copy of data from a source database used to update data in a target database, or for use in an application.
2. *Verb.* To copy data from a source for data movement and data transformation.

data extract date

The date data was extracted from a source database.

data extract frequency

The latency of data extracts, such as daily versus weekly, monthly, quarterly, etc. The frequency that data extracts are needed in the Data Warehouse is determined by the shortest frequency requested through an order, or by the frequency required to maintain consistency of the other associated data types in the source Data Warehouse.

data extract specification

The standard expectations of a particular source Data Warehouse for data extracts from the operational database system-of-record. A system-of-record uses an extract specification to retrieve a snapshot of shared data, and formats the data in the way specified for updating the data in the source Data Warehouse. An extract specification also contains extract frequency rules for use by the data access environment.

data extraction software

Software that reads one or more sources of data and creates a new image of the data. SEE ALSO Extract-Transform-Load.

data federation

A method of transparently joining or linking data from multiple physical locations and/or multiple platforms.

data file

A physical file of data that exists in a Database Management System, such as a computer file, or outside a database management system, such as a manual file. It is referred to as a table in a relational database. A data file generally represents a data entity, subject to adjustments made during formal data denormalization. (Brackett 2011)

data file-relation diagram

A diagram that represents the data files and the relations between those data files in a database. (Brackett 2011)

data flow

The transfer of data between systems, applications, or data sets.

Data Flow Diagram (DFD)

A visual representation of how data moves or is moved between logical processes or application services (i.e., how the output data from a process serves as the input data for other processes). Essentially a process model, complementary to a data model.

data governance

The exercise of authority, control, and shared decision-making (planning, monitoring, and enforcement) over the management of data assets. SEE governance; data stewardship.

Data Governance Council (DGC)

The highest tier data governance organization in an enterprise. The DGC includes senior managers serving as executive data stewards, along with the DM Leader and the CIO. A business executive may formally chair the council as chief data steward with the DM Leader serving as facilitator for council meetings and other activities.

Data Governance Office (DGO)

A staff organization of full-time data analysts found in larger enterprises whose mission is to support the Data Governance Council, Data Stewardship Coordinating Committees, and data stewardship teams.

data heritage

Documentation of the source of the data and their original meaning at the time of data capture. (Brackett 2011)

data hoarding

The process of restricting access to data based on concerns regarding proprietary content, economic impact, security implications.

data identification

The data that have been identified thus far for potential inclusion in the information system. The process of specifying which data should or will be sought to fulfill user needs. A description of the different types of data and their applicable tools for analysis is also included.

data in a cloud

Data that is stored in a distributed network of systems, where the location of the data is unknown and transparent to the user.

data in context

Individual facts that have meaning and can be readily understood. They are raw facts wrapped with meaning. (Brackett 2011)

data independence

1. The ability to change the logical or physical structure of data without changing the application program and its view of the data.
2. On a large scale, the independence of the data architecture from the business activity architecture, the platform architecture, and the information system architecture. On a smaller scale, the independence of the logical design from the physical platform where data will be stored.

data instance

A specific set of data values for the characteristics in a data occurrence that is valid at a point in time, or for a period of time. Many data instances can exist for each data occurrence, particularly when historical data are maintained. One data instance is the current instance and the others are historical instances. (Brackett 2011)

data instant

The point in time or the timeframe the data represent in the business world. (Brackett 2011)

data integration

The planned and controlled:

a) merge using some form of reference,
b) transformation using a set of business rules, and
c) flow of data from a source to a target,

for operational and/or analytical use. Data needs to be accessed and extracted, moved, validated and cleansed, standardized, transformed, and loaded.

data integration architect

An IT professional responsible for data integration processes, practices and software programs across an enterprise.

data integration architecture

A part of a master plan for how data is selected, transformed and flows across databases. The data integration architecture is an important part of enterprise data architecture. It may include database architecture, Master Data Management architecture, Business Intelligence architecture, and meta-data architecture.

data integration developer

A software developer responsible for data integration programming.

data integrity

1. Data that complies with all rules regarding definitions, relationships, lineage, and heritage.
2. In data movement, data that is provably not changed unexpectedly through transmission between systems.

data intermediary

A role in which individuals transform data from one form, not created by them, into another form. For example, a data entry clerk enters data from a paper form into a database.

data inventory

A comprehensive list of all data objects in a system or an organization, including electronically stored data such as databases and files, and non-electronic data.

data item

An individual field in a data record, referred to as a column in a relational database. A data item represents a data attribute, subject to adjustments made during formal data denormalization. (Brackett 2011)

data key

Any data attribute or set of data attributes used to identify a data occurrence within a data entity. (Brackett 2011)

data latency

The time delay for data to be updated in a system compared to the real world. When data is displayed in real time, data latency is eliminated.

data lifecycle

A conceptualization of how data is created and used which attempts to define a "birth-to-death" value chain for data, including acquisition, storage and maintenance, use, movement to archive, and destruction. (DAMA-DMBOK Guide, 1st edition, pg. 3.)

data lineage

A description of the pathway from the data source to their current location and the alterations made to the data along that pathway. (Brackett 2011)

data loading

The process of populating more than one row at time into database, typically a Data Warehouse.

Data Management (DM)

1. The business function that develops and executes plans, policies, practices, and projects that acquire, control, protect, deliver, and enhance the value of data.
2. A program for implementation and performance of the data management function.
3. The field of disciplines required to perform the data management function.
4. The profession of individuals who perform data management disciplines.
5. In some cases, a synonym for a Data Management Services organization that performs data management activities.

Data Management Association, The (DAMA)

SEE DAMA International.

Data Management Body of Knowledge (DAMA-DMBOK)

SEE Body of Knowledge, Data Management.

data management center of excellence

SEE Center of Excellence, Data Management.

data management community of interest

All the data management professionals, data stewards and other stakeholders with an active interest and role in data management.

data management function

One of the ten business processes within data management, according to the functional decomposition in the DAMA-DMBOK Functional Framework:

- Data Governance
- Data Architecture
- Data Development
- Data Operations Management
- Data Security Management
- Data Quality Management
- Reference & Master Data Management
- Data Warehousing & Business Intelligence Management
- Document and Content management
- Meta-data Management

DAMA-DMBOK Guide, 1st edition, pg. 6.)

data management leader **Alternate form: DM Leader**

A generic term used in the DAMA-DMBOK Guide for the highest-level manager of Data Management Services organizations. The DM Leader is the manager most directly responsible for data management, including coordinating data governance and data stewardship activity, overseeing data management projects, and supervising data management professionals. May be a manager, director, Associate VP, or VP.

data management professional

A professional specializing in one or more data management functions, and may or may not be part of IT organizations.

data management services (DMS)

An organization of data management professionals performing data management functions. One or more units of data management professionals responsible for data management within an organization. A centralized DMS organization is sometimes known as a Data Management Center of Excellence.

data management strategy

Selected courses of actions setting the direction for data management within the enterprise, including vision, mission, goals, principles, policies, and projects.

Data Manipulation Language (DML)

A language used to insert, retrieve, update, delete, and otherwise manipulate data in a database. The SELECT statement in SQL is an example of a retrieval operation. (Everest 2010)

data map

SEE chart, data map.

data mapping

The assignment of source data entities and attributes to target data entities and attributes, and the resolution of disparate data.

data marking

A term used for the classifying data at a deep meaningful level for its sensitivity (secret, etc.) and appropriate release. For example, some data will not be sensitive on its own, but will not be releasable to certain countries, or in combination with other data, which then makes it sensitive.

Data Mart (DM)

A decision support database supporting Business Intelligence in a limited subject area, using a dimensional data model design. Typically, data marts source their data from an Enterprise Data Warehouse or Operational Data Store.

data mashup

SEE mashup, data.

data migration

The process of transferring data from one database to another. SEE ALSO conversion.

data mining

The process of sifting through large amounts of data using pattern recognition, fuzzy logic, and other knowledge discovery statistical techniques to identify previously unknown, unsuspected, and potentially meaningful data content relationships and trends. SEE ALSO predictive analysis.

data model

A model that includes formal data names, comprehensive data definitions, proper data structures, and precise data integrity rules. A complete data model must include all four of these components. (Brackett 2011)

data model diagram

The visual presentation of the structural portion of a data model with icons for entity records and lines between them to represent relationships. SEE ALSO Data Structure Diagram.

Data Model, Conceptual (CDM)

A data model that is presented at a high level of abstraction, hiding the underlying details, and making it easier for people to comprehend. A conceptual model should reflect the phenomena in the users' world being modeled as directly as possible, as close to the way the users think. For example, many-to-many relationships are common in conceptual models.

data model, dimensional

A data model that represents data in a star-like structure of only one-to-many relationships, where each entity has either all relationships having the 'one' side or the 'many' side. SEE ALSO schema, star.

Data Model, Enterprise (EDM)

A conceptual data model or logical data model providing a common consistent view of shared data across the enterprise, however that is defined, at a point in time. It is common to use the term to mean a high-level, simplified data model, but that is a question of abstraction for presentation. SEE ALSO data model, conceptual.

data model, hierarchical

A data model that represents data in a tree-like structure of only one-to-many relationships, where each entity may have a 'many' side when related to a parent, and a 'one' side when related to a child. SEE ALSO structure, hierarchical.

Data Model, Logical (LDM)

A entity-relationship data model including data attributes that represents the inherent properties of the data, including names, definitions, structure, and integrity rules, independent of software, hardware, volumetrics, frequency of use, or performance considerations.

data model, network

A representation of objects and their participation in one or more owner-member sets. In such a model, a both owners and members may participate in multiple sets, affecting a network of objects and relationships.

Data Model, Physical (PDM)

The definition or representation of a data model for implementation and realization in a particular DBMS, including naming convention and physical data types. It may be denormalized for performance and access simplification. A high-level description of a database design without specific physical layout (how the data is stored on disk) information.

Data Model, Semantic (SDM)

A conceptual data model that provides structure and defines meaning for non-tabular data, making that meaning explicit enough that a human or software agent can reason about it. SEE ALSO ontology.

data modeler

A person who builds data models.

data modeling

1. An analysis and design method, building data models to
   a) define and analyze data requirements,
   b) design logical and physical data structures that support these requirements, and
   c) define business and technical meta-data.
2. The act of creating a data model.

data modeling notation, Barker

One of several notation conventions for modeling data, developed by Richard Barker and others in 1986.

data modeling notation, IDEF1X (IDEF1X)

A style of notation for entity relationship diagrams in data models, developed by Robert G. Brown in 1979, and extended by the U. S. Air Force in 1985. The 'X' stands for eXtensions to the original IDEF1 specification, the extensions were due to Dan Appleton. This data modeling scheme is one variant of Entity Relationship modeling. It was originally embodied in ERwin®, which has since evolved to include additional modeling notations. SEE ALSO Integrated DEFinition.

data modeling notation, Information Engineering (IE)

A record-based data modeling scheme and notation developed by Clive Finkelstein in the 1970s and later popularized by James Martin.

data modeling scheme

The formalism, technique, style, notation, etc. used to guide the Data Modeling activity to create a data model. The scheme encompasses the notational conventions (syntax) for representing the semantics of the data model. Examples of data modeling schemes include single file, flat file, multi-file, relational, hierarchical, record-based, ER, EER, fact oriented (no file), IE, UML, IDEF1X, Barker, multi-dimensional, star, object-oriented.

data modeling scheme, no file

A data modeling scheme that is not record-based - does not use the constructs of file or entity tables, and consequently does not suffer from table think. (Everest 2010) SEE ALSO Fact Oriented Modeling; object role model.

data modeling scheme, record-based

A data modeling scheme in which records are formed by clustering attributes. Used to represent an entity type population. One or more attributes may serve as an identifier. In general, a record could have a hierarchical structure, thus allowing multi-valued data items and repeating groups of items. (Everest 2010)

data modeling scheme, relational

A data modeling scheme that uses the constructs of entity, attribute, identifier, and foreign key to represent relationships. Attributes are represented by data items or columns. Entities are represented by tables, which is a cluster of one or more attributes. Relationships between entities are represented by foreign keys. The major distinguishing characteristic of a relational data model is that all attributes must be single valued (atomic). SEE ALSO flat file.

data movement

The process of extracting data from one system and loading it onto another system. SEE ALSO Extract-Transform-Load.

data name

A label for a fact or a set of related facts contained in the data resource, appearing on a data model, or displayed on screens, reports, or documents. (Brackett 2011)

data name abbreviation

The shortening of a primary data name to meet some length restriction. (Brackett 2011)

data normalization

The process that brings data into a normal form that minimizes redundancies and keeps anomalies from entering the data resource. It provides a subject-oriented data resource based on business objects and events. (Brackett 2011)

data occurrence

A logical record that represents the existence of a business object or the happening of a business event in the business world, such as an employee, a vehicle, and so on. (Brackett 2011)

data operations management

Providing support from data acquisition to purging. (DAMA-DMBOK Guide, 1st edition, pg. 6.)

data overload

A deluge of data coming at a recipient that is not relevant and timely. It is a deluge of unwanted non-information.

data owner

An individual responsible for definitions, policy, and practice decisions about data within their area of responsibility. For business data, the individual may be called a business owner of the data.

data policy

Short statements of management intent and fundamental rules governing the creation, acquisition, integrity, security, quality, and use of data and information. (DAMA-DMBOK Guide, 1st edition, pg. 47.)

data preparation

The process which involves checking or logging the data in; checking the data for accuracy; entering the data into the computer; transforming the data; and developing and documenting a database structure that integrates the various measures. This process includes preparation and assignment of appropriate metadata to describe the product in human readable code/format.

data presentation quality

The degree to which information products (reports, screens, charts) are easy to understand and use without misinterpretation by the intended audience.

data privacy

The limitation of data access to only those authorized to view the data. SEE ALSO confidentiality.

data processing

The operation performed on data through capture, transformation, and storage, in order to derive new information according to a given set of rules.

data producer

A person, organization, or software service creating or providing data. SEE ALSO data creator.

data professional

SEE data management professional.

data profile

A collection of statistics about a data attribute that shows patterns of usage, patterns of contents, and any other patterns that may be interesting.

data profiler

Someone who performs data profiling.

data profiling

An approach to data quality analysis, using statistics to show patterns of usage, and patterns of contents, and automated as much as possible. Some profiling activities must be done manually, but most can be automated.

data propagation

The distribution of data from one or more source databases to one or more local target databases, according to defined rules. Typically used in reference to distributed databases. SEE ALSO data replication.

data provenance

Provenance applied to the organization's data resource. (Brackett 2011)

data quality

The degree to which data is accurate, complete, timely, consistent with all requirements and business rules, and relevant for a given use. SEE ALSO information quality.

data quality analysis

The evaluation of data quality; the identification of inaccurate, incomplete, inconsistent, and untimely data and its causes.

data quality assessment

SEE data quality audit; quality assessment.

data quality assurance

Quality inspection and review processes for data, data models, and database designs, including testing for application data controls and edits, testing of data integration programs, data quality analysis, and data quality audits. SEE ALSO quality assurance.

data quality audit

The random sampling of data and testing it against its valid data values to determine its accuracy and reliability.

data quality certification

A declaration that a database has met a set of defined data quality requirements (service levels), based on data quality analysis and audits.

data quality decay rate

The rate that a data attribute loses accuracy over time if not updated. For example, if age is stored, the entire dataset's age attribute will be incorrect after one year because everyone will have aged by then.

data quality management

The application of total quality management concepts and practices to improve data and information quality, including setting data quality policies and guidelines, data quality measurement (including data quality auditing and certification), data quality analysis, data cleansing and correction, data quality process improvement, and data quality education. One of the ten data management functions identified in the DAMA-DMBOK Functional Framework.

data quality process improvement

System analysis and redesign to eliminate or prevent data errors and defects. Data quality process improvement is a proactive, preventive approach to improving data quality.

data quality requirement

Application requirements that eliminate or prevent data errors, including requirements for domain control, referential integrity constraints, and edit and validation routines.

data reconciliation

The process of adjusting data derived from two different sources to remove, or at least reduce, the impact of differences identified.

data record

A physical grouping of data items that are stored in or retrieved from a data file. It is referred to as a row or tuple in a relational database. A data record represents a data instance. (Brackett 2011)

data redundancy

The unknown and unmanaged duplication of business facts.

data re-engineering

The process of analyzing, standardizing, and transforming data from non-standard files and databases into a standardized database that is part of the enterprise data architecture.

data reference set

A specific set of data codes for a general topic, such as a set of management level codes in an organization. (Brackett 2011)

data refresh

The process of applying updates as a group to a data set, then allowing users access to the updated data.

data relation

An association between data occurrences in different data subjects or within the same data subject. It provides the connections between data subjects for building the proper data structure and for navigating in the database. (Brackett 2011)

data remanence

The residue of data that has been nominally erased or removed.

data replication

The consistent copying of data from one primary data site to one or more secondary data sites. The copied data are kept in synch with the primary data on a regular basis. (Brackett 2011)

data repository

A loose term for a collection of multiple databases. Something entirely different from a meta-data repository. Not recommended for use.

data requirement

Statements describing the data needs of a person or organization. Business meta-data (data names and meanings) and Logical Data Models are structured ways of defining data requirements, in addition to more traditional requirement specifications.

Data Resource Management (DRM)

SEE data management.

data rule

A subset of business rules that deals with the data column of the Zachman Framework. (Brackett 2011)

data scrubbing

SEE data cleansing.

data security

1. The safety of data from unauthorized and inappropriate access or change.
2. The measures taken to prevent unauthorized access, use, modification, or destruction of data.

data security audit

Testing of data security measures by an objective party.

data security management

The process of ensuring that data is safe from unauthorized and inappropriate access or change. Includes focus on data privacy, confidentiality, access, functional capabilities and use. One of the ten data management functions identified in the DAMA-DMBOK Functional Framework. (DAMA-DMBOK Guide, 1st edition, pg. 6.)

data service

An interface to a business process that receives or delivers data attributes, usually via a web application.

data set

Any organized collection of data.

data sharing

Exchange of data and/or meta-data in a situation involving the use of open, freely available data formats, where process patterns are known and standard, and where not limited by privacy and confidentiality regulations.

data sharing agreement

An agreement between parties that describes the allowed activities, uses, and restrictions regarding data shared between the parties.

Data Source Name (DSN)

Connection information for a database used in an Open DataBase Connectivity connection setup.

data staging

The process of moving data from one system into intermediate storage before final processing into a target.

data staging area

A database that stands between the operational source databases and the target databases (typically an Operational Data Store, Data Warehouse or Data Mart). The data staging area is considered the "back room" portion of the Data Warehouse environment. The data staging area is where the extract, transform, and load effort takes place, and is out of bounds for end users. Most data in the data staging area is transient, although typically there is some relatively small amount of persistent data.

data steward

A business leader and/or subject matter expert designated as accountable for:

a) the identification of operational and Business Intelligence data requirements within an assigned subject area,
b) the quality of data names, business definitions, data integrity rules, and domain values within an assigned subject area,
c) compliance with regulatory requirements and conformance to internal data policies and data standards,
d) application of appropriate security controls,
e) analyzing and improving data quality, and
f) identifying and resolving data related issues.

Data stewards are often categorized as executive data stewards, business data stewards, or coordinating data stewards. SEE ALSO data owner; data stewardship; data governance.

data stewardship

1. The formal, specifically assigned, and entrusted accountability for business (non-technical) responsibilities ensuring effective control and use of data and information resources. SEE ALSO data steward; stewardship; data governance.
2. The formal accountability for business responsibilities ensuring effective control and use of data assets. (DAMA-DMBOK Guide, 1st edition, pg. 39.)

Data Stewardship Committee (DSC)

A permanent cross-functional group of coordinating data stewards responsible for

a) supporting the Data Governance Council, and
b) integrating the work of Data Stewardship Teams.

The Data Governance Council may delegate responsibilities to the Data Stewardship Committee. The DSC may be led by the Chief Data Steward, DM Leader, and/or the Enterprise Data Architect. In a large organization, there may be additional Data Stewardship Committees at one more levels lower than the enterprise DSC.

data stewardship council

A generic term for any committee of data stewards. May be synonymous with Data Governance Council (DGC) with both executive data stewards and coordinating data stewards, or may be a working committee of coordinating data stewards below the DGC.

data stewardship team

A temporary or permanent focused group of business data stewards collaborating on data modeling, specification, and data quality improvement, typically in an assigned subject area, led by a coordinating data steward and facilitated by a data architect.

data storage

The means of recording or archiving data so that they are available for future use.

data store

A place where data is stored; data at rest. A generic term that includes databases, flat files, and non-electronic data files.

data strategy

A business plan for leveraging an enterprise's data assets to maximum advantage. SEE ALSO enterprise data strategy.

data structure definition

A set of structural meta-data associated to a data set, which includes information about how concepts are associated with the measures, dimensions, and attributes of a data structure along with information about the representation of data and related descriptive meta-data.

data structure diagram

The visual presentation of a data model with icons for entities with attributes and lines between them to represent relationships and roles. First known published article to propose such diagrams was by Charles Bachman (1969). (Everest 2010) SEE ALSO data model diagram; entity-relationship diagram.

data subject

A person, place, thing, concept, or event that is of interest to the organization and about which data are captured and maintained in the organization's data resource. Data subjects are defined from business objects and business events, making the data resource subject oriented toward the business. (Brackett 2011)

data supply chain

The flow of data across business processes.

data synchronization

The continuous harmonization of data attribute values between two or more different systems, with the end result being the data attribute values are the same in all of the systems.

data technology management

The evaluation, selection, implementation, inventory and maintenance of hardware and software products in support of data management, including Database Management Systems, data modeling and database administration tools, Meta-data Management tools, data integration tools and Business Intelligence tools.

data tracking

The process of documenting data provenance. (Brackett 2011)

data transfer

The process of moving data from one system or operating environment to another.

data transformation

Changing the format, structure, integrity, and/or definitions of data from the source database to comply with the requirements of a target database.

data transport

The mechanism that moves data from a source to target environment.

data type **Alternate form: datatype**

1. A category of physical data structures with common physical properties and uses, such as numeric, alphanumeric, packed decimal, floating point, datetime, etc.
2. A set of distinct values characterized by properties of those values and by operations on those values. [ISO/IEC 11404:1996, 4.11]

data update

The process of inserting or modifying a data attribute in a database

data validation

The process of monitoring the results of data compilation and ensuring the quality of the computational results.

data value

The specific representation of a value for an attribute as of a point in time.

data value chain

The flow of data across processes in support of the enterprise's business value chain.

data value chain analysis

The identification of which functions, processes, applications, organizations, and roles create, read, update, and delete different kinds of data (subject areas, entities, attributes), expressed in CRUD matrices, particularly when the compared items are arranged in value chain sequence.

data versioning

The process of identifying and ordering snapshots of data as it changes over time according to certain criteria. Each version becomes an independent instance.

data visualization

Techniques for graphical representation of trends, patterns and other information.

Data Warehouse (DW)

1. An integrated, centralized decision support database and the related software programs used to collect, cleanse, transform, and store data from a variety of operational sources to support Business Intelligence. A Data Warehouse may also include dependent data marts. (DAMA-DMBOK Guide, 1st edition, pg. 197.)
2. A subject oriented, integrated, time variant, and non-volatile collection of summary and detailed historical data used to support the strategic decision-making processes for the corporation. ("What is a Data Warehouse?" W.H. Inmon, Prism, Volume 1, Number 1, 1995)
3. A copy of transaction data specifically structured for query and analysis. (Ralph Kimball, The Data Warehouse Toolkit, pg. 310.)

data warehouse appliance

A system containing integrated servers, storage, and software specifically optimized for Data Warehouse processing.

data warehouse architecture

SEE architecture, Business Intelligence.

data warehouse audits and controls

A collection of checks and balances to assure the right data is extracted from the right sources, then transformed, cleansed and summarized correctly and finally loaded to the right target database tables.

data warehouse bus architecture

The Data Warehouse Bus Architecture is composed of "a master suite of conformed dimensions" and standardized definitions of facts. [1, P. 156]

data warehouse engine

A Relational DataBase Management System or Multi-Dimensional DataBase Management System. Data Warehouse engines require strong query capabilities, fast load mechanisms, and large storage requirements.

data warehouse infrastructure

SEE infrastructure, data warehouse.

data warehouse network

An integrated network of Data Warehouses that contain sharable data propagated from a source Data Warehouse based on information consumer demand. The warehouses are managed to control data redundancy and to promote effective use of the sharable data.

data warehouse, active

Implementation of a Data Warehouse that enables real time or near-time data analysis.

data warehouse, federated

1. A conceptual Data Warehouse made up of multiple decision support databases, potentially on multiple servers, but presented transparently to Business Intelligence users as a unified schema for query, analysis, and reporting.
2. An Enterprise Data Warehouse fed by extracts from departmental Data Warehouses and/or legacy Data Warehouses prior to their incorporation and/or retirement.

data warehouse, functional

A Data Warehouse that draws data from nearby operational systems and supports a distinct organization, functional area (such as manufacturing), or geographic unit within the enterprise. Distinct from an Enterprise Data Warehouse.

Data Warehousing (DW)

1. The operational extract, cleansing, transformation, and load processes, and associated control processes, that maintain the data containing within a Data Warehouse.
2. The storage of evaluational data for the analysis of trends and patterns in the business. (Brackett 2011)

Data Warehousing and Business Intelligence management

The operational, administrative and control processes that provide access to Business Intelligence data and support to knowledge workers engaged in reporting, query, and analysis. One of ten data management functions identified in the DAMA-DMBOK Functional Framework. (DAMA-DMBOK Guide, 1st edition, pg. 7.)

data, analytical

Subject oriented, integrated, time variant, non-volatile collections of data in support of Business Intelligence activities. SEE ALSO OnLine Analytical Processing.

data, derived

A data set created through a computational step applied to atomic data. Derived data is the result either of relating two or more attributes of a single transaction (such as an aggregation), or of relating one or more attributes of a transaction to an external algorithm (formula) or rule. SEE ALSO data attribute, derived.

data, non-tabular

Data not structured in a relational database table or grid format. Includes unstructured data, which has different internal structures, but can include links as well as classification tags as part of the tabular data attributes. SEE ALSO data, unstructured.

data, operational

Process oriented, non-integrated, time current, volatile collections of data used to support the daily activities of an enterprise. SEE ALSO OnLine Transaction Processing.

data, structured

Data that can be described using a discrete domain of vocabulary terms, organized by inherent patterns into semantic groups or entities, presented by context rather than content.

data, tabular

Data stored in grid (or table) format (records or rows, and columns).

data, unstructured

Any document, file, graphic, image, text, report, form, video, or sound recording that has not been tagged or otherwise structured into rows and columns or records. This term has some inaccurate connotations, as there is usually some structure (for instance, paragraphs and chapters) in these formats.

data.gov

A U.S. government website launched by the Federal Chief Information Officer of the U.S. in order to make available government collected data for use by the public.

data-at-rest

Data that is written to and contained in static storage.

database **Alternate form: data base**

An organized collection of data stored in a structured way to enable rapid search and retrieval by a computer.

database administration

The function of managing the physical aspects of data resources, including database design and integrity, backup and recovery, performance and tuning, generally within the context of a particular DBMS.

DataBase Administrator (DBA)

The IT professional role responsible for database administration, usually in the context of a particular DBMS, hence often prefixed with the name of the DBMS, e.g., Oracle DBA. Functional responsibilities vary based on further definitions.

DataBase Administrator, application

A DBA who supports application systems, sometimes focusing on development and test environments, database design, and SQL tuning as opposed to the entire application stack. Contrasts with operational DBA and procedural DBA.

DataBase Administrator, operational

A DBA focused on support of production environments, including performance tuning, backup and recovery, high availability, job scheduling, data delivery, security access levels, etc. The Operational DBA has a specific responsibility for change management regarding implementation.

DataBase Administrator, procedural

1. A DBA that specializes in development and support of procedural logic controlled and executed by the DBMS: stored procedures, triggers, and user-defined functions. (DAMA-DMBOK Guide, 1st edition, pg. 149.)
2. A DBA that supports the development of data management applications.

database auditing

The logging, monitoring, analysis, and reporting on database activity.

database definition

SEE schema, database.

database design

1. The process of developing a physical data model, followed by definition of all physical database objects, including tables, indexes, and sequences.
2. The physical data model and the detailed DDL for a database. The database design addresses physical constraints such as storage and performance.

database designer

SEE data modeler.

database integrity

1. The degree to which data in a database conforms to logical integrity constraints through the implementation of physical DBMS constraints.
2. The degree to which data in a database can be recovered in the event of a hardware or software failure.

database inventory

A comprehensive list of all databases within a system or an organization.

database management

The development and support of structured data resources. Database management is broader in scope than database administration, including the responsibilities beyond those of database administrators.

DataBase Management System (DBMS)

The computer software program used to manage and query a database.

database management system, hierarchical

A type of Database Management System, where parent-child relationships are established between data segments.

DataBase Management System, Multi-Dimensional (MDDBMS)

A specialized Database Management System that supports OnLine Analytical Processing, enabling users to analyze large amounts of data. An MDDBMS captures and presents arrays of data that can be arranged in multiple dimensions.

DataBase Management System, Object-Oriented (OODBMS, ODBMS)

Database software that stores data as objects, instead of storing the data in a relational format, and then instantiating objects in memory.

DataBase Management System, Object Relational (ORDBMS)

An Object Relational DBMS to manage an Object Relational Data Structure, which is a hybrid of OO and Relational.

DataBase Management System, Relational (RDBMS)

Database management software controlling the creation, storage, manipulation, access, and performance of relational databases.

database marketing

The use of information about customers and prospects to strengthen customer relationships by identifying new opportunities and improving customer service. Uses methods for creating, testing, and executing marketing strategies based on analysis of customer data. Includes the mass customization of marketing campaigns to decrease costs, improve response, build customer loyalty, reduce attrition, and increase customer satisfaction.

database reorganization

The process of rearranging physical storage for a database in order to optimize performance.

database schema

SEE schema, database.

database server

In a distributed application architecture, the DBMS software, related data integration and access services and associated hardware supporting access and manipulation of data, separate from application logic and user interfaces.

database transaction

A unit of work; a set of statements to read, create, modify, or delete business data, which the Database Management System must complete performance of all the statements or reverse the changes.

database, archival

An exact copy of a database, along with any specific software necessary for managing that database, saved for purposes of historical research, recovery, or restoration.

database, columnar

A database structure that serialized values by columns then by rows, rather than conventional databases which serialize values by rows and then by columns.

database, column-oriented

A Database Management System that stores its content by column rather than by row.

database, correlation

A Database Management System that is data model independent and designed to efficiently handle unplanned, ad hoc queries in an analytical system environment. Unlike relational database management systems (records-based storage) or column-oriented databases (column-based storage), a correlation database uses a value-based storage architecture in which each unique data value is stored only once and an auto-generated indexing system maintains the context for all values.

database, distributed

A database that contains objects residing on independent systems in a network, but can be accessed as though all objects resided on the same system.

database, hierarchical

A database in which all relationships among data entities and attributes are hierarchical (SEE relationship, hierarchical). Sometimes used to refer to databases that have hierarchical record structures but allow more general network relationships between record types. Examples include UML, most OO data models, Kroenke's Semantic Object Model, the SQL:99 standard (and later versions), and nested relations. There is increasing interest in moving away from the restrictions of the relational model, which allow only flat record structures. SEE ALSO structure, hierarchical.

database, historical

A database that provides an historical perspective on the data; that is, a database that can be used to show how facts about an entity have changed over time.

DataBase, Multi-Dimensional (MDDB)

A data structure with three or more independent dimensions.

database, network

A type of database where records are stored with links or pointers to other records. Distinguished from a hierarchical database in the sense that a child record may have relationships with multiple parent records.

DataBase, Object-Oriented (OODB)

A database based on the object-oriented paradigm instead of the relational model.

database, operational

A database supporting one or more transactional applications. Operational databases are the sources of data for data Operational Data Stores and Data Warehouses. They contain detailed data used to run the day-to-day operations of the business. The data continually changes as updates are made. SEE ALSO OnLine Transaction Processing.

database, relational

1. The most common form of database today, storing data in tables made of up of columns and rows, created using the relational data modeling scheme.
2. A database conforming to Codd's rules:

    Rule 0: The system must qualify as relational, as a database, and as a management system.

    Rule 1: The information rule.

    Rule 2: The guaranteed access rule.

    Rule 3: Systematic treatment of null values.

    Rule 4: Active online catalog based on the relational model.

    Rule 5: The comprehensive data sublanguage rule.

    Rule 6: The view updating rule.

    Rule 7: High-level insert, update, and delete.

    Rule 8: Physical data independence.

    Rule 9: Logical data independence.

    Rule 10: Integrity independence.

    Rule 11: Distribution independence.

    Rule 12: The non-subversion rule.

database, source

A database that feeds into a target database. May be an operational database, ODS, data staging area or Data Warehouse.

database, target

The database in which data will be loaded or inserted.

database, temporal

A database with built-in time aspects, including valid time and transaction time.

data-in-motion

Data that is carried across networks between systems.

date

1. A point in time with the granularity of a day.
2. A class word, abbreviated usually to dt.
3. DCMI element in element set Instantiation: a timeframe for an event. SEE ALSO Dublin Core Metadata Initiative.

datum

Historically, has been defined as the singular form of data related to one fact. (Brackett 2011)

deadlock

A scenario where a set of multiple simultaneous actions within a set wait for others within the set to complete and release the resources being held. The waiting processes are "locked out" from the resources held by the other processes. A true deadlock lasts forever, is never resolved.

decision rights

In Data Governance, information about the who, when and how a data-related decision is made.

decision support

SEE Business Intelligence.

Decision Support System (DSS)

An application that uses data to support managerial decisions through ad hoc query, summarization, drill-down analysis, trend analysis, exception identification and "what if" scenario modeling. SEE ALSO Business Intelligence.

decision tree

SEE chart, decision tree.

declarative

Adjective. Describes a type of programming language in which the programmer does not define the flow of control at execution time.

decryption

The process of reversing encryption; decoding back into original format.

deduction

1. The process of reasoning from one state to another, such as from cause to effect, or from general to specific.
2. Subtraction.

deduplication

The process of elimination of redundant copies of data from storage or during a merge of multiple datasets.

default data value **Alternate term: default value**

A data value that is automatically assigned when no other data values are selected or applied.

defect

A data value that does not conform to its quality requirements. SEE ALSO error.

defect prevention

Improving systems to eliminate or minimize data errors in a database or information product.

defect rate

The percentage of data that is incorrect, inaccurate, or no longer true. The number of defects found compared to the total number of data values.

Defense Advanced Research Projects Agency (DARPA)

The U.S. federal funding source for development of the semantic web.

Define-Measure-Analyze-Design-Verify (DMADV)

A Six Sigma process improvement method, used for projects to design and create new product or processes.

Define-Measure-Analyze-Improve-Control (DMAIC)

A Six Sigma process improvement method, used for projects to improve existing business processes.

definition

1. A statement conveying a fundamental character or the meaning of a word, phrase, or term. It is a clear, distinct, detailed statement of the precise meaning or significance of something. (Brackett 2011)
2. The process of assigning names, description, and specification.

degenerate dimension

SEE dimension, degenerate.

degenerate fact table

SEE fact table, factless.

degree

The number of attributes (columns) in a record or relation including those making up the identifier. (Everest 2010)

delete

1. To remove or erase.
2. A SQL statement (command) that specifies removal of data in a relational database.

deliverable

An expected output or outcome from a project, function, activity, or task. Usually an information delivery product, such as a document or database.

delta

1. A Greek letter (Δ) signifying the difference between two statistical values.
2. The term used to identify rows that have changed between time periods, used in ETL processing.

delta update

A dataset containing only the data that was updated between the last extraction or snapshot process and the current execution of the extraction or snapshot.

Deming Cycle

The "plan-do-check-act" cycle of continuous improvement developed by Walter Shewhart and popularized by W. Edwards Deming. SEE ALSO Shewhart Cycle.

demographics

A segment of a population delineated by certain shared inherent characteristics.

demography

The study of human populations through statistics.

denormalization

The process of reversing the decomposition resulting from applying the rules of normalization; recombining records. (Everest 2010)

dense index

SEE index, dense.

density-equalizing map

SEE chart, area cartogram.

Department of Defense Architecture Framework (DODAF)

An architecture framework developed by the U.S. Department of Defense in the 1990s.

dependency

Characteristic of a relationship that expresses "must have at least one." Also called mandatory, required, exhaustive, or NOT NULL. Opposite of optional, orphan, or nullable. (Everest 2010)

dependency, functional

1. In a relationship, a constraint between any two attributes, where one attribute value matches to one and only one value of the other attribute.
2. Used in the context of an attribute in an entity record, an attribute instance cannot exist without being related to an entity instance (the dependency part) and there can be at most one instance (value) for that attribute for each entity instance (the function part where A = fn(X) - given a value for X, fn uniquely determines a value for A. In this case, X is called the determinant of A.).

dependency, multi-valued

In a relationship, a constraint between sets of attributes where the values of one set of attributes match to one and only one other set of attribute values. Contrast with functional dependency where the constraints involve only one attribute from each set.

dependency, partial

A type of dependency in which the value of a non-key field is determined by a part of a composite key, thus violating second Normal form.

dependency, transitive

A type of dependency in which the values of non-key attributes are determined by another non-key attribute, rather than the entity key. It is a functional dependency but between two non-key attributes, hence violating third Normal Form. SEE ALSO dependency, functional.

dependent data mart

A data mart whose tables are sourced from an Enterprise Data Warehouse.

dependent entity

SEE data entity, dependent.

deployment

The act of putting information technology into productive use. Installation puts the system into the production environment. Deployment includes installation, but also includes efforts to train and encourage effective use.

deployment diagram

A visual representation of the configuration of a system deployed in a production environment, including hardware, software, data objects, and all processes that use them, including processes that only exist while executing.

derived attribute

SEE data attribute, derived.

derived data

SEE data, derived.

description

1. A textual representation of a thing.
2. A class word, abbreviated usually to desc.
3. DCMI element in element set Content: a textual, tabular, or graphical portrayal of a resource. SEE ALSO Dublin Core Metadata Initiative.

descriptive meta-data

SEE meta-data, descriptive.

descriptive model

A model that describes how a system actually works.

design

1. A deliberate, purposeful plan, layout, delineation, arrangement, and specification of the component parts and interfaces of a product or system. A logical design is an abstract design for fulfilling requirements without consideration for physical constraints. A physical design considers the requirements along with physical constraints.
2. *Verb.* To conceive, plan, define, arrange, and specify a product or system.

Design For Six Sigma (DFSS)

SEE Define-Measure-Analyze-Design-Verify.

design review

A process where all aspects of a system design are reviewed publicly before code construction starts.

Desktop OLAP (DOLAP)

SEE OnLine Analytical Processing, Desktop.

determinant

The entity domain that determines the value of an attribute. SEE ALSO dependency, functional.

deterministic matching

A type of matching that relies on defined patterns and rules for assigning weights and scores for determining similarity. (DAMA-DMBOK Guide, 1st edition, pg. 310.)

developer

A person who designs, codes and/or tests software. Different types are known as software developer, systems developer, application developer, software engineer, or application engineer.

development activity

In the DAMA-DMBOK Functional Framework, an activity undertaken with projects and recognized as part of the Systems Development LifeCycle, creating data deliverables through analysis, design, building, testing, and deployment. SEE ALSO activity group.

deviation

The measure of difference between expected and observed values, or more generally, between any two values.

diagram

A visual representation of relationships between multiple things, i.e., how a system works, how parts are related to the whole. SEE ALSO chart.

dialect

A subset of language used or agreed to by a group of people. An ontology defines the precise meaning of the vocabulary in a dialect and the relationship between these terms.

dice

A slice operation on more than two dimensions of a data cube, or more than two consecutive slices. (DAMA-DMBOK Guide, 1st edition, pg. 236.) SEE ALSO slice.

dictionary

A collection of definitions for words, terms, and phrases that differentiate closely related words. SEE ALSO data dictionary.

Digital Elevation Model (DEM)

A digital representation of a topography or terrain, using regular shapes (squares or triangles) to approximate roughness of a surface.

digital preservation

The management of data on digital media over time. As digital media storage mediums and storage applications change, either data must be moved to new media, or old storage retrieval mechanisms and applications must be kept operational.

digital rights management

A generic term for technologies that can be used to impose limitations on usage of digital content and/or devices.

Digital Terrain Model (DTM)

SEE digital elevation model.

digitize

Verb. To convert something into a binary representation for computer storage and/or use.

dimension

1. Generally, an axis from which you can regard or summarize something.
2. In architecture, one of a series of properties that together are used to uniquely identify a location or a component of a system.
3. In Business Intelligence, a category for summarizing or viewing data (e.g., time period, product, product line, geographic area, organization).
4. In dimensional modeling, a type of table, or a structural attribute of a data cube containing a list of members, all of which are of a similar type in the user's perception of the data. For example, all months, quarters, years, etc., make up a time dimension; likewise all cities, regions, countries, etc., make up a geography dimension. A dimension acts as an index for identifying values within a multi-dimensional array. Dimensions offer a very concise, intuitive way of organizing and selecting data for retrieval, exploration, and analysis.

dimension table

In dimensional modeling, a table containing a row for each occurrence of a dimension list, linked to one or more fact tables through use of the dimension table key as a foreign key in each related fact table.

dimension, conformed

A dimension that exists once but is used in multiple star schemas, so that the dimension content and meaning is the same regardless of which fact table is joined.

dimension, degenerate

A dimension where there are no valid dimensional attributes other than a unique identifier in a one-to-one relationship with a fact table.

dimension, junk

A dimension that consists of multiple loosely-related codes and indicators collected into one table in order to reduce the number of keys and indexes needed in a star schema.

dimension, mini

A dimension that includes attributes of another dimension that change over time more frequently than is desired. This sometimes greatly enhances load performance by concentrating the write operations to a small subset of attributes.

dimension, slowly changing

A dimension containing data that changes over time, such that the rate of change is a small percentage of the total row count (i.e., 1% per quarter). Dimensions of type 0, 1, 2, 2A, 3, 4, and 6 are all types of slowly changing dimensions.

dimension, slowly growing

A dimension that slowly increases in the number of rows.

dimension, type 0

A dimension where no updates occur. All rows stay as they were when initially written to the table.

dimension, type 1

A dimension in which all attributes are type 1, so all attributes are overwritten with new data.

dimension, type 2

A dimension in which all attributes are type 2, so any attribute that changes for the business key requires generation of a new row.

dimension, type 2A

Similar to a type 2 dimension, a type 2A writes a new row for any change in the data for the row and is time-date stamped. However, the old row is retired to a history table; it is not left in the current table. So in effect, the type 2A table resembles a type 1 in its contents. However, it can be joined to the history table to get a full type 2 view.

dimension, type 3

A dimension in which all attributes are type 3, so that any attribute that changes for the business key will require copying attribute values to other attributes before the original attributes are overwritten.

dimension, type 4

A dimension table where the data is physically split into two tables, one with the current value rows, and the other with only historical value rows.

dimension, type 6

A dimension table which combines the attributes of types 1, 2 and 3 (1+2+3=6).

dimensional aggregate

A computed value derived from the calculation of a fact measure at the intersection of one or more dimensions at non-granular levels.

dimensional model

A specialized type of physical data model particular to a retrieval-only database design, commonly used in Data Warehouses and data marts, where de-normalized fact tables are linked to dimension tables. Star schemas and snowflake schemas are examples of dimensional models.

direct access file system

A protocol for data access across systems using data files instead of blocks.

Direct Access Storage Device (DASD)

A type of storage device where access is directly to the device, rather than through a cache or other interface.

Direct Attached Storage (DAS)

A storage device attached to a server or workstation without the use of a storage network.

Direct Marketing Association (DMA)

The largest and oldest international trade association that seeks to advance the efficacy of all forms of direct marketing.

directory

1. Generally, information heavily optimized for searching and reading.
2. In data storage, a table, index or folder containing addresses and locations of data or relationships between data objects.
3. In operating systems, a synonym for a folder in Windows and other operating systems, used to organize stored files and other folders.
4. A type of meta-data store that limits the meta-data to the location or source of data in the enterprise. (DAMA-DMBOK 1st edition, pg. 282.)

dirty data

Data with a high degree of inaccuracy, incompleteness, inconsistency, or that fail some edit criteria.

disaggregation

The breakdown of computations usually within a common branch of a hierarchy, to a more detailed level for which detailed measures can be attributed.

disambiguate

Verb. To clarify the meaning of a term by selecting between alternate interpretations.

disambiguation

The process of identifying attributes to differentiate or clarify between alternate interpretations.

disaster recovery

A protocol and associated execution to recover lost computing-system usage (applications, data, and data transactions) committed up to the moment of system loss.

disparate

Adjective. Fundamentally dissimilar in kind, or containing or including dissimilar or unlike attributes. Opposite of similar.

disparate data

Data that are essentially not alike, or are distinctly different in kind, quality, or character. They are unequal and cannot be readily integrated to meet the business information demand. They are low quality, defective, discordant, ambiguous, heterogeneous data. (Brackett 2011)

distance cartogram

SEE chart, distance cartogram.

distributed database

SEE database, distributed.

Distributed Relational Database Architecture (DRDA)

An IBM architecture for coordinating data across multiple relational Database Management Systems.

document

1. Generally, any information delivery vehicle, paper or electronic.
2. In data management, the content and structure in an electronic file.
3. In document or record management, a paper object in the real world, which may include signatures.

document and content management

Managing data found outside of standard structured databases. One of ten data management functions identified in the DAMA-DMBOK Functional Framework. (DAMA-DMBOK Guide, 1st edition, pg. 7.)

document management

The storage, inventory, and control of electronic and paper documents. (DAMA-DMBOK Guide, 1st edition, pg. 239.)

Document Management System (DMS)

An application used to track and store electronic documents and/or images of paper documents. Document management systems commonly provide storage, versioning, meta-data, and security, as well as indexing and retrieval capabilities.

Document Object Model (DOM)

A platform and language neutral application programming interface that allows programs and scripts to dynamically access nodes in an XML document and update the content, structure and style of these documents.

Document Type Definition (DTD)

A text file that specifies the meaning of each tag.

document, record, and content management

Control over capture, storage, access and use of data stored outside structured databases. An older name for one of ten data management functions identified in the DAMA Functional Framework.

documentation

Descriptive text and images used to define or describe an object, design, specification, instructions, or procedure.

domain

1. Generally, a set of things that have a common definition, such as the set of possible values for an attribute, or the population of an entity.
2. In data modeling, a type of attribute with common properties and purposes, such as key, code, date, indicator, amount, name, or description.
3. In an ontology, a constraint limiting the classes that can use a property.

domain chaos

A characteristic of multiple attributes using a domain where the domain of valid values used are not internally consistent from attribute to attribute, or are not applied consistently. Example: a unit of measure code domain where one attribute uses the code to show quantity on hand as "doz", and another shows reorder point quantity in numerals.

domain constraint

SEE constraint, domain.

domain key

SEE key, business.

Domain Name System (DNS)

A hierarchical naming system, built on a distributed database, to associate various information with domain names assigned to each of the participating entities. The DNS serves as the phone book for the Internet by translating human-friendly computer hostnames into IP addresses. This system is managed by Internet Corporation for Assigned Names and Numbers (ICANN).

Domain Name System server **Alternate form: DNS server**

The Domain Name System uses a distributed database system architecture based on the client/server model. The nodes are the name servers. Each top-level domain has at least one authoritative DNS server that publishes information about that domain and the name servers of any domains subordinate to it.

domain study

The study of a domain of values for a data item, to determine if that item is similar to another item and a candidate for integration or merging.

Domain/Key Normal Form (DKNF)

SEE Normal Form, Domain/Key.

dot.com

Internet-based companies that rely on digital technology and the use of the Web as the primary communication and interaction media.

downtime **Alternate form: down-time**

A general condition wherein users cannot use or access computing systems, applications, data, or information for a broad variety of reasons.

drill across

Data analysis performed across multiple dimensions.

drill anywhere

The ability to "drill down" to any dimension without having to follow predefined drill paths.

drill down

A method of exploring detailed data that was used in creating a summary level of data. Drill down levels depend on the granularity of data within a dimension.

drill through

An OLAP function often used to imply the ability to navigate from dimensionally aggregated data to relational transaction source data. Typically, the transaction set returned is constrained by multiple filters in accordance with the starting dimensional aggregate.

drill up

Data analysis performed on a data set with applied mathematical functions, associated with fewer dimensions, higher levels of hierarchy in one or more dimensions, or both.

Dublin Core

A standard core ontology for meta-data about documents, originating in Dublin Ohio and managed by the Dublin Core Metadata Initiative.

Dublin Core Metadata Initiative (DCMI)

The Dublin Core Metadata Initiative is an open forum engaged in the development of interoperable online meta-data standards that support a broad range of purposes and business models.

dummy key

SEE key, surrogate.

duplex

Adjective. Describes a system that has communication paths in both directions between two parties.

duplicate identification match rule

SEE rule, duplicate identification match.

DW 2.0

DW 2.0 - Advanced Data Warehouse architecture that includes the life cycle of data in the Data Warehouse, the integration of unstructured data, and enterprise metadata.

dynamic data dictionary

A data dictionary that an application program accesses at run time.

Dynamic Data Exchange (DDE)

An industry standard widely accepted by application software for exchanging data among different software programs.

dynamic SQL

Dynamically constructed SQL queries that are not pre-processed, and whose access paths are determined at run time prior to execution.

E

e-business

Simply doing business electronically, usually over the Internet. The two main types of e-business are business-to-consumer (B2C) and business-to-business (B2B).

e-commerce

Consumers doing business with a commercial enterprise directly through computers and without other human intermediaries. SEE ALSO Business-to-Consumer; e-business.

Economic Value Added (EVA)

A value-based metric for performance measurement, value-based planning, and incentive compensation developed by Joel Stern and G. Bennett Steward III. EVA is calculated by taking operation profits and deducting a charge for the cost of capital.

edge

In graph theory, a connection between two nodes in a graph. Also known as an arc.

Edgeworth box chart

SEE chart, Edgeworth box.

edit and validate

Assuring data is created in conformance with business rules. Database integrity controls and software routines can enforce business rules.

Electronic Data Interchange (EDI)

Standards-driven technology for high-volume B2B e-business transaction exchange, linking application systems across enterprises, so that a transaction on one system at one company generates a like transaction on a system at another company. More sophisticated EDI implementations transform the way business procedures are executed to gain optimal productivity.

Electronic Data Interchange for Administration, Commerce, and Transport (EDIFACT)

The international EDI standard developed by the United Nations, and maintained by the United Nations Center for Trade Facilitation and Electronic Business. EDIFACT provides a set of syntax rules for data structures, an exchange protocol for interaction, and standard communication messages that allow multi-country and multi-industry exchange. Can be compared to XML, however EDIFACT data is very cryptic, whereas XML is human-readable.

Electronic Document Management System (EDMS)

A system used to track and store electronic documents or images of paper documents.

Electronic Health Record (EHR)

The systematic collection of individual patient or population health information.

Electronics Record Archive (ERA)

A strategic initiative of the U.S. National Archives and Records Administration (NARA) to preserve and provide long-term access to Federal, Presidential, and Congressional records.

element

1. SEE component.
2. For use with data, SEE data attribute.

elementary fact sentence

A sentence having one predicate (verb phrase) and one or more nouns or noun phrases which serve as subject(s) or objects; can also include modifiers with the verb or nouns, such as must, only, at most one, at least one. The basis for Object Role Modeling or Fact Oriented Modeling (formerly called NIAM). (Everest 2010)

Elementary Key Normal Form (EKNF)

SEE normal form, elementary key.

emulation

The process of providing results of one system using another different system, such that the results are identical even if the processes are not.

encapsulation

1. A method of communication protocol design which separates network functions from underlying structures.
2. In object-oriented design, the combination of structure (data and values) and operations (processes; program code) associated with an object. The processes use the data to act on objects.

encryption

The conversion of a recognizably meaningful character stream to an unrecognizable character stream by means of a cipher code, in order to secure data and prevent unauthorized access of personally identifiable information, and/or company confidential information.

encryption, private key

An encryption method where both the writer and reader use the same key to encrypt and decrypt messages or character strings, respectively.

encryption, public key

An encryption method where the key to encode the information is different from the key to decode the information.

encyclopedia/tool encyclopedia

A non-definable meta-data store used by an application development tool.

Engineers as Builders

Zachman Framework row name, matches Technology Physics.

enterprise

The scope of an organization as defined by that organization based on a purpose or point of view. An enterprise may be a business, not-for-profit, government agency, or educational institution. An enterprise has a purpose, goals, and objectives.

Enterprise Application Integration (EAI)

Technology that allows data sharing between unrelated systems in the organization, providing a single point of interface to which all applications and databases connect, resolving differences between systems, triggering processes and delivering data in the proper format to the proper destination.

enterprise architecture

SEE architecture, enterprise.

enterprise BI portal

A web-based approach to distributing business information, consolidating Business Intelligence objects (reports, documents, spreadsheets, data cubes, etc.) and making them easily accessible, subject to security authorization, to non- technical users via standard browser technology.

Enterprise Content Management (ECM)

SEE content management.

enterprise data

Data that is shared across more than one function within an enterprise, or is created and used by one function but still considered essential to the enterprise.

enterprise data architecture

Part of the complete enterprise architecture, including

a) an enterprise data model, and
b) the information value chain analysis that identifies the linkages and alignment of the data model with enterprise views of business functions and processes, organizations, applications and enterprise goals.

SEE ALSO architecture, data.

Enterprise Data Fabric (EDF)

A data layer that separates data sources from applications, providing the means to solve the potential gridlock prevalent in distributed environments such as grid computing and service-oriented architecture.

Enterprise Data Management (EDM)

A structured program for managing physical data resources as they are used by the enterprise.

Enterprise Data Model (EDM)

SEE Data Model, Enterprise.

enterprise data modeling

The development of a common consistent view and understanding of data entities and attributes, and their relationships across the enterprise.

enterprise data strategy

A data strategy supporting the entire enterprise.

Enterprise Data Warehouse (EDW)

A centralized Data Warehouse designed to service the Business Intelligence needs of the entire enterprise. An EDW adheres to an enterprise data model to ensure consistency of decision support data across the enterprise.

enterprise information architecture

An architecture for managing information contained in multiple formats across an enterprise. SEE ALSO enterprise data architecture.

Enterprise Information Integration (EII)

Technology providing custom views into multiple databases transparently to enable applications to more easily provide integrated real time read and write access across databases.

Enterprise Information Management (EIM)

A structured program for managing information as a strategic asset.

Enterprise JavaBeans (EJB)

A server application component architecture defined by Sun. EJB is used to create application objects, and related content may be sent using Java server pages (JSPs).

enterprise model

The collection of enterprise data models, enterprise process models, and any other model addressing the entire enterprise in scope. The complete set of enterprise models is commonly called the enterprise architecture.

Enterprise Performance Management (EPM)

An enterprise-wide program that provides a structured approach for deploying and evaluating a company's strategy in a consistent and continuous manner. It gives an organization the capability to effectively communicate strategy and ensure that business processes are aligned to support the deployment of that strategy.

enterprise process architecture

Process models of the entire enterprise at the contextual and conceptual level, typically including

a) a functional decomposition,
b) process flow diagrams,
c) business process modeling (BPM) diagrams and
d) value chain analysis linking processes to data (subject areas or entities), organizations, roles, goals, existing and planned applications and/or implementation projects and programs.

enterprise reporting

1. The process of producing reports using unified views of enterprise data.
2. A category of software tools used to produce reports; a term for what were simply known as reporting tools.

Enterprise Resource Planning (ERP)

Systems that tie together many of an enterprise's functions, including finance, manufacturing, sales and human resources. ERP systems enable analysis of integrated data to plan production, forecast sales, and analyze product and process quality. Many organizations extend the ERP architecture through Data Warehousing to support of more advanced reporting, analytical and decision support capabilities.

Enterprise Risk Management (ERM)

The process of planning, organizing, leading, and controlling the activities of an organization in order to minimize the effects of risk on its capital and earnings. ERM includes not only risks associated with accidental losses, but also financial, strategic, operational, and other risks.

Enterprise Service Bus (ESB)

A software layer that provides data between services on an event-driven basis, using standards for data transmission between the services.

enterprise storage

Storage designed for large-scale, high availability environments.

entity

1. Any concrete or abstract thing that exists, did exist, or might exist, including associations among these things e.g. a person, object, event, idea, process, etc.
2. In mathematics, is a single existent, such as an employee John J. Smith. (Brackett 2011)

Entity Attribute Relationship (EAR)

The presentation of a data model diagram which shows Entities, Relationships between (among) entities, and Attributes of entities, hence EAR.

entity extraction

The process of scanning unstructured documents to find identifiable entities, based on contextual clues.

entity generalization

SEE generalization, entity.

entity hierarchy

The set of connected parent-child relationships of which an entity is a connected part. SEE ALSO hierarchy.

entity instance

1. Generally, the existence of a thing or the happening of an event.
2. In data modeling, a single specimen or member of an entity type population. SEE ALSO object.

entity life history

The changes to the entity occurrence over its lifecycle.

entity lifecycle

The phases and distinct states through which an entity moves through time. A state transition diagram documents the entity lifecycle.

entity occurrence

SEE entity instance.

Entity Relationship (ER)

Any relationship or connection between two entities, concepts, or objects.

Entity Relationship Diagram (ERD) **Alternate form: ER Diagram, E-R Diagram**

The graphical diagram for an Entity Relationship data model. The underlying data model generally includes more semantics than is or can be represented in the view shown on the diagram, e.g., some business rules.

entity relationship model

1. Generally, a record-based data modeling scheme that focuses on entities and relationships in the presentation of data model diagrams, thus suppressing the display of attributes. A true ER model allows multi-valued data items and repeating groups of items (nested relations, thus violating first normal form), retains M:N relationships, attributed relationships, subtypes/supertypes, ternary and higher-order relationships, none of which can be represented directly in a relational data model. A true ER model generally excludes (defers) the representation of entity identifiers and foreign keys. Originally proposed and named by Peter Chen (1976).
2. In relational modeling, the most popular style of data model, defining entities and the business relationships between the entities. Some more detailed models include also some of the attributes of these entities, usually those involved in the relationships as keys.

entity set

In mathematics, is a group of like entities, such as Employee. (Brackett 2011)

entity type

A population of entity instances which conform to the same data definition or schema, often synonymous with object type or class. An entity type represents a class of objects in the users' universe of discourse, their world represented in a data model. They may be persons, places, things, abstract concepts, events, etc. of interest to the enterprise. (Everest 2010)

entity, business

Something of interest to an organization. It may be concrete or an abstract concept. May be represented by a data entity in a data model. (Everest 2010) SEE ALSO entity type.

entity, event

Discrete occurrences that are noted by time stamps or other ordering attributes.

entity, kernel

An entity that is at the top of a hierarchy, the basic high-level entity.

entity, reference

An entity that classifies something else, or that something else refers to for clarity.

entropy

The measurement of uncertainty in an outcome, or randomness in a system.

environment

1. In the computer technology context, it refers to the conditions surrounding data, such as databases, data formats, servers, network, and any other components that affect the data.
2. In a business context, the influencing factors on business performance.

environmental element

An aspect of an organization and its business processes defined in the DAMA-DMBOK Functional Framework. The seven environmental elements are Goals & Principles, Activities, Deliverables, Roles & Responsibilities, Practices & Techniques, Technology, and Organization & Culture.

epistemology

A branch of philosophy that studies the nature of truth and knowledge.

equivalence

A relationship where each side implies or replaces the other; interchangeable.

ergonomics

The study of how technology affects the health of the human body. Also known as biotechnology.

error

1. An incorrectly stated, inaccurate, or no longer valid fact.
2. An incorrect action taken in a process, usually resulting in a defect.

error rate

1. The frequency with which errors occur in transactions. Also called the failure rate.
2. In data quality, the percentage of data that is incorrect, inaccurate, or no longer true. Also called the data defect rate.

essential

Adjective. Required, critical.

estimate

The particular value yielded by an estimator or an estimate process in a given set of circumstances.

Ethernet

A local area network protocol developed by Xerox in cooperation with DEC and Intel. Ethernet uses a bus topology and supports transfer rates of 10 Mbps. The Ethernet specification served as the basis for the IEEE 802.3 standard, which specifies the physical and lower software layers.

ethics

In general, a social system's rules of behavior with which all members of that social system are expected to comply. Contrast with morals. SEE ALSO professional ethics.

evaluational data

Subject oriented, integrated, time variant, non-volatile collections of data in support of management's decision-making process. They are used to evaluate the business and usually contain summary data with some capability to drill down to detail data. (Brackett 2011)

event

The occurrence of some action of interest to the enterprise, usually characterized at a point in time. For a period of time, recognizing that a process may span a duration of time, the start and stop of the process would be the events. SEE ALSO transaction.

event analysis

A process of analyzing notifications and taking action based on the notification content.

event data

Data about business events (often system transactions) that have historic significance, or are needed for analysis by other systems. Event data is atomic data that may be aggregated.

event entity

SEE entity, event.

event tree

SEE chart, event tree.

Event-driven Process Chain (EPC)

A type of flowchart used for Business Process Modeling, Enterprise Resource Planning, and Business Process Improvement. Consists of a sequence of events in a process, the functions that execute following that event, the inputs, supporting systems, outputs and organization units supporting that function, the control flows between events and functions, and logical decision points (branch/merge, fork/join, and OR).

Exabyte (Eb)

One thousand Petabytes.

EXCEPT

A SQL set operator that returns one tabular SELECT answer sets with consistent column structures from two answer sets where rows in the 'left' table do not have matches in the 'right' table using the join conditions.

eXchangeable Faceted Metadata Language (XFML)

An open XML specification for defining and sharing faceted classifications.

exclusivity

Characteristic of a relationship that expresses “at most one.”

executive data steward

A role held by a senior manager sitting on the Data Governance Council, accountable for the data quality and data practices within a department, for planning and oversight of data management programs, and appointment of other data stewards. Sometimes referred to as a strategic data steward.

Executive Information System (EIS)

Business Intelligence software products provide sets of reports (“briefing books”) to top-level executives. They offer strong reporting and drill-down capabilities, along with ad hoc query against a multi-dimensional database, and most offer analytical applications along functional lines such as sales or financial analysis.

Executive Leaders as Owners

Zachman Framework row name, matches Business Concepts.

expert system

An artificial intelligence system driven by rules based on the skills and experience of one or more experts in a given field, so the system processes information the same way an expert person does. Expert systems are deterministic, versus neural networks, which are non-deterministic.

explicit

Adjective. Describes a formal expression of knowledge.

Exploratory Data Analysis (EDA)

The process of analyzing data to suggest hypotheses using statistical tools, which can then be tested.

Extended Binary Code Decimal Interchange Code (EBCDIC)

An 8-bit character encoding used by IBM. SEE ALSO ASCII.

Extended Entity Relationship (EER)

An Entity Relationship model developed by Toby Teorey, which includes more information, such as for ternary relationships and supertype/subtype relationships.

eXtended Intelligent Enterprise Architecture (XIE)

Foundational architecture composed of three core components: a zero-latency ODS, an enterprise portal as an access mechanism and extensive integration capabilities.

extensibility **Alternate form: extendibility**

The ability to easily add new functionality to existing services without major software rewrites or without redefining the basic architecture.

eXtensible Business Reporting Language (XBRL)

An XML-based markup language developed for financial reporting. It provides a standards-based method to prepare, publish (in a variety of formats), reliable extract and automatically exchange financial statements according to GAAP standards.

eXtensible Markup Interface (XMI)

A specification that contains rules for generating an XML document containing meta-data. (DAMA-DMBOK Guide, 1st Edition, pg. 252.)

eXtensible Markup Language (XML)

A tag-based markup language (a subset of SGML) containing a set of rules for encoding documents in machine-readable form, defined by W3C with a tag set that can be extended. The tags enable XML documents to be self-describing data structures.

eXtensible Stylesheet Language (XSL)

A tag language that describes how data is presented. XSL may also be used to transform XML data into HTML/CSS documents on the Web servers.

eXtensible Stylesheet Language Transformation (XSLT)

A language for transforming XML documents into other XML documents. XSLT is designed for use as part of XSL.

extensional

Adjective. Defined by a specific and finite list of values, not by conformity to any rule or requirement. Opposite of intensional.

external data tracking

The process of monitoring the flow of data between data sites in different organization. (Brackett 2011)

Extract-Transform-Load (ETL)

1. Generally, an approach to data integration from multiple source databases to integrated target databases (Operational Data Stores, Data Warehouses, or Data Marts).
2. Commonly, a software product or tool that extracts data from a data source, converts data to a new format, and loads the data to a target database. SEE ALSO data integration.

extranet

An internal network or intranet opened to selected business partners. Suppliers, distributors, and other authorized users can connect to a company's network over the Internet or through private networks.

eXtreme Programming (XP)

An updated approach to Rapid Application Development using object-oriented techniques and a minimum of specifications.

extrinsic

Adjective. Describes a property that is nonspecific and unessential to a thing or event.

F

facet taxonomy

SEE taxonomy, facet.

fact

1. A verifiably true data point.
2. In dimensional modeling, an attribute that can be measured.

Fact Oriented Modeling (FOM)

A data model that is built up from elementary facts. SEE Object Role Model. The term used primarily in Europe, and considered more generic. SEE ALSO elementary fact sentence.

fact table

In dimensional modeling, a central table that contains numerical measures and keys relating facts to dimension tables. Fact tables contain data that describes specific events or transactions (such as bank transactions) or results from mathematical functions applied to the events or transactions (such as the net summary of a day's transactions against a single account).

fact table, accumulating snapshot

A fact table that contains data from multiple events on one row in order to track progression of steps within a process.

fact table, factless — **Alternate form: degenerate fact table**

A fact table that contains only events with no other inherent measurements. Some have a count variable set to 1, which allows summing of these events using more optimal aggregation functions. An example is a fact table that records the attendance of a student in a class.

fact table, snapshot

A fact table that contains data showing the state of something at a point in time.

fact table, transaction

A fact table that contains data showing a change of some kind. Common transaction fact tables include data on sales, assignment changes, etc.

factless fact table

SEE fact table, factless.

Fagan inspection — **Alternate form: Fagan's domain key criterion**

A structured process named for Michael Fagan that evaluates activities or operations that have entry and exit criteria for compliance with those criteria.

failure rate

The frequency with which errors occur in transactions. SEE ALSO defect rate.

failure transparency

The extent to which errors and recoveries within a distributed system are invisible to users and applications.

failure tree

SEE chart, fault tree.

false negative

An incorrect result, which fails to detect a condition or return a result that is actually present.

false positive

An incorrect result, which detects a condition or returns a result that is not actually present.

fault tree

SEE chart, fault tree.

Federal Information Processing Standard (FIPS)

A numeric code that identifies U.S. states, districts, and protectorates with 2 digit codes and counties with 3 digit codes.

federated data warehouse

SEE data warehouse, federated.

federated database

A set of databases that are documented and then interconnected to operate as one database, even when those databases are on different platforms. A person desiring data goes to the federation and gets the data they need without knowing where those data reside. (Brackett 2011)

field

The physical container for values of an attribute.

fifth Normal Form (5NF)

SEE Normal Form, fifth.

file

A collection of information either on paper, or electronically in the form of data fields (or more complex structures) which describe a set of entities possessing some common characteristics or attributes; a collection of zero or more records which may have an arbitrarily complex structure (flat, hierarchical, etc.).

File Allocation Table (FAT)

A table on a disk that catalogs the location and size of files on disk, as well as free and unusable areas.

File Transfer Program/File Transfer Protocol (FTP)

A service that allows you to transfer files to and from other computers. Anyone who has access to FTP can transfer publicly available files to his or her computer.

filter

A saved set of selective criteria specifying a subset of data in a database.

Financial Accounting Standards Board (FASB)

A private organization whose mission is to "establish and improve standards of financial accounting and reporting for the guidance and education of the public, including issuers, auditors and users of financial information." FASB publishes the Generally Accepted Accounting Principles (GAAP).

financial consolidation

The process of combining and aggregating data from different financial systems to create integrated financial analytic views and comprehensive financial statements compliant with accounting and financial reporting standards.

financial integrity

Compliant and reliable financial data, achieved through quality integrated systems and processes, strong internal control, validations to ensure accuracy and conformance with accounting and reporting standards.

firewall

A combination of specialized hardware and software set up to monitor traffic between an internal network and an external network (i.e. the Internet). Its primary purpose if for security and is designed to keep unauthorized outsiders from tampering with or accessing information on a networked computer system.

First In, First Out (FIFO)

A method of posting a transaction in "first-in-first-out" order. In other words, transactions are posted in the same order that the data producer entered them.

first Normal Form (1NF)

SEE Normal Form, first.

first valid date

The first date that an attribute or entity instance is valid.

fishbone diagram

SEE chart, cause-and-effect diagram.

flag

An attribute of a cell in a data set representing qualitative information about the value of that cell, either positive or negative. SEE ALSO indicator.

flat file

A file in which all the attribute fields are atomic, that is, single valued. SEE table. SEE ALSO database, relational.

flat taxonomy

SEE taxonomy, flat.

flatten

Verb. In a hierarchical data structure, to absorb all child records into their parent records (flattening up) or copying a parent record into each of its children (flattening down). In flattening up, each child type must be given a different name in the parent record, so that the parent record becomes a flat file with atomic fields. For example, in a hierarchical structure you may have a nested repeating group called address with a type attribute on each address instance (i.e., home, school, vacation, summer cabin). When flattened, each of the repeating attributes must be named differently, such as home street, summer street, etc. This is a technique to convert a hierarchical structure into a single flat file or relation that can be implemented more easily in a relational DBMS.

floating point

A system for using significant digits and exponents to represent numbers too large or small to display using the existing format or display criteria.

flying bricks chart

SEE chart, waterfall.

folksonomy

A system of classification that originates from collaboration of users to categorize (tag) and organize information; a usage-generated taxonomy.

force field diagram

SEE chart, force field diagram.

Foreign Key (FK)

SEE key, foreign.

fork

A graphical symbol used to represent manyness in the multiplicity characteristic of a relationship, preferred because it visually and intuitively communicates manyness. First proposed by Gordon Everest in a 1976 paper. Also called inverted arrow, chicken feet, crow's foot, or trident.

format

1. The specifications for layout or display of information, such as in a document or on a disk.
2. *Verb.* To apply display or configuration specifications to a document or data set.
3. DCMI element in element set Instantiation: physical characteristics of a resource. SEE ALSO Dublin Core Metadata Initiative.

formula **Alternate form: formulae**

A set of rules or instructions that, when applied to a specific input, will provide an expected output.

forward engineering

The process of generating physical structures from concepts and logical descriptions. SEE ALSO reverse engineering.

Fourth Generation Language (4GL)

A high-level language for manipulating a database, characterized by operations on sets of instances, that is, multiple records at a time. Contrast with low-level, one-record-at-a-time languages such as COBOL and Fortran, which are 3GL.

fourth Normal Form (4NF)

SEE normal form, fourth.

framework

1. Generally, a basic skeletal structure.
2. Conceptually, a classification scheme used to better understand a topic; a defined and documented paradigm, used as a lens to view a complex problem.
3. In software development, a reusable object-oriented design, including a library of reusable classes and other components, along with standards for designing additional components and how they interact.

fraud detection

The process of detecting patterns, trends, or correlations in consumer or corporate behavior that might indicate that fraudulent activity is taking place; e.g., identifying potential or existing fraud through analysis and comparison of standard and aberrant behaviors. SEE ALSO data mining.

frequency distribution

A tabulation of values output from a function given a set of inputs.

Frequently-Asked Questions (FAQ)

A list of questions and answers that are commonly seen regarding a topic.

Friend of a Friend (FOAF)

FOAF is describes social networks - people including activities and relationships between them. FOAF is a descriptive vocabulary using the RDF and the OWL. Computers use these FOAF profiles to find, for example, all people living in Illinois, or to list people both you and a friend of yours have in common, by defining relationships between people. Each profile has a unique identifier used to define relationships.

full duplex

Adjective. Describes a system that allows communication between two endpoints simultaneously. SEE ALSO half duplex; simplex.

full join

SEE join, outer.

full table space scan

The process of searching a table space or storage file rather than using the actual table structure.

function

1. Generally, the acts, operations, and duties expected of a person or thing.
2. In process design, a high-level process consisting of a group of closely related lower-level activities that together contribute to the overall purpose and health of an organization or person.
3. In mathematics, a transformation that operates on one or more independent variables, and produces a value for the dependent variable. Generally written as D=Fn(I). SEE ALSO dependency, functional.

function point

A unit of measurement expressing business functionality provided to a user by an information system, calculated using data from past projects.

functional data warehouse

SEE data warehouse, functional.

functional decomposition

SEE chart, functional decomposition.

functional dependency **Alternate form: functional dependence**

SEE dependency, functional.

functional requirement

SEE requirement, functional.

funnel chart

SEE chart, funnel.

fuzzy matching

A technique of decomposing words into component parts and comparing the parts to find an acceptable level of correspondence.

G

Gantt chart

SEE chart, Gantt.

gap analysis

An assessment of a system in comparison with another system or a set of requirements, listing those items that are not common between them.

Gartner Magic Quadrant

SEE chart, Magic Quadrant.

gateway

A software product that allows SQL-based applications to access relational and non-relational data sources.

gateway exchange

An organized set of bilateral exchanges, in which several data and meta-data sending organizations or individuals agree to exchange the collected information with each other in a single, known format, and according to a single, known process.

General Morphological Analysis (GMA)

A method for identifying and investigating configurations or relationships that affect a given problem by identifying all possible combinations, and then removing those that are impossible or inapplicable.

generalization

The process of recognizing commonalities, and combining similar types of entities or objects into a less specialized type based on common attributes and behaviors, creating a supertype for two or more specialized subtypes. Contrast with specialization.

generalization, attribute

The process of evaluating attributes in multiple related entities for commonalities and possibly moving specialized attributes from a child or subtype entity to a parent or supertype entity where the specialization applies to more than one of the children.

generalization, entity

The process of evaluating multiple entities in a set for commonalities and then possibly combining some of those entities into one larger entity that covers the topics represented by the subsumed entities.

generalization, relationship

The process of evaluating multiple relationships between entities in a set into fewer relationships. Usually necessary after other generalization activities have taken place, which carry the relationships of the specialized entities into the generalized entities. For example, two 1:M relationships between two entities, each having a different parent, can be generalized into a M:N relationship.

Generally Acceptable release (GA)

A release of software for general use; it has passed the quality gates of alpha and beta releases.

Generally Accepted Accounting Principles (GAAP)

The standard framework of guidelines for financial accounting in the United States; the standards, conventions, and rules accountants follow in recording and summarizing transactions, and in the preparation of financial statements, including definitions of what the categories in financial statements mean and what practices are commonly allowed. Managed by the Financial Accounting Standards Board.

Generally Accepted Data Management Principles (GADMP)

A term coined by The DAMA Foundation for principles documented in the DAMA-DMBOK Guide.

geodesy **Alternate form: geodetics**

The science of measuring the shape of a planet and geographical point placement. This science makes global positioning systems possible.

geodetic data

Data used in navigation and surveying to translate positions to a position on a planet.

Geographic Information System (GIS)

A system or tool for creating, storing, editing, analyzing, and managing geospatial data entities and associated attributes.

Geography markup language (GML)

An XML grammar used to express geographical features and attributes.

geomatics

The discipline of gathering, storing, processing, and delivering of geospatial data. The use of geospatial technology to survey and capture geospatial measurements.

geospacial

Adjective. Pertaining to data about locations on, in, above, or below a planet's surface.

geospatial data

Data pertaining to locations and regions on the earth, generally expressed as latitude and longitude (and sometimes altitude); can be located and reasoned about in terms of area.

Gigabyte (Gb)

A billion bytes of storage; a thousand Megabytes.

Global Data Synchronization Network (GSDN)

An internet-based network of data sets and a registry that enables exchange of standardized and synchronized data.

global index

SEE index, global.

Global Positioning System (GPS)

A fully-functional satellite navigation system. More than two dozen GPS satellites broadcasts precise timing signals by radio to GPS receivers, allowing them to accurately determine their location (longitude, latitude, and altitude) in any weather, day or night, anywhere on Earth. GPS has become a vital global utility, indispensable for modern navigation, as well as an important tool for map-making and land surveying. GPS also provides an extremely precise time reference, required for telecommunications and some scientific research. Officially named NAVSTAR GPS, the US Department of Defense developed the system. However, GPS is available for free use in civilian applications worldwide for the public good. SEE ALSO geospatial data; geographic information system.

Globally Unique Identifier (GUID)

A special type of identifier used in software applications to provide a unique reference number. The value is represented as a 32 character hexadecimal string, and usually stored as a 128 bit integer. Ideally, a GUID will never be generated twice by any computer or group of computers in existence. The term GUID usually, but not always, refers to Microsoft's implementation of the Universally Unique Identifier standard.

glossary

1. Generally, a dictionary covering a limited subject area.
2. In Meta-data Management, a glossary may be an extract of business meta-data (terms and their meanings) from a meta-data repository.

goal

A desired state or statement of general direction for long-term improvement. SEE ALSO objective.

Goal-Question-Metric method (GQM)

An approach which defines development efforts by starting with measurable goals at the conceptual level and drilling through operational processes into metrics, and then designing the resulting system to match.

goals and principles

One of the DAMA Functional Framework Environmental Elements. The directional business goals of each function and the fundamental principles that guide performance of each function. (DAMA-DMBOK Guide, 1st edition, pg. 12.)

gold data set **Alternate form: gold standard, gold source**

A data set with perfect contents according to requirements. Used to describe sources of record or data sets used for testing purposes. SEE ALSO system of record.

governance

1. Generally, the exercise of authority and control over a process, organization, or geopolitical area.
2. In data management, the process of setting, controlling, administering, and monitoring conformance with policy. SEE ALSO data governance.

grain **Alternate form: granularity**

The degree of summarization of data in a data set, representing the most detailed information available. All aggregations would result from mathematical functions using this data set, without any additional data.

grammar

The rules by which the syntact components of a language (whether linear or graphical) are assembled into meaningful sentences, command statements, or graphical structures based on semiotics.

graph

1. Generally, a set of homogeneous nodes (vertices) and edges (arcs) between pairs of nodes.
2. In Business Intelligence, a visual representation using references to a set of axes to illustrate the relationship between functions or sets of quantities. SEE ALSO chart.

graph theory

The study of mathematical structures used to model relations between items within a data set.

graphical data editing

The use of graphs to identify anomalies in data.

Graphical User Interface (GUI)

The dominant style for desktop and client/server computer applications.

Gregorian calendar

Internationally accepted civil calendar used in the western world, with additional rules regarding application of leap days, and other minor adjustments.

grid computing

A web-based operation allowing companies to share computing resources on demand.

Guide to the Project Management Body of Knowledge (PMBOK®)

SEE Body of Knowledge, Guide to the Project Management.

H

half duplex

Adjective. Describes a system that allows communication between two endpoints where only one may transmit at a time. SEE ALSO simplex; full duplex.

Hamming code

A class of binary linear codes used for parity calculation that can detect up to two simultaneous bit errors, rather than just odd numbers of errors. Named for Richard Hamming. Used in computer memory (RAM) and telecommunications for validating data transmission.

hash **Alternate form: hashing**

1. Data allocated in an algorithmically randomized fashion in an attempt to evenly distribute data and smooth access patterns.
2. *Verb.* To calculate a hash key for data.

hash key **Alternate form: hashed key**

SEE key, hash.

hash partitioning

SEE partitioning, hash.

Health Insurance Portability and Accountability Act, The (HIPAA)

A law enacted by the U.S. Congress in 1996. Title I of HIPAA protects health insurance coverage for workers and their families when they change or lose their jobs. Title II requires the establishment of national standards for electronic health care transactions and national identifiers for providers, health insurance plans, and employers. Title II also addresses the security and privacy of health data. The standards are meant to encourage use of electronic data interchange in US healthcare.

heat map

SEE chart, heat map.

heaven and hell chart

SEE chart, heaven and hell.

help desk

SEE call center.

heterogeneous

Adjective. Describes multiple members in a set that have differences in nature or structure. Opposite of homogeneous.

heuristics

"Rules of thumb" and approximation methods for obtaining a goal, a high quality solution, or improved performance. It sacrifices completeness to increase efficiency, as some potential solutions would not be practicable or acceptable due to their 'rareness' or 'complexity'. This method may not always find the best solution, but it will find an acceptable solution within a reasonable timeframe for problems that will require almost infinite or longer than acceptable times to compute.

hexadecimal

A numbering system using a base of 16, using letters A through F to represent 10 through 15 decimal. A byte is generally 8 binary digits, so that 1 hexadecimal representation represents 4 binary digits. Core dumps are expressed in hexadecimal for example.

hierarchical data model

SEE data model, hierarchical.

hierarchical database

SEE database, hierarchical.

Hierarchical Query Language (HQL)

A high-level language on a hierarchical data structure, similar to SQL on a multi-file data structure.

hierarchical relationship

SEE relationship, hierarchical.

hierarchical structure

SEE structure, hierarchical

hierarchical taxonomy

SEE taxonomy, hierarchical.

hierarchy

1. Generally, a classification structure arranged in levels of detail from the broadest to the most detailed level. Each level of the classification is defined in terms of the categories at the next lower level of the classification.
2. In dimensional modeling and dimensional databases, the organization of a dimension's members based on parent-child relationships, typically where a parent member represents the consolidation of child members.

high availability

A protocol and associated execution that ensures a certain relative degree of computing-system operational continuity in any down-time event.

histogram

A chart that shows quantities of data points that occur within various numeric ranges.

historical database

SEE database, historical.

historical revisionism

The reinterpretation of historical data based on new data, validated or invalidated assumptions about the data, or different perspectives on the environment that generated the data.

homogeneous

Adjective. Describes multiple members in a set that have no differences in nature or structure. Opposite of heterogeneous.

homogeneous nodes

A set of nodes conforming to the same definition (or of the same type).

homonym

A term that has the same or nearly same spelling or sound as another term, but has a different meaning. Contrast with synonym.

horizontal abstraction

SEE abstraction, horizontal.

horizontal partitioning

SEE partitioning, horizontal.

host-driven

Adjective. Describes a processing method in which the host computer controls the session. A host-driven session typically includes terminal emulation, front ending, or client/server types of connections. The host determines what is displayed on the desktop, receives user input from the desktop, and determines how the application responds to the input.

hot backup

SEE backup, hot.

house of quality chart

SEE chart, house of quality.

householding

Consolidating related names and addresses into groups.

How

Zachman Framework column name, matches Process Transformations.

human interface

An interface from a system to a human that enables the human to interact with and receive information from that system. SEE ALSO interface.

Hybrid OLAP (HOLAP)

SEE OnLine Analytical Processing, Hybrid.

hype-cycle chart

SEE chart, hype-cycle.

hyperbolic tree

SEE chart, hyperbolic tree.

hypercube

An OLAP product that stores all data in a single data cube which has all the application dimensions applied to it.

hyperlink

A one-way reference from one electronic document to another. Most frequently implemented as navigational links from one web page to another.

hypertext

Electronically stored text data organized into documents and logical sections that can be accessed randomly via hyperlinks as well as sequentially.

Hypertext Markup Language (HTML)

A tag set used to create a web page document; a subset of SGML (standard generalized markup language). The tags or elements tell the browser how to display the information. The tags are used to "mark," in a hierarchical format, the different components of the document.

HyperText Transfer Protocol (HTTP)

A system of communicating between a web browser application and a document stored on a web server.

I

iceberg diagram

SEE chart, iceberg diagram.

IDEF0 function modeling notation (IDEF0)

A specific style of notation for business process flow diagrams in process models. SEE ALSO Integrated DEFinition.

IDEF1X data modeling notation (IDEF1X)

SEE data modeling notation, IDEF1X.

IDEF2 simulation modeling notation (IDEF2)

A style of notation for modeling resource behavior over time in a simulation. SEE ALSO Integrated DEFinition.

IDentifier (ID)

1. The label (value, name, handle, ...) used to unambiguously refer to individual instances of a population. It is represented by a key in the records or relations of a database. There must be a 1:1 relationship between the values of the key, and the members of the population in the user world. Identifiers define keys (primary keys, candidate keys).
2. A class word assigned to attributes or columns containing unique identity values for that instance or row.
3. DCMI element in element set Instantiation: a unique reference to a resource. SEE ALSO Dublin Core Metadata Initiative.

identifying relationship

SEE relationship, identifying.

IE data modeling notation (IE)

SEE data modeling notation, Information Engineering.

image

A class word, abbreviated usually to img.

image management

The process of managing image files stored electronically.

impact analysis

Identifying the potential consequences of changing an object to its related objects.

implementation

Installing and converting to use of a software application.

inaccurate

Adjective. Not complying with a standard, model, or rule. Having defects or errors.

inconsistent

Adjective. Having disagreement or disparity among things or parts of things. Having internal contradictions.

increment

A portion of a complete implementation, considered as its own discrete project, but part of an overall implementation program.

incremental implementation

SEE Phased Implementation.

incremental load

Data propagation to a target database limited to the data that has changed in the source database since the last load.

index

1. Generally, a cross-reference created to find something that matches some selection criteria.
2. In data management, a data structure which cross references a set of values from the same domain to the places (records or rows) where each value appears, generally within a single file (SEE join index). An index is usually ordered according to the values in the domain. In general, an index can have multiple references (or pointers) for each value, unless the index is on an identifier, in which case there is a one-to-one relationship between the values and the record identifiers. An index is used to improve retrieval performance on a file; it does not add any new information to the database.
3. *Verb.* To create a cross-reference list.

index, bitmap

An indexing technique in which a separate structure stores the references to the data as bit arrays.

index, block

Describes an index where every key relates to a block in a data file, using the lowest search key in the block.

index, b-tree

A binary search tree index that stores index pointers in block partitions according to the values themselves. It simulates a binary search tree and uses corresponding search methods to give performance of the order of Log(base2)N, rather than N as in conventional indexes.

index, clustered

An indexing technique in which the actual data is physically stored in the order of the index values, rather than having the index in a separate structure pointing to the data rows. Only one clustered index may exist on an object at a time.

index, covering

An index where the values of the data are stored in the index, allowing data retrieval from the index itself, instead of the data object.

index, dense

Describes an index where every row in the indexed structure relates to a value in the index.

index, global

A type of index that either is related to a non-partitioned table, or is not partitioned even though the underlying table is partitioned.

index, inverted

An index structure that stores locations of keywords within a set of files, and possibly the location within the file, rather than a list of possible values, in order to provide speedy searches for words or phrases. Mostly used for content searches through multiple files, such as a search for the term "DAMA" within several web pages or documents.

index, local

A type of partitioned index where the index block corresponds to one and only one data block.

index, non-clustered

An indexing technique in which the actual data is stored in random order, not physically in the order of the index. Files can have multiple non-clustered indexes, and each non-clustered index will take up space as an object.

index, reverse

An indexing technique in which the value being indexed is reversed (reversing the characters or reversing the digits) before being sorted. This is especially useful for indexing sequence numbers, where the most significant digit rarely changes, but the least significant digit always does.

index, sparse

Describes an index where every possible value in the indexed object relates to a pointer in the index, and few of those values actually appear in the indexed file or object, so that the index is mostly empty. See also index, block.

index, unique

An index on an identifier, or attribute(s) defined as unique, in which case there can only be one pointer for each value entry in the index.

indexed file organization

A method of storing data such that the index key controls the physical order of the data within the file.

Indexed Sequential Access Method (ISAM) **Alternate form: block index**

A form of disk file management that uses indexes to assign storage information and retrieve data from the disk. Originally the name IBM assigned to its partial or block indexing scheme. Has since taken on a more generic usage.

indicator

1. An attribute type that is considered to be binary: On or Off, True or False, Yes or No.
2. A class word, abbreviated usually to ind.

induction

In data management, the process of creating categories from instances.

inference

Reasoning from known propositions.

inferential model

A model in which some of the data is inferred by actual data points.

information

1. Generally, understanding concerning any objects such as facts, events, things, processes, or ideas, including concepts that, within a certain context and timeframe, have a particular meaning.
2. The interpretation of data based on its context, including the
   a) the business meaning of data elements and related terms,
   b) the format in which the data is presented,
   c) the timeframe represented by the data, and
   d) the relevance of the data to a given usage.

   (DAMA-DMBOK Guide, 1st edition, pg. 2.)

Information and Communication Technology (ICT)

Synonymous with Information Technology, used predominantly in the United Kingdom, particularly in the UK education system.

information architecture

SEE architecture, information.

information asset

Data in any form or media placed into meaningful context for users, collected in relation to business or research activity.

Information Asset Management (IAM)

Formal management of data, and organization of the users of that data, that provide context and create information assets.

Information Awareness Office (IAO)

Established by the U.S. DARPA to collect and integrate personal information of U.S. citizens and residents, primarily targeted for data mining to detect threats to the country.

information chaos

Chaos in information that may be relevant and timely, but is interpreted incorrectly, inconsistently, or incompletely.

information consumer

A person or group that receives data and uses it to create information. A more descriptive term for a data consumer, since the consumer creates and uses information by interpreting data in context.

information directory

A collection of the meta-data that relates to Data Warehouse and Business Intelligence systems within an organization, providing some context to the meta-data to make it usable and searchable by business professionals in natural language terms. The directory includes business meta-data including definitions, domains, examples, relationships, functions, rules, advisories, and equivalents in other environments. It also may include technical meta-data about datatypes, lengths, number of distinct values, transformation rules, and replication schedules.

Information Engineering (IE)

In data modeling, a record-based data modeling scheme and notation developed by Clive Finkelstein in the 1970s and popularized by James Martin.

information engineering objective

To get the right data, to the right people, in the right place, at the right time, in the right form, at the right cost, so they can make the right decisions, and take the right actions. The operative term is the right data. (Brackett 2011)

information flow modeling

Depicts the complete flow of information from source to target. In Data Warehousing, shows the flow of data from all sources through intermediate structures into final targets where the data is turned into information.

Information Lifecycle Management (ILM)

An approach to manage the flow of a system's information from creation through usage to purge.

Information Management (IM)

The management of data in context, with relevance and timeframes, for business benefit.

information mapping

A technique of dividing and categorizing information for ease of comprehension and recall.

information model

A model showing information structure, usually at a conceptual or logical level.

information needs analysis

The identification and study of the information needs required to satisfy a particular business driver.

information overload

The state where the rate or amount of input to a system or person outstrips the capacity or speed of processing that input successfully.

information policy

A statement of principles and guidelines for information management.

Information Quality (IQ)

1. The degree to which information consistently meets the requirements and expectations of knowledge workers in performing their jobs. Larry English, Improving Data Warehouse and Business Information Quality, p. 478.
2. In the context of a specific use, the degree to which information, as prepared from the data, meets the requirements and expectations for that use.

information quality decay rate

The rate that information loses relevance over time if not refreshed and reviewed.

information quality management

A form of data quality management, although with an added emphasis on managing the quality of the context in which data appears as well as the quality of the data itself.

Information Resource Management (IRM)

SEE information management.

Information Services (IS)

SEE Information Technology.

information stewardship

SEE data stewardship.

Information Supply Chain (ISC)

The full set of data and processes - technical, procedural, and organizational - that

a) collect,
b) transform, and
c) distribute information appropriately.

Information System (IS)

1. Generally, an automated or manual organized process for collecting, manipulating, transmitting, and disseminating information. SEE ALSO application.
2. In data management, a system that supports decision-making concerning some piece of reality (the object system) by giving decision-makers access to information concerning relevant aspects of the object system and its environment.

Information Systems (IS)

SEE Information Technology.

information systems architecture

SEE architecture, information systems

Information Systems Planning (ISP)

The first phase in an Information Engineering methodology. The goal of an ISP is to define an enterprise architecture. ISP is usually performed as a separate project, defining several subsequent projects. SEE ALSO Business Systems Planning.

Information Technology (IT)

1. A broad subject concerned with technology and other aspects of managing and processing information, especially in large organizations. IT deals with the use of electronic computers and computer software to convert, store, protect, process, transmit, and retrieve information.
2. The department of an organization that deals with computer hardware, application software systems, and data. SEE ALSO Management Information Systems.

Information Technology Infrastructure Library (ITIL)

A framework of supplier independent best practice management procedures for delivery of high quality IT services.

information value chain analysis

A process to link conceptual and logical data models to process models, applications, organizations, roles and/or goals, to provide context, relevance, and timeframes.

information warehouse

IBM's approach to data warehousing that supports the implementation of either central, functional, or decentralized warehouses. It may provide information, but it does not contain information by itself. SEE ALSO Data Warehouse.

infrastructure

The underlying foundation of a system or organization. SEE ALSO infrastructure, IT.

infrastructure, data warehouse

A combination of technologies and the interaction of technologies that support a Data Warehousing environment.

infrastructure, IT

1. The complete set of hardware, operating system, and software products implemented in support of the application software of an enterprise.
2. The IT organization responsible for design, implementation, maintenance, operation, and support of the IT infrastructure.

inheritance

1. Generally, to receive by succession.
2. In data modeling, the sharing of the attributes and behaviors of parent class (supertype entity).

in-memory architecture

SEE architecture, in-memory.

inner join

SEE join, inner.

inner query

SEE subquery.

INSERT

A SQL statement (command) that specifies addition of rows of data in a relational database.

installation

Moving a software product or application into a production computing environment.

instance

1. An individual member of a population, such as a value in the domain of values for an attribute, or an individual entity record in a file. (Everest 2010) SEE ALSO entity instance; attribute; object.
2. A set of facts describing an actual entity occurrence at a point in time or during a period of time. The data about an occurrence may vary in different instances.

instantiate

Verb. To create an instance of a software object or database row/record.

instantiation

1. An instance of a software object or database row/record.
2. The name of a DCMI element set (Date, Format, Identifier, Language). SEE ALSO Dublin Core Metadata Initiative.

Institute for Certification of Computing Professionals (ICCP)

A nonprofit consortium of professional associations (including DAMA International) with the common goal of assessing, credentialing, and improving the skills and standards of students and individuals employed in the Business, Computer, Information, and Communications Technology industries. The ICCP handles exam administration and delivery of the CDMP exams and recertification.

Institute for Electric and Electronic Engineers (IEEE)

A professional organization for engineers, including software engineers.

institutional mandate

Set of rules or other formal set of instructions assigning responsibility as well as the authority to an organization for the collection, processing, and dissemination of information

intangible asset

SEE asset, intangible.

integer

A natural whole number (positive or negative) or zero. From the Latin *integer* for "intact, untouched". Contrast with real number.

integrate

Verb. To form or blend into a whole; to unite with something else; to incorporate into a larger unit; to bring into common organization. (Brackett 2011)

integrated data resource

A data resource that is fully integrated within a single, organization-wide, common data architecture and is deployed as necessary to meet the business information demand. It contains one version of truth about the business(Brackett 2011)

Integrated DEFinition (IDEF)

ICAMS (Integrated Computer-Aided Manufacturing) DEFinition Languages, developed for the U.S. Air Force. There are several of these modeling languages.

IDEF0 describes functional modeling notation.

IDEF1X describes data modeling notation.

IDEF2 describes simulation model notation.

IDEF3 describes process description capture.

IDEF4 describes object-oriented design.

IDEF5 describes ontology description capture.

IDEF6 describes design rationale capture.

IDEF7 describes information system auditing (not developed).

IDEF8 describes user interface modeling.

IDEF9 describes business constraint discovery.

IDEF10 describes implementation architecture modeling (not developed).

IDEF11 describes information artifact modeling (not developed).

IDEF12 describes organization modeling (not developed).

IDEF13 describes three schema mapping design (not developed).

IDEF14 describes network design.

Integrated Development Environment (IDE)

A software application or suite of integrated applications that are used to design, develop, and test application code.

Integrated Drive Electronics (IDE)

A disk system where the disk controller is integrated into the drive itself, rather than remotely.

integration

1. The unified state of multiple components into one whole, complex system.
2. The process of unifying multiple components into one complex system.

integration test

SEE test, integration.

intellectual capital

SEE intellectual property.

Intellectual Property (IP)

1. Intangible assets of an enterprise created by its knowledge workers including information about tangible assets, documents, ideas, patents, inventions, trade secrets, brands, software and databases, and generally expressed in some copyable storage form.
2. The name of a DCMI element set (Contributor, Creator, Publisher, Rights). SEE ALSO Dublin Core Metadata Initiative.

intelligence

1. *Verb.* The ability to understand and apply to practice.
2. In common use, a collection of data about something or someone.

intelligent agent

A software routine that waits in the background and performs an action when a specified event occurs. For example, agents could transmit a summary file on the first day of the month or monitor incoming data and alert the user when certain transactions have arrived.

intelligent key

SEE key, intelligent.

intensional

Adjective. Describes a set of valid values defined by conformity to rules. Each time the rules are executed, the result set may be different from the time before. For instance, the set of customers with overdue balances is an intensional set. SEE ALSO domain; extensional; Master Data Management.

intensional set

A set where membership is defined by explicit rule(s) applied to members of a larger set. The operands of the rule would be attributes of the (entity) instance being considered for membership. Opposite of extensional set.

interactive query

A query formed through the interaction between a human and the (computer) system. The system can assist the user in formulating a query. The query may then be executed (usually is) or stored for later execution.

interdependency

1. The degree to which a set of attributes influence each other's values.
2. In data quality, the degree to which one attribute or row influences the values of other attributes or rows.

interface

The connection to and means of communication between people and systems, or between different systems.

Interface Definition Language (IDL)

The standard API for calling CORBA services.

International Accounting Standards Board (IASB)

The international standards organization that determines generally accepted accounting principles (GAAP).

International Organization for Standardization (ISO)

A global network that identifies what international standards are required by business, government, and society, develops them in partnership with the sectors that will put them to use, and delivers them to be implemented worldwide. ISO is the world's leading developer of international standards. ISO is a network of the national standards institutes of 163 countries, one member per country, with a Central Secretariat in Geneva, Switzerland, that coordinates the system. Some 50,000 experts contribute annually to a portfolio of over 15,000 standards. In collaboration with its partners the International Electrotechnical Commission (IEC) and the International Telecommunication Union (ITU-T), ISO established the World Standards Cooperation (WSC) effort as the focus for standards in the field of information technology.

International Standard Book Number (ISBN)

A unique commercial book identification number based on the Standard Book Numbering code that is applied to books and book-like products that are published internationally.

International Telecommunications Union (ITU)

International Telecommunications Union (formerly CCITT), a branch of the United Nations that sets and manages the representation of phone numbers (among other things in the industry). It specifies that the universal representation of phone numbers shall only use dots (periods) as a separator, and be in the form of nnn.nnn.nnnn within each country. That number is then preceded by numeric country and region codes. Hyphens and parentheses are to be discontinued.

internet archive

A non-profit digital library offering free access to uploaded books, music, and archived web pages.

internet bookmark

The address to an Internet site that has been saved with a name or a tag.

Internet Protocol (IP)

A set of standard mechanisms for routing and communication used for transmitting data across networks.

internet tagging

The process of adding attributes to sites on the internet in order to enable grouping or filtering.

Internet, The

The global set of computers linked over public networks addressing each other through DNSs and URL addresses, using HTTP for their primary access protocol and HTML to display information.

interoperability

The ability of various types of computers and programs to work together and share data across different platforms.

interpolation

The use of a formula to estimate an intermediate data value.

interpretive language

A computer language that compiles source instructions one at a time as needed at run time.

interrogative

1. Generally, a question; a sentence that generates a reply.
2. In language, a part of speech that is used to show a question: Who, What, When, Where, How, Why are all interrogatives.
3. *Adjective.* Of or relating to questions.

INTERSECT

A SQL set operator that intersects two tabular SELECT answer sets with consistent column structures into one answer set table where only rows that match using the join conditions are included.

intersection entity

SEE data entity, associative.

interval number

A numeric scale in which the numbers have no arithmetic zero point or origin. Thus, it is only meaningful to add and subtract them, not multiply or divide. We cannot say that 60 degrees is twice as hot as 30 degrees. Examples are date, time, and temperature, except for Kelvin, which does have a meaningful absolute zero.

intranet

A subset of the Internet used internally by an organization. Unlike the larger Internet, intranets are private and accessible only from within the organization. The use of Internet technologies over a private network.

intrinsic

Adjective. Describes a property which is specific and essential to, and inseparable from, only one thing or event, and which is independent of any other property.

Inventory Configuration

Zachman Framework cell name, intersection of What/Inventory Sets and Component Assemblies/Technicians as Implementers.

Inventory Definition

Zachman Framework cell name, intersection of What/Inventory Sets and Business Concepts/Executive Leaders as Owners.

Inventory Identification

Zachman Framework cell name, intersection of What/Inventory Sets and Scope Contexts/Strategists as Theorists.

Inventory Instantiation

Zachman Framework cell name, intersection of What/Inventory Sets and Operations Instance Classes/Workers as Participants.

Inventory Representation

Zachman Framework cell name, intersection of What/Inventory Sets and System Logic/Architects as Designers.

Inventory Sets

Zachman Framework column name, matches What.

Inventory Specification

Zachman Framework cell name, intersection of What/Inventory Sets and Technology Physics/Engineers as Builders.

inverted index

SEE index, inverted.

inverted list

An index structure that stores locations to records in a database file by mapping the contents of the database file itself as a list.

Ishikawa diagram

SEE chart, cause-and-effect diagram.

ISO 9000

International standards for quality management, specifying guidelines and procedures for documenting and managing business processes, and providing a system for third-party certification to verify those procedures are followed in actual practice.

ISO/IEC 11179

International ISO/IEC Standard on meta-data registries addressing the semantics of data, the representation of data, and the registration of the descriptions of data.

isodemographic map

SEE chart, area cartogram.

IT Architect Body of Knowledge (ITABOK)

SEE Body of Knowledge, IT Architect.

IT governance

The process of making decisions about IT investments, the IT application portfolio, and the IT project portfolio. (DAMA-DMBOK Guide, 1st edition, pg. 38.)

IT infrastructure

SEE infrastructure, IT.

IT portfolio management

1. The budgeting, funding, issue and risk management, and overall tracking mechanism for all IT projects and programs.
2. The formal process for managing IT assets including application software, infrastructure software and hardware, internal staff, and external consulting, and how they support business processes and strategies, outside of program or project management.

IT Steering Committee

The governing body of senior executives responsible for aligning IT goals, objectives, strategy, architecture and projects with enterprise goals, objectives and strategy, for oversight of IT functions and projects, including project prioritization and funding.

iterative

Adjective. Describes an approach to building something by repeating a procedure.

J

jargon

Words in a dialect intended to keep nonmembers from knowing what is happening.

Java

A cross-platform source object-oriented programming language that allows applications to be distributed over networks and the Internet.

Java Database Connectivity (JDBC)

A standard API for accessing relational data from Java programs.

Java Messaging Service (JMS)

The standard API for sending and receiving messages for Java programs.

Java OLAP (JOLAP)

SEE OnLine Analytical Processing, Java.

Java Server Page (JSP)

A way to create dynamic Web content. They may also be used to generate and consume XML between n-tier servers or between servers and clients.

Java2 Platform Enterprise Edition (J2EE)

An acronym for, a standard for developing multi-tier applications, particularly for middleware and application servers.

job

A series of scripts or programs that run at a predefined schedule without manual intervention for the manipulation, movement, transformation, archiving or backing up a set of data.

join

In relational databases, an operation in which the data from two sets is combined into a larger result set based on common or matching data values in each set.

join index

An index in which the values appear in two (or more) different files (or tables). It can then be used for the rapid production of the join between the two on that domain without searching either of the joined files, and without pre-storing the join. (Everest 2010)

join, inner

A form of join where only rows with the join conditions matching are returned. Where A.JC = B.JC, only return rows where each row in A matches a row in B, and vice versa.

join, left

A form of table join where rows from the table on the left side of the join conditions are returned, regardless of whether there is a match in the other table. Where A.JC = B.JC, return all rows in A plus rows in B where B's join conditions match A's join conditions.

join, outer

A form of table join where data from both tables is included regardless of whether there is a match to a row in the other table. Where A.JC = B.JC, returns all rows in A plus all rows in B, matching where A's join conditions match B's join conditions.

join, partial **Alternate form: partial outer join**

A join in which some entries are included in the join which do not appear in both of the joined files. If all entries in each of the two joined files are included, it is called a full outer join, or simply outer join.

join, right

A form of table join where rows from the table on the right side of the join conditions are returned, regardless of whether there is a match in the other table. Where A.JC = B.JC, return all rows in B plus rows in A where A's join conditions match B's join conditions.

Joint Application Design (JAD)

A group process for defining requirements and designing a computer-based system. JAD sessions are highly focused bringing together business professionals and IT professionals under the leadership of a skilled facilitator. JAD sessions can be used to draft, review, and refine data models. They are generally held over one or more contiguous days. JAD sessions are more valuable as brain storming sessions, getting a sense of the attendees, taking straw polls, etc.

joint Bayes classifier

A modeling technique in which some attributes describe a class in conjunction with other attributes that also describe that class. SEE ALSO predictive modeling.

Joint Photographic Experts Group (JPEG)

A standard method of compression of photographic images.

journal

1. Generally, a written record of observations and experiences.
2. In data management, a file that contains database activity details for rollback and recovery. SEE ALSO log.

Julian calendar

A solar calendar that established the months and years, with a leap day every four years. Was supplanted by the Gregorian calendar in AD 1582.

Julian date

The date expressed as a simple number, used by astronomers and historians due to the simple math involved. The Julian calendar started on January 1, 4713 BCE at noon. The Julian date for noon on CE 2011 February 20 is JD 2455613.000000.

junction entity

SEE data entity, associative.

junk dimension

SEE dimension, junk.

just-in-time

Information delivered at the time it will be used, not before and not after.

K

Kagi chart

SEE chart, Kagi.

kaizen

The Japanese word for "continuous improvement".

kernel entity

SEE entity, kernel.

key

1. A data item or combination of data items designated to uniquely identify a particular entity instance or table row. SEE ALSO identifier.
2. *Adjective.* Critically important.

key constraint

SEE constraint, key.

Key Performance Indicator (KPI)

A business calculation (metric) with associated target values or ranges that allows macro level insights into the business process to manage profitability and monitor strategic impact.

key, alternate — **Alternate form: secondary key**

A unique identifier for an entity instance other than the primary key. Usually an alternate key is a unique natural key.

key, business — **Alternate form: domain key, natural key**

1. An identifier familiar to and used by data consumers, using existing attributes, which has a logical relationship to the attributes within the row.
2. A primary key that uses attributes that have meaning to the business. Opposite of a surrogate key.

key, candidate

A key that can uniquely identify occurrences of an entity. Each occurrence must have a different key value, and every attribute in the key is needed to uniquely identify each occurrence. Such identifiers are "candidates" to become a primary key, and candidate keys not selected as the primary key are considered alternate keys.

key, composite

A key that is made up of more than one attribute.

Key, Foreign (FK)

1. An attribute (or attributes) in a relational table which is from the same domain as the identifier of the same or another table; can be thought of as a logical pointer from the "referencing" entity table (with the foreign key) to the "referenced" entity table (with the identifier). It is used to represent a many-to-one relationship between the referencing and referenced tables. It is not necessary for a foreign key to have a value; that is determined by the independently defined dependency characteristic.
2. The preferred primary key of a parent data subject that is placed in a subordinate data subject to identify the relevant parent data occurrence in that parent data subject.

key, hash

A number based on the hash value of a string.

key, intelligent

A key value that has some meaning assigned to the values other than just as a link to rows in other tables. For example, the key of a CALENDAR_DIM could be of the format "CCYYMMDD" in order to enable truncation of the key for partitioning into time-based segments.

key, partial

A portion of a key, in which each value of the partial key may identify more than one unique instance (record) in the file or data set.

Key, Primary (PK)

A set of one or more data attributes whose values are used to uniquely identify an entity instance or relational database table row. The primary key will have a unique value for each record or row in the table and is the means of navigation across entities and tables. Primary key attributes and values of parent entities and tables appear as foreign key attributes and values in child entities and tables.

key, secondary

A key whose value identifies a set of occurrences in a data structure that share common characteristics. Access by secondary keys may return multiple occurrences, where access by a primary key is assured to find no more than one occurrence.

key, superkey

A set of attributes in a dataset such that there are no repeated value sets. Each combination of the values in the attributes in a superkey are unique.

key, surrogate **Alternate form: dummy key**

A single-part, artificially established, physical identifier for a data set, usually not visible to business users, and used for database management and performance. Surrogate key assignment is a special case of derived data - one where the primary key is derived. A common way of deriving surrogate key values is to assign integer values sequentially. Sometimes referred to as a dummy key, sequential key, or auto-number field.

keyword

A term found in a document, indexed to enable document search and location.

Kilobyte (Kb)

A thousand bytes of storage.

k-nearest neighbor algorithm

A modeling technique that assigns values to points based on the values of the k nearby points, such as average value, or most common value. SEE ALSO predictive modeling.

knowledge

1. Generally, expertise; familiarity gained through experience or association; cognizance, the fact or condition of knowing something; the acquaintance with or the understanding of something; the fact or condition of being aware of something, of apprehending truth or fact.
2. Understanding; awareness, cognizance, and the recognition of a situation and familiarity with its complexity. Understanding of the significance of information; information in perspective, integrated into a viewpoint based on the recognition of patterns (such as trends and causes) based on other information and experience. (DAMA-DMBOK Guide, 1st edition, pg. 3.)

knowledge base

A database of rules, usually expressed in an if/then format, used in an expert system.

Knowledge Discovery in Databases (KDD)

SEE data mining.

Knowledge Interchange Format (KIF)

A standard format for exchanging rules between artificial intelligence (AI) systems.

Knowledge Management (KM)

1. The management of an environment where people generate tacit knowledge, render it into explicit knowledge, and feed it back to the organization. The cycle forms a base for more tacit knowledge, which keeps the cycle going in an intelligent learning organization. (Brackett 2011)
2. The discipline that fosters organizational learning and the management of intellectual capital as an enterprise resource. (DAMA-DMBOK Guide, 1st edition, pg. 3.)

knowledge worker

Anyone who works for a living by understanding information. A type of information consumer. Knowledge workers seek to gain expertise though the understanding of information, and then apply that expertise by making informed and aware decisions and actions.

knowledge, explicit

Knowledge that is easily codified, shared, documented, and explained.

knowledge, tacit

Knowledge that is based on experience and not easy to share, document, or explain.

L

label

A title or tag applied to a data attribute that concisely describes the entity or attribute type and/or content for ease of sorting, filtering, or scanning for relevance.

language

1. A system of communication using sounds (spoken language) or symbols (written language).
2. DCMI element in element set Instantiation: the terminology set used to describe a resource. SEE ALSO Dublin Core Metadata Initiative.

last valid date

The last date that an attribute or entity instance is valid.

latency

The measure of time between two events, such as the initiation and completion of an event, or the read on one system and the write to another system.

layer

A group of functionally related components within an architecture representing a level of abstraction different from other layers within the architecture.

layer chart

SEE chart, layer.

learning curve

The average time it takes a person to learn how to use or master a tool or technique.

left join

SEE join, left.

legacy data

Data that comes from production files and databases that stand outside of, or came from a previous form of, the organization's data architecture.

legacy system

An application implemented outside of, or from a prior version of, an organization's application architecture. Usually an older application that may be slated for eventual replacement. Legacy systems are often frustrating because they are difficult to change, few people know exactly what they do and how they do it, and/or the technology on which they are dependent is becoming obsolete and unsupportable.

level

A group of codes that are characterized by homogeneous coding, and where the parent of each code in the group is at the same higher level of the hierarchy.

leverage

Taking full advantage of a resource to effectively achieve a desired outcome.

lexicon

1. In general, a glossary or dictionary.
2. In data management, a computer-readable data dictionary of attributes.

liability

A possession and responsibility for current economic costs, such as a debt; the opposite of an asset.

lie factor

In charts, a ratio of the size of a graphical representation of an item or effect to the size of the effect within the data itself. The lie factor describes how far off the graphic representation shown is in respect to the actual data driving the chart.

lifecycle

1. The set of valid states of an object, arranged in sequence from "birth" to "death." Usually depicted in a state transition diagram.
2. A shorthand reference for the software development lifecycle (SDLC).

lifecycle diagram

SEE chart, lifecycle diagram.

lifetime value (LTV) **Alternate form: customer lifetime value**

The 'present' value of 'future' cash flows expected from a something (equipment or property) or someone (customer or citizen) over an anticipated timeframe, computed using the costs of acquisition and retention, in order to estimate profitability.

line chart

SEE chart, line.

lineage

The relationship path from a start point to a finish point.

lineage, data

The path that a data attribute travels between systems, and the alterations made during that journey.

lineage, meta-data

The path that meta-data travels between the source systems and the meta-data repository.

linear

Relating to a line, or with a progression that strongly resembles a line.

list partitioning

SEE partitioning, list.

literal

1. A constant value provided for a variable.
2. *Adjective.* Describes conformance with strict meaning.

Local Area Network (LAN)

A computer network covering a limited physical area, such as an office or a building.

local index

SEE index, local.

location transparency

A mechanism that keeps the specific physical address of an object from a user. The physical location is resolved within the system so that operations can be performed without knowledge of the actual physical location.

lock

A means of preventing access to data while a process is updating that data.

lock contention

Occurs when a one process requests and is denied a lock to a resource because it is held by another process.

lock granularity

The level of data that is involved in a lock. Lock granularity can be at any level of physical data: database, block, set of tables, row, or column level, and include any amount of data contained within those objects.

log

In data management, a collection of records that describe the sequence of events that occur during DBMS execution, recorded for use in database recovery in the event of a DBMS failure. SEE ALSO journal.

log shipping

The process of sending transaction log backups to other servers for reapplying the logs to replicate the state of a system.

Logical Data Model (LDM)

SEE data model, logical.

logistic regression

A modeling technique where unknown values are predicted by known values of other valuables where the dependent variable is binary type. SEE ALSO predictive modeling.

Logistics

The management of flows of goods, information, resources, etc. in a logical progression between points of origin, consumption, and destruction.

log-write-ahead

A process of writing data where modifications are written to a log before being applied to the stored data at rest.

loose coupling

An arrangement whereby components can be easily attached and detached, enabling easier configuration changes. SEE ALSO design.

lower control limit

SEE control limit, lower.

M

Machine-Readable Cataloging (MARC)

A standard for representation and communication of bibliographic and related information in machine-readable form, created by the U.S. Library of Congress.

macro

A stored sequence of commands or instructions which, when invoked, will execute a series of commands or keypresses. Commonly used to automate repetitive tasks within applications such as word or number processors.

Magic Quadrant

SEE chart, Magic Quadrant.

magnetic north

The point on the earth's surface at which the magnetic field points vertically down from the northern hemisphere. Not the same as true north.

mainframe

A centralized computer architecture, once dominant but still widely used and supporting a very large number of applications.

majority classifier

A modeling technique that includes rules that result in non-outlier data directly into the model calculations. SEE ALSO predictive modeling.

Malcolm Baldrige National Quality Award

An award given by the United States National Institute of Standards and Technology to recognize total quality management achievements of U.S. business, health care and educational organizations. It was established in 1987 and named for Malcolm Baldrige, who was U.S. Secretary of Commerce from 1981 until his 1987 death in a rodeo accident. The purposes of the award are to promote quality awareness, recognize quality achievements of the US companies, and publicize successful quality strategies.

manageability

1. The possibility of something being controllable and supportable.
2. Describes the ability to create and maintain an effective environment. (DAMA-DMBOK Guide, 1st edition, pg. 134.)

managed availability

The ability to deliver consistent, predictable access to data whenever users need it.

Managed Meta-data Environment (MME)

The operational implementation of a meta-data architecture, including a meta-data repository, meta-data sources, integration procedures, management processes, delivery procedures to meta marts, and access interfaces.

managed replication

Planning for and control of replicated data, ensuring there is a master record and that copies of that record are consistent, and that minimal redundant and non-productive replication occurs.

Management Information System (MIS)

A reporting or Business Intelligence system. SEE ALSO Information System.

Management of Information Systems (MIS)

SEE Information Technology.

mandatory

1. *Adjective.* Required, not optional. A dependency must be fulfilled.
2. In SQL, and many DBMSs, mandatory equates to "NOT NULL" or "NOT NULLABLE" constraints.

mandatory relationship

SEE relationship, mandatory.

Many-to-Many (M:N) **Alternate form: M-N, M-M**

The characteristic of a relationship in which a member of one population can be related to multiple members of the other population, and vice versa. (Everest 2010) SEE ALSO cardinality; relationship.

Many-to-one (M:1)

The reverse of one-to-zero-or-Many or one-to-one-or-Many.

map

Verb. To associate mathematically every member in a given set with at least one member of another set.

mapping

A list of source and target entities and attributes linked by a set of instructions.

marimekko chart

SEE chart, marimekko.

Mario chart

SEE chart, waterfall.

market basket analysis

The use of a fixed list of items used specifically to track the progress of inflation in an economy or specific market. The list used for such an analysis would contain a number of the most commonly bought food and household items. The variations in the prices of the items on the list from month to month give an indication of the overall development of price trends.

market segmentation

The process of identifying groups of potential customers with similar needs and/or characteristics who are likely to exhibit similar purchase behavior.

market share

A company's sales expressed as a percentage of the sales for the total industry.

Marketing Resource Management (MRM)

Software that helps with the upfront planning of a marketing function and the coordination and collaboration of marketing resources.

markup

Verb. To annotate documents by inserting tags to offset and identify sections.

markup language

A set of symbols or rules that describe format, structure, or display of a document or file separate from the actual contents.

mashup

A combination of application outputs, content objects, or data attributes that create new structures from the parts.

mashup, content

Content that collects from multiple external sources to create a new object.

mashup, data

A display of non-integrated data attributes from multiple sources that can be combined to form new display objects.

mass customization

The definition and delivery of customized products and services on a wide-scale and cost-effective basis, typically by leveraging information technology. A concept defined and developed by Joseph Pine of IBM.

Massively Parallel Processing (MPP)

In computer architecture, the "shared nothing" approach to parallel computing. Describes a distributed memory computer system of multiple nodes where each node has data, processors, memory, a network link so that each node may process a part of a task independently on its data, and then send the results back to a collector. Growth is achieved by adding more nodes. Possible bottlenecks include network bandwidth. Requires specialized partitioning to spread the data effectively and efficiently across the nodes based on expected usage. Contrast with Symmetrical Multi-Processing.

master data

The data that provides the context for business activity data in the form of common and abstract concepts that relate to the activity. It includes the details (definitions and identifiers) of internal and external objects involved in business transactions, such as customers, products, employees, vendors, and controlled domains (code values).

Master Data Management (MDM)

Processes that control management of master data values to enable consistent, shared, contextual use across systems, of the most accurate, timely, and relevant version of truth about essential business entities. (DAMA-DMBOK Guide, 1st edition, pg. 171.)

master data, financial

Master data about an organization's financial configuration including business units, cost centers, profit centers, general ledger accounts, budgets, projections, and projects.

master data, location

Master data about locations specifically related to a business, in the form of geographic data, such as business party addresses and facility locations. (DAMA-DMBOK Guide, 1st edition, pg. 180.)

master data, party

Master data about individuals, organizations, and the roles they play in business relationships. May include customer, employee, vendor, partner, and competitors; citizens; suspects, witnesses, and victims; members and donors; patients and providers; or students and faculty. (DAMA-DMBOK Guide, 1st edition, pg. 178.

master data, product

Master data that focuses on an organization's internal products or services, or an entire industry's shared products or services, including competitor products and services.

master file

An old term for database, used before relational databases were commonplace. Now used as a concept in Master Data Management regarding the official version of master data.

matching

The process of comparing rows in data sets to determine which rows describe the same thing and are therefore either complimentary or redundant. SEE ALSO similarity analysis.

match-link rule

SEE rule, match-link.

match-merge rule

SEE rule, match-merge.

materialized view

A view that is actually stored as a separate object in order to optimize performance.

matrix

A set of arrays of the same type, where each array is seen as a dimension. Matrices are used to analyze and document the linkages and relationships between the occurrences of one dimension with the occurrences of the other dimensions. SEE ALSO array; scalar.

maturity model

A structured collection of characteristics of effective processes at progressive levels of quality and effectiveness. A maturity model provides a common language and a shared vision for process improvement, a standard for benchmarking, and a framework for prioritizing actions. A maturity model assumes a natural evolutionary path for organizational process improvement.

mean

The result of dividing the sum of all values within a set by the count of all values included.

Mean Time Between Failures (MTF, MTBF)

The predicted elapsed time (arithmetic mean) between system failures. Used to evaluate system stability.

Mean Time To Recover (MTR, MTTR)

The predicted elapsed time (arithmetic mean) between a failure and restoration of a system. Used to evaluate system support efficacy.

measure **Alternate form: measurement**

1. Loosely used, a metric.
2. In data modeling, a quantified characteristic; the unit used to quantify the dimensions, capacity, or amount of something.
3. *Verb.* To quantify one or more dimensions, capacity or amounts of something.

median

The center-most value in an ordered set of values. If the set quantity is even, then the average of the two center-most values.

Medical Subject Heading (MeSH)

A comprehensive set of descriptors used to index medical and life sciences journal articles.

Megabyte (Mb)

A million bytes of storage; a thousand Kilobytes.

member

An individual instance of a population.

membership

The state of belonging to a set.

memory block allocation

A system and method for placing, locating, and indexing blocks of data.

message

An electronic request or reply expressed in data. Messages can be expressed in the form of XML documents.

message broker

A software intermediary function that dispatches messages to the correct sites.

Message Oriented Middleware (MOM)

Software that enables inter-component communication through messages and message routing through a message broker.

meta muck

An environment created when meta-data exists in multiple products and repositories (DBMS catalogs, DBMS dictionaries, CASE tool encyclopedias, BI information directories).

meta-data **Alternate forms: meta data, metadata**

Literally, "data about data"; data that defines and describes the characteristics of other data, used to improve both business and technical understanding of data and data-related processes. Because the term 'metadata' is a trademark of The Metadata Company, DAMA specifically uses the term meta-data.

meta-data architecture

SEE architecture, meta-data.

meta-data integration

The process of joining differing attributes in multiple meta-data repositories to allow for easier access.

Meta-data Management (MM)

Processes that create, control, integrate, access, and analyze meta-data. One of ten data management functions identified in the DAMA-DMBOK Functional Framework. (DAMA-DMBOK Guide, 1st edition, pg. 7.)

meta-data repository

1. Generally, any structured database of meta-data, often in support of a particular tool.
2. Specifically, an integrated database of meta-data, considered the official representation of meta-data in an enterprise. A repository contains business and technical meta-data from multiple sources. It may be updated in real time or in batch.

meta-data synchronization

The process of consolidating and relating data attributes with the same or similar meaning from different systems.

meta-data, administrative

Meta-data that records lifecycle attributes of a resource, including acquisition, access rules, locations, version control/differentiations, lineage, and archival/destruction.

meta-data, business

The names and business definitions of entities and tables, attributes and columns, and defined domain data values that establish the consistent shared meaning of data. Non-technical meta-data of interest to business professionals, ideally defined by business data stewards. Business meta-data includes the names and definitions of business entities and their data attributes in a conceptual or logical data model, as well as the equivalent business definitions for tables and columns in a physical data model or implemented database. Business meta-data also includes the descriptions of business relationships between business entities, the business rules that govern those relationships, the logical business names and definitions of domain values (code values), and the descriptions of rules governing use of these code values.

meta-data, data stewardship

Data stewardship meta-data is data about data stewards, stewardship processes, and responsibility assignments.

meta-data, descriptive

Meta-data that characterizes and catalogs the actual resource.

meta-data, preservation

Meta-data that describes the physical condition of stored resources, and changes to that physical condition over time (such as copying to different media).

meta-data, process

Meta-data is that defines and describes the characteristics of other systems (processes, business rules, programs, jobs, tools, etc.).

meta-data, rights management

Meta-data that represents rules regarding the use of that resource with respect to intellectual property rights.

meta-data, structural

Meta-data that describes resources at atomic levels, and at higher levels including how the atomic data attributes are related.

meta-data, technical

The physical characteristics of data found in a database, including physical names, datatypes, lengths, precision and scale of numeric data attributes, statistics, source locations (lineage), and code values. It may also include data about programs and other technology.

meta-data, usage

Meta-data that represents how the resource is accessed, processed, and output.

metamart **Alternate forms: meta mart, meta-data mart, meta-data mart**

A data store for meta-data fed from a meta-data repository, created for a specialized audience or tool, such as an information directory.

metamodel

1. Generally, a model that specifies one or more other models.
2. In Meta-data Management, a model of a meta-data system or a data model for a meta-data repository.

method

1. Generally, a formalized system of principles, practices, and procedural methods used to build systems, perform a process, or solve a problem, including organizational arrangements, deliverables, and time lines.
2. In object-oriented design and programming, a function bound to a class as part of its overall behavior, executed in response to a message.

methodology

The study of methods.

metric

1. Generally, a unit of measure selected used to monitor and control a process.
2. In Business Intelligence, a calculated value based on measurements used to monitor and control a process or business activity. Most metrics are ratios comparing one measurement to another.

metro map

SEE chart, metro map.

microdata

SEE atomic data.

middleware

Software that allows applications to interact across hardware and network environments.

milestone

Used in project management, marking the end of a task or set of tasks, usually accompanied by some sort of event or a record of approval.

Million Instructions Per Second (MIPS)

A measurement of processing speed. The concept is mistakenly considered a relative measure of computing capability among models and vendors. It is a meaningful measure only among versions of the same processors configured with identical peripherals and software.

minimart — **Alternate forms: mini mart, mini-mart**

A data store presenting a small subset of a Data Warehouse used by a small number of users. A minimart is a very focused slice of a larger Data Warehouse. SEE ALSO Data Mart.

MINUS

SEE EXCEPT.

MIP-o-suction

The consumption of a high percentage of CPU cycles by a database query.

mirror — **Alternate form: mirroring**

An exact copy of a data set, kept up-to-date in real time. SEE ALSO data replication.

misclassification

Erroneous classification of a subject into a category in which the subject does not belong

mobile Business Intelligence — **Alternate form: Mobile BI**

SEE Business Intelligence, mobile.

mode

The value occurring most frequently in a range of values.

model

An abstract representation of how something is built (or is to be built), or how something works (or is observed as working).

model management

The storage and configuration management of models (including change control).

model, conceptual

A model of any kind that is independent of implementation and usage context, consisting solely of basic entities and relationships at a high level.

model, contextual

Generally, a very high-level block diagram listing the main terms and definitions for a business or system.

Model-Driven Development (MDD)

A software development process that creates models or abstractions of a system or data in order to increase basic compatibility between systems.

Model-View-Controller (MVC)

An application design paradigm for object-oriented applications that separates the underlying "model" of business objects from the "view" presentation interface objects and the "controller" events that users perform. By overlaying the controller functions on the view, it creates the illusion of direct manipulation.

morals

In general, a person's internal rules of behavior. Contrast with ethics. SEE ALSO professional ethics.

morphological box **Alternate form: Zwicky box**

A problem-structuring and problem-solving technique that reduces the parameters to a finite number with a finite number of possible values, and then compares them to each other. Similar to construction of a dense cube with each parameter being a dimension.

Motivation Configuration

Zachman Framework cell name, intersection of Why/Motivation Reasons and Component Assemblies/Technicians as Implementers.

Motivation Definition

Zachman Framework cell name, intersection of Why/Motivation Reasons and Business Concepts/Executive Leaders as Owners.

Motivation Identification

Zachman Framework cell name, intersection of Why/Motivation Reasons and Scope Contexts/Strategists as Theorists.

Motivation Instantiation

Zachman Framework cell name, intersection of Why/Motivation Reasons and Operations Instance Classes/Workers as Participants.

motivation model

In architecture, describes reasons for establishing organized business plans, their attributes, priorities, and inter-relationships.

Motivation Reasons

Zachman Framework column name, matches Why.

Motivation Representation

Zachman Framework cell name, intersection of Why/Motivation Reasons and System Logic/Architects as Designers.

Motivation Specification

Zachman Framework cell name, intersection of Why/Motivation Reasons and Technology Physics/Engineers as Builders.

multi-dimensional

1. *Adjective.* In physics and mathematics, describes an item that has a greater-than-two minimum number of coordinates necessary to specify it.
2. *Adjective.* In data analysis, describes a data attribute that must be described by two or more distinct parameters.

multi-dimensional array

A group of data cells arranged by the dimensions of the data. For example, a spreadsheet exemplifies a two-dimensional array with the data cells arranged in rows and columns, each being a dimension. A three-dimensional array can be visualized as a cube with each dimension forming a side of the cube, including any slice parallel with that side. Higher dimensional arrays have no physical metaphor, but they organize the data in the way users think of their enterprise. Typical enterprise dimensions are time, measures, products, services, geographical regions, etc.

Multi-Dimensional DataBase (MDDB)

SEE database, multi-dimensional.

Multi-Dimensional DataBase Management System (MDDBMS)

SEE DataBase Management System, Multi-dimensional.

Multi-Dimensional eXtensions to SQL (MDX)

A language used to access a multi-dimensional data structure.

Multi-dimensional OLAP (MOLAP)

SEE OnLine Analytical Processing, Multi-dimensional.

Multi-dimensional Query Language (MQL)

A computer language that allows one to specify which data to retrieve out of a multi-dimensional structure. The user process for this type of query is usually called slicing and dicing. The result of a multi-dimensional query is a cell, a two- dimensional slice, or a multi-dimensional sub-cube.

multi-file data structure

A data structure consisting of multiple files that may also include the explicit definition of relationships between/among the files. SEE ALSO data model, physical.

multimedia storage

Storage devices for multimedia files that also contain applications to display or play the multimedia files.

multiplicity

Characteristic of a relationship as either at most one (exclusive) or more than one. (Everest 2010)

multi-tier architecture

SEE architecture, multi-tier.

multi-valued attribute

SEE data attribute, multi-valued.

multi-valued dependency

SEE dependency, multi-valued.

multi-variable model

A model showing evaluation based on multiple variables.

munge

To transform data such that the original data is unrecognizable without knowing the transformation rules and sequence, which is unpredictable or inconsistent. Sometimes accomplished with substitution of characters in order to obfuscate the original data. Occasionally explained as "modify until not guessed easily".

N

naïve Bayes classifier

A modeling technique where each attribute describes a class independent of any other attributes that also describe that class. SEE ALSO predictive modeling.

name

1. Generally, the designation of an object by a linguistic expression.
2. In data modeling, a class word, abbreviated usually to nm.

namespace

A defined domain within which a name is guaranteed to be unique and findable. A reusable reference glossary of XML attributes found at a URL address. Entity and attribute names used in XML documents can be easily qualified by associating them with namespaces identified by URL references.

naming convention

SEE naming standard.

naming standard

A pattern of assigning names, words, or parts of words to objects, often intended to convey meta-information that promotes consistency and ease-of-use while avoiding conflicts.

N-ary

Adjective. Relating to N (some number) of entities in a relationship, the number of attributes or columns in an entity table, the number of arguments or operands that a function requires, or more specifically, the number of objects in a predicate in ORM.

National Institute for Standards and Technology (NIST)

Formerly known as The National Bureau of Standards, a non-regulatory agency of the United States Department of Commerce. The institute's mission is to promote U.S. innovation and industrial competitiveness by advancing measurement science, standards, and technology in ways that enhance economic security and improve quality of life. As part of this mission, NIST awards the Malcolm Baldrige National Quality Award.

natural key

SEE key, business.

natural language modeling

The process of describing information using proper sentences, not abbreviations or sentence fragments.

near real time

Transmission with a minimal amount of propagation and buffering delays.

nearline storage

Data that is not on line but is capable of being accessed and placed on line within 15 seconds of the access request. Archived data may be kept in nearline storage. SEE ALSO archive.

nested query

SEE subquery.

nested relation

An attribute of a relation, itself representing a relation. In a relational DBMS, a column that contains a table in each row.

Net Present Value (NPV)

A comparison of the current value of a dollar versus the value of a dollar at some future time, after allowing for future influences such as inflation and expected rates of return. Positive NPV is said to indicate a good investment.

network

1. Visually, a graph of nodes and connections where more than one entry point for each node is allowed.
2. In architecture, a topological arrangement of hardware and connections to allow communication between nodes and access to shared data and software.

Network Configuration

Zachman Framework cell name, intersection of Where/Network Nodes and Component Assemblies/Technicians as Implementers.

network data model

SEE data model, network.

network database

SEE database, network.

Network Definition

Zachman Framework cell name, intersection of Where/Network Nodes and Business Concepts/Executive Leaders as Owners.

Network Definition Language (NDL)

Network Definition Language, the ANSI standard (first adopted in 1986) based on the CODASYL Network data structure. It was substantially rolled into the SQL:1999 ANSI standard, which is no longer relational.

Network File Share (NFS)

A folder (directory) on a server that is shared out to users on a local area network (LAN) or intranet. Users attach to this file share and can drag and drop files/folders or modify the files/folder within the file share. A file share is typically mapped to a user's local computer as a logical drive, such as X:. It is accessed just like the other drives on your computer, such as the A: or C: drives. File shares are a fast and secure method for managing content on a remote server.

Network Identification

Zachman Framework cell name, intersection of Where/Network Nodes and Scope Contexts/Strategists as Theorists.

Network Instantiation

Zachman Framework cell name, intersection of Where/Network Nodes and Operations Instance Classes/Workers as Participants.

network node

1. An addressable device or connection point attached to a network.
2. Zachman Framework column name, matches Where.

Network Representation

Zachman Framework cell name, intersection of Where/Network Nodes and System Logic/Architects as Designers.

Network Specification

Zachman Framework cell name, intersection of Where/Network Nodes and Technology Physics/Engineers as Builders.

network taxonomy

SEE taxonomy, network.

Network-Attached Storage (NAS)

A form of storage that attaches to a network but does not provide server functions such as file management.

niche marketing

A marketing segmentation strategy in which the firm focuses on serving one segment of the market. Similar to segmented marketing, but a niche is a small distinguishable segment that can be uniquely served.

Nijssens Information Analysis Method (NIAM)

A data modeling technique, the predecessor to object role modeling. Has also been called "Natural Information Analysis Method".

no file data modeling scheme

SEE data modeling scheme, no file.

node

In graph theory, a generic representation of something in a graph; could be a type (representing a population), or an individual instance. Usually represented by some icon (e.g., box, circle) in the diagram.

noise

Unwanted sound or data included with or around wanted sound or data.

nomenclature

A systematic naming of things or a system of names or terms for things. In classification, nomenclature involves a systemic naming of categories or items.

nominal number

A number system that has no arithmetic or ordering significance, hence can only be compared as match or no match. Other operators are meaningless - multiply, divide, add, subtract, comparative (<, =,...), or Boolean. This is probably the most commonly occurring type of numerical data in database. Examples include account numbers. Often used as codes for particular characteristics or values in the real world.

non-clustered index

SEE index, non-clustered.

Non-Disclosure Agreement (NDA)

An agreement between parties to not share specific confidential information without proper authorization from other involved parties.

non-functional requirement

SEE requirement, non-functional.

non-identifying relationship

SEE relationship, non-identifying.

non-information

A set of data in context that is not relevant or timely to the recipient. (Brackett 2011)

non-tabular data

SEE data, non-tabular.

normal distribution

A mathematical distribution of points around an axis that represents the mean of the data set values, which resembles a bell (low at both ends and high in the middle).

normal form

A characteristic of a file or table that indicates that it satisfies one or more of the rules of normalization. Not all rules must be satisfied in order. SEE ALSO normalize.

Normal Form, Boyce/Codd (BCNF)

A level of normalization where every attribute or combination of attributes that can uniquely identify an instance is identified as a candidate key. Violations are known as overlapping keys.

Normal Form, Domain/Key (DKNF)

A level of normalization that requires that a database only contains key constraints and domain constraints.

Normal Form, Elementary Key (EKNF)

A level of normalization where there are no candidate keys that re-use the same attribute.

Normal Form, fifth (5NF)

An advanced level of normalization where all attributes of a concatenated key are independent of each other and cannot be derived from the remainder of the key. Violations are commonly known as inter-entity dependencies.

Normal Form, first (1NF)

1. A level of normalization where exist no multi-valued dependencies within a record or row; all attributes are atomic (single valued) for each entity instance. Multi-valued attributes and repeating groups must be removed from the record. In practice, any relational database table with a primary key assumes first normal form.
2. A table structure is in 1NF when it satisfies the six properties of a relation:
   i. All rows are unique
   ii. Order of rows is unimportant
   iii. All columns have unique names
   iv. Order of columns is unimportant
   v. All values in a column are the same type
   vi. No column contains multiple values in the same row

Normal Form, fourth (4NF)

An advanced level of normalization where no instance contains two or more independent multi-valued facts. Violations are commonly known as derived data.

Normal Form, Project Join (PJNF)

SEE Normal Form, fifth.

Normal Form, second (2NF)

A level of normalization where every non-key attribute is fully dependent on the key in its entirety. In practice, when entities have compound keys, seek out any attribute that is dependent upon only part of the key and create a separate entity for what is identifiable by anything less than the whole key. Violations are commonly known as partial key dependencies.

Normal Form, sixth (6NF)

1. An advanced level of normalization that adds temporal constraints upon relations, such as a range of time when a relationship was effective. SEE ALSO database, temporal.
2. Sometimes used incorrectly to refer to Domain/Key Normal Form; not the same as definition 1.

Normal Form, third (3NF)

A form of normalization where every entity has no transitive dependencies, that is, every data item must be directly determined by the identifier, and not indirectly determined through some other non-key attribute. For example, if the boss of a department were determined by the department, then it would be incorrect to store both the department ID and the boss name in the employee record. Violations are commonly known as inter-attribute dependencies. Sometimes colloquially referred to as "the key, the whole key, and nothing but the key."

normalize

1. *Verb.* Generally, to impose standards or regulations, or bring to a desired state.
2. *Verb.* In data modeling, to apply rules to a record-based data structure to reduce redundancy, such that each data attribute is stored
   a) as few times as necessary, and
   b) with its determinant as the identifier.

The rules of normalization are applied only within a record or table, and cannot be applied until an identifier is first designated for the table. Even though the rules of normalization are numbered, there is no necessary ordering -- they can be applied in any order, and some may be satisfied while others are not. For example, a record may have no transitive dependencies (thus not violating the condition for 3NF) but may have a partial dependency (thus failing 2NF).

normative model

A model that describes how a system should work according to assumptions or pre-defined standards.

North American Industrial Classification System (NAICS)

A taxonomy of business classification, replacing the Standard Industry Code. The North American Industry Classification System is the standard used by Federal statistical agencies in classifying business establishments for the purpose of collecting, analyzing, and publishing statistical data related to the U.S. business economy. NAICS was developed jointly by the U.S. Economic Classification Policy Committee, Statistics Canada, and Mexico's Instituto Nacional de Estadistica y Geografia, to allow for a high level of comparability in business statistics among the North American countries.

Not Only SQL (NoSQL)

A type of database that is distributed to enable large-scale data access.

noun

A type of word that describes a person, a place, a thing, or an idea. One of the syntactic components used to construct sentences according to a grammar.

n-tier architecture

SEE architecture, multi-tier.

null

The absence of any value. A null value tells you the value does not exist. It does not denote why the value is missing. Placing a zero or blank in the row would not reflect the accurate state of the row, because zero and blank are values. In ASCII, null is hex 00, blank is hex 20, and zero is hex 30. In EBCDIC, null is hex 00, blank is hex 40, and zero is hex F0. SQL supports the notion of null values as a way to search for missing data.

null hypothesis

1. Generally, the prediction that an observed result is not due to any inherent systemic cause.
2. In data analysis, the prediction that one variable has no association with and responds independently of another variable.

number

A class word, abbreviated usually to num.

obfuscate

1. Generally, to conceal through confusion.
2. In data security, the process of permanently scrambling or replacing data with unrelated values in order to conceal the original data permanently. Used to remove sensitive information from data when being transferred to unsecure systems.

object

1. In the real world, a person, place, thing, or concept. SEE ALSO entity; instance.
2. In an object-oriented design, an instance of a class or a population of objects or events.
3. In an object-oriented program relating to object type, the code in memory that describes the attributes and allowable behavior of a business object, interface object or control object.

object class

1. Generally, a set of ideas, abstractions, or things in the real world that can be identified with explicit boundaries and meaning, and whose properties and behavior follow the same rules.
2. Specifically, the definition of a set of objects that conforms to that definition.
3. In an object-oriented design, a collection of objects (instances) that conform to the same definition of structure and behaviors.

Object Identifier (OID)

A unique value assigned to an object in order to track it simply and efficiently. OIDs are generally system assigned, immutable, and not visible to the user/programmer (unlike keys in a relational or ER database). They are used to establish and maintain the integrity of defined relationships within the database.

Object Management Group (OMG)

A non-profit organization that promotes object-oriented technology and open systems standards.

object model

1. A collection of objects or classes.
2. The description of an object's properties.

Object Relational DataBase Management System (ORDBMS)

SEE DataBase Management System, Object Relational.

Object Role Model (ORM)

A data model that is built up from elementary fact sentences; could also be thought of as a "no file" modeling scheme because it is not record-based. The main modeling constructs are objects and relationships. Objects encompass both entities and attributes. An object has attributes by virtue of the role that it plays in relationship with other objects. SEE ALSO table think; NIAM.

objective

A specific, quantified target of achievement against which progress towards attainment can be measured. Achieving an objective contributes to achievement of a more general goal. A good objective is "SMART" (simple, measurable, attainable, realistic, and timely).

objectivity

The practice of not including personal biases or preferences during an evaluation; evaluating on the agreed-to standards and facts alone.

Object-Oriented (OO)

1. *Adjective.* Generally, a form of design organized around objects (instances) where objects can be built (re)using other similar objects. For efficiency, the notion of object class was added to define a set of objects only once. SEE ALSO object.
2. *Adjective.* In data management, a style of software development (analysis, design, programming and testing) organized around classes of objects in which the code encapsulates the data. Object-oriented approaches promote data hiding, cohesion, class inheritance, and reuse.

Object-Oriented DataBase (OODB)

SEE database, object-oriented.

Object-Oriented DataBase Management System (OODBMS, ODBMS)

SEE DataBase Management System, Object-Oriented.

Object-Oriented Programming System (OOPS)

A development environment for design, building, and testing software using object-oriented languages and techniques.

occurrence

1. Generally, an event; the fact that an event happened.
2. In data management, a physical record, row or document representing an entity instance.

occurrence group

In the data resource, a set of entities in mathematics. (Brackett 2011)

occurrence of record

A specific record selected from a set of redundant records as the authoritative record, into which data from the other records can be consolidated.

octal

A numbering system using a base of 8.

one-to-Many (1:M)

SEE one-to-zero-or-Many; one-to-one-or-Many.

one-to-one (1:1)

The characteristic of a relationship in which a member of population A must be related to only one member of population B, and vice versa. SEE ALSO cardinality; relationship.

one-to-one-or-Many (1:1..M)

The characteristic of a relationship in which a member of population A must be related to one or more members of population B, but not vice versa. SEE ALSO cardinality; relationship.

one-to-zero-or-Many (1:0..M)

The characteristic of a relationship in which a member of population A may be related to one or more members of population B, but not vice versa. SEE ALSO cardinality; relationship.

OnLine Analytical Processing (OLAP)

The collection of structures and processing routines to store and manipulate a dimensional data model (whether stored as a cube or a star) to enable multi-dimensional analysis of business trends and development of business projections. The term was originally coined by E.F. Codd. Opposite of OnLine Transaction Processing.

OnLine Analytical Processing client **Alternate form: OLAP client**

An end user application that can request slices from OLTP servers and provide two-dimensional or multi-dimensional displays, user modifications, selections, ranking, calculations, etc., for visualization and navigation purposes. OLAP clients may be as simple as a spreadsheet program retrieving a slice for further work by a spreadsheet-literate user or as high-functioned as a financial modeling or sales analysis application.

OnLine Analytical Processing, Desktop (DOLAP) **Alternate form: Desktop OLAP**

OnLine Analytical Processing where the data to be analyzed is stored on a desktop computer rather than on a conventional storage system.

OnLine Analytical Processing, Hybrid (HOLAP) **Alternate form: Hybrid OLAP**

OnLine Analytical Processing that can provide multi-dimensional analysis simultaneously of data stored in a Multi-Dimensional DBMS and in a Relational DBMS.

OnLine Analytical Processing, Java (JOLAP) **Alternate form: Java OLAP**

A Java application programming interface (API) for the Java 2 Platform Enterprise Edition environment that supports the creation, storage, access, and management of data in an OLAP application. Hyperion, IBM, and Oracle initiated the development of JOLAP intending it to be a counterpart to Java Database Connectivity specifically for OLAP.

OnLine Analytical Processing, Multi-dimensional (MOLAP) **Alternate form: Multi-dimensional OLAP**

OnLine Analytical Processing that only uses a Multi-Dimensional Database Management System to drive analysis.

OnLine Analytical Processing, Real Time (RTOLAP) **Alternate form: Real Time OLAP**

A version of OnLine Analytical Processing where data is stored in RAM memory rather than on disk, and calculations are performed on-the-fly, rather than stored. RTOLAP has a limitation of size since all data must be stored in RAM, and therefore space is at a premium; calculation results are therefore not stored.

OnLine Analytical Processing, Relational (ROLAP) **Alternate form: Relational OLAP**

OnLine Analytical Processing that performs multi-dimensional analysis on data stored in an RDBMS. The multi-dimensional processing may be done within the RDBMS, a mid-tier server or the client. A 'merchant' ROLAP is one from an independent vendor that can work with any standard RDBMS.

OnLine Analytical Processing, Spatial (SOLAP) **Alternate form: Spatial OLAP**

OnLine Analytical Processing where the spatial data is included in the data to be analyzed.

OnLine Analytical Processing, Web-based (WOLAP) **Alternate form: Web OLAP**

OnLine Analytical Processing where the interaction with the data is through a web browser, and may include the addition of web-based applications when analyzing or displaying the data.

OnLine Transaction Processing (OLTP)

The application systems used to support the daily business operations (transactions) of an enterprise. Opposite of OnLine Analytical Processing.

ontology

1. Generally, the grammar rules for usage of a controlled vocabulary to create meaningful expressions within a domain or subject area.
2. In data management, a semantic data model defining structure and meaning, typically used to model non-tabular data. SEE ALSO schema.

Ontology Inference Layer (OIL)

In semantic modeling, a standard for defining ontologies.

open architecture

SEE architecture, open.

open data

A philosophy and practice requiring that some data be freely available to everyone, without restrictions from copyright, patents, or other mechanisms of control.

Open Database Connectivity (ODBC)

A standard to allow programmers to write to an abstract relational database layer and delay binding until run time. Developed by the SQL Access Group consortium, ODBC has been widely adopted with modifications by Microsoft.

Open Educational Resource (OER)

Free learning materials available via the Internet.

Open Geospatial Consortium (OGC)

An international voluntary standards group with over 300 commercial, governmental, nonprofit and research member organizations worldwide, collaborating to develop and implement standards for geospatial data and services, GIS data processing and exchange. Previously known as Open GIS Consortium. OGC specifications include the Web Map Service (WMS), Simple Features SQL (SFS) and Geography Markup Language (GML).

Open Software Foundation (OSF)

An organization that promotes the adoption of standards for UNIX operating systems.

open source

Software code that is freely available - meaning the customer can download it, install it, begin using it, or customize it without paying.

Open Source Intelligence (OSINT)

A form of data acquisition and analysis that focuses on publicly available data.

OpenCourseWare (OCW)

The process of making course materials from learning institutions available on the Internet.

Open-High-Low-Close chart (OHLC)

SEE chart, Open-High-Low-Close.

operational activity

In the DAMA-DMBOK Functional Framework, a service and support activity performed on an on-going basis. SEE ALSO activity group.

Operational Business Intelligence **Alternate form: Operational BI**

The application of BI tools to provide BI to the front lines of the business, where analytical capabilities guide operational decisions. Operational BI is used to manage and optimize business operations. (DAMA-DMBOK Guide, 1st edition, pg. 209.)

operational data

SEE data, operational.

Operational Data Store (ODS)

An integrated database of operational data. Its sources include legacy databases and other operational databases. An ODS contains current or near term data. An ODS may contain 30 to 60 days of information, while a Data Warehouse typically contains years of data. Like a Data Warehouse, data in an ODS is extracted from sources, cleansed, consolidated ,and transformed into a standard format. An ODS supports enterprise reporting, Master Data Management and application integration as the enterprise source for shared operational data. An ODS may serve as the primary source for a Data Warehouse, or be used to audit a Data Warehouse.

Operational Data Store, Class I

An ODS where data is moved from sources almost immediately after being written in the source system, without any integration or transformation.

Operational Data Store, Class II

An ODS where data is moved from sources within a few hours after being written in the source system, allowing for some integration and transformation.

Operational Data Store, Class III

An ODS where data is moved from sources overnight following being written in the source system, allowing for integration and transformation.

Operational Data Store, Class IV

An ODS where summary data is moved from a Data Warehouse into the ODS for operational use.

operational database

SEE database, operational.

operational DBA

SEE DataBase Administrator, operational.

operational performance

Measurable outcomes relative to stated enterprise-wide operational goals.

operational system

Application that runs the business on a day-to-day basis using real time data (typically OLTP databases).

Operations Instance Classes

Zachman Framework row name, matches Workers as Participants.

Optical Character Recognition (OCR)

Technology that can scan typed or handwritten characters and convert them to digital text (usually ASCII).

Optical Mark Recognition (OMR)

The process of capturing data from document forms that have been human-generated rather than computer-generated, such as highlights and margin notes.

optimize

To configure a system to perform more in accordance with some expected measurement than another configuration.

optional

1. *Adjective.* Generally, not required. Opposite of mandatory.
2. *Adjective.* Characteristic of an attribute, where a value is not required by an entity constraint (NULLs allowed in SQL).
3. *Adjective.* Characteristic of a relationship in which an entity or object instance need not relate to any member of the other entity type population, i.e., can be an orphan.

optional relationship

SEE relationship, optional.

order

1. Generally, the sequence of items or events in time or ranked by some quality, such as importance.
2. In data services, a message sent which trigger the delivery of required data. There are three types of orders: select order, transform order, and propagate order.

ordinal number

A number that signifies sequence within a set, or a rank, solely for comparison or matching. Does not signify quantity, and cannot be meaningfully added or subtracted.

organization

In general, an arrangement of people dedicated to common goals, who control the organization's performance, and have a clear delineation of what is included in the organization.

organization and culture

One of the DAMA Functional Framework Environmental Elements. Includes management; critical success factors; reporting structures; contracting strategies; budgeting and related resource allocation issues; teamwork and group dynamics; authority and empowerment; shared values and beliefs; expectations and attitudes; personal style and preference differences; cultural rites, rituals and symbols; organizational heritage; and change management recommendations. (DAMA-DMBOK Guide, 1st edition, pg. 13.)

organization chart

SEE chart, organization.

Organization Configuration

Zachman Framework cell name, intersection of Who/Organization Groups and Component Assemblies/Technicians as Implementers.

Organization Definition

Zachman Framework cell name, intersection of Who/Organization Groups and Business Concepts/Executive Leaders as Owners.

Organization for the Advancement of Structured Information (OASIS)

A non-for-profit consortium that advances e-business by promoting open, collaborative development of interoperability specifications.

Organization Groups

Zachman Framework column name, matches Who.

Organization Identification

Zachman Framework cell name, intersection of Who/Organization Groups and Scope Contexts/Strategists as Theorists.

Organization Instantiation

Zachman Framework cell name, intersection of Who/Organization Groups and Operations Instance Classes/Workers as Participants.

Organization Representation

Zachman Framework cell name, intersection of Who/Organization Groups and System Logic/Architects as Designers.

Organization Specification

Zachman Framework cell name, intersection of Who/Organization Groups and Technology Physics/Engineers as Builders.

organizational intelligence

The collected data of the enterprise about itself and its environment, in current context.

organizational knowledge

Information that is of significance to the organization, is combined with experience and understanding, and is retained. It is information in context with respect to understanding what is relevant and significant to a business issue or business topic-what is meaningful to the business. (Brackett 2011)

organizational model

A model showing the organization of a particular system or company.

orthogonal

Adjective. Literally, to be at right angles. Typically refers to characteristics that are as independent of each other as possible. For example, data and processes are considered orthogonal to each other.

outer join

SEE join, outer.

outlier

A data instance that is extremely deviated from the mean of the rest of the data set.

outrigger dimension

SEE table, outrigger.

outrigger entity

SEE table, outrigger.

outrigger table

SEE table, outrigger.

outsourcing

The process of arranging services to be done by an external party, to replace the need for an internal party to perform those services.

P

package

1. In software, a pre-developed application software product available for purchase.
2. In object-oriented software, a unit of deployment, usually consisting of many related object-oriented classes.

packaged analytic application

Value-added solutions with embedded knowledge of business processes and specific functional metrics based on industry best practices, available for purchase.

paging

1. The process of splitting data sets into finite blocks (pages) for optimal storage performance.
2. The process of retrieving and/or swapping parts of data sets (pages) as they are required.

paradigm

An example of pattern that represents an acquired way of thinking about something that consciously and/or unconsciously shapes thought and action.

parallel coordinates diagram

SEE chart, parallel coordinates.

parallelism

The ability to perform multiple functions in parallel.

paralysis by analysis

A process of ongoing analysis and modeling to make sure everything is complete and correct. People want to analyze a situation to the nth degree, working the problem forever, before moving ahead. (Brackett 2011)

parameter

In data management, a data attribute provided as input to a system or process.

Pareto diagram

SEE chart, Pareto.

parity

A single bit that represents the count of the preceding bits that equal 1 in value. Used to check data transmission - if the parity bit says there were an odd number of 1 values, and the data shows an even number of 1 values, then there is an error in transmission.

parse

To analyze a sequence using pre-determined rules to determine content or value.

partial key

SEE key, partial.

partition

1. *Verb.* In general, to split into parts according to some rule or condition.
2. *Verb.* To logically and/or physically segregate data in a single table into multiple files each containing groups of similar rows that are more easily maintained or accessed. Relational DBMSs typically provide this functionality. Partitioning of data aids in performance and utility processing.
3. One segment of a dataset identified by a specific condition.

partitioning condition

An attribute or expression used to differentiate parts of data sets.

partitioning, composite

A method of partitioning a table horizontally using one partitioning method first, and then partitioning the resulting set using another partitioning method. Common types are range-list and range-hash.

partitioning, hash

A method of partitioning a table horizontally where the partitions are identified by a hash value derived from one or more columns in the table.

partitioning, horizontal

A method of partitioning that divides a single logical table into multiple physical tables based on the row values of the primary key column. All columns generally appear in each table, but each table contains a subset of the logical table's rows (either discrete or overlapping subsets). Employed when there is a regular need to access, or to isolate, a readily identifiable subset of the rows to meet security, distribution, and performance optimization needs. Note: It is only horizontal because of the convention used to represent a table, namely, columns across the top, and rows down.

partitioning, list

A method of partitioning a table horizontally where the partitions are identified by presence of a column's value in a list of possible values.

partitioning, range

A method of partitioning a table horizontally where the partitions are identified by the upper and lower bounds of one or more columns in the table.

partitioning, vertical

A method of partitioning that segregates the columns of a single logical table into multiple physical tables. All logical rows may appear in each new table, but each new table contains a subset of the original table's columns. Some columns may be redundant across tables, and will necessarily be so for primary key columns. Vertical partitioning is employed when there is a regular need to access, or to isolate, a readily identifiable subset of the "parent" table's columns. This technique may be effective to meet security, distribution, and usability requirements. Note: It is only vertical because of the convention used to represent a table, namely, attributes across the top, and entity instances down. SEE ALSO table, outrigger.

password

A string of characters used to help authenticate a user logging into a system.

path

A series of one or more arcs between nodes in a graph.

Payment Card Industry Data Security Standard (PCI DSS)

A worldwide information security standard assembled by the Payment Card Industry Security Standards Council.

performance

Measurable outcomes relative to stated goals.

performance accountability

Assuming responsibility for achieving objectives and disclosing present and future variances against those objectives.

performance alert

Notification via email, portal or wireless device of a key trend or business event that is associated with an objective.

performance charting

SEE chart, performance charting.

performance monitoring and tuning

Activities related to understanding and improving computer hardware and software performance (response time and throughput), including database performance.

performance scorecarding

A strategic management process designed to translate an organization's mission statement and overall business strategy into specific, quantifiable objectives and to monitor the organization's performance in terms of achieving those objectives.

performance test

SEE test, performance.

period

1. Generally, the interval of single repetition of a varying quantity or a motion, or phenomenon that repeats itself regularly.
2. Specifically, a quantity of time.

periodicity

Refers to the frequency of compilation of the data (e.g., a time series could be available at annual frequency but the underlying data are compiled monthly, thus have a monthly periodicity).

persistence

A state or status that lasts beyond the process that created it.

persistent data

Data that outlasts the execution of a particular program, stored in the records of the enterprise and available for reuse.

Personal Health Information (PHI)

The Privacy Rule, a Federal law, gives individuals rights over their health information and sets rules and limits on who can look at and receive your health information. The Privacy Rule applies to all forms of individuals' protected health information, whether electronic, written, or oral. The Security Rule, a Federal law that protects health information in electronic form, requires entities covered by HIPAA to ensure that electronic protected health information is secure. (www.hhs.gov)

Personal Identifying Information (PII)

Information that refers to a specific individual. Includes name, address, telephone number, Governmental ID numbers, U.S. Social Security Numbers, etc.

Personal Software Process Body of Knowledge (PSPBOK)

SEE Body of Knowledge, Personal Software Process.

perspectives chart

SEE chart, perspectives.

pervasive computing

A ubiquitous, wireless, always-on, networked world.

Petabyte (Pb)

One thousand Terabytes.

petri net

SEE chart, petri net.

Physical Data Model (PDM)

SEE data model, physical.

physical database design

The act of developing a physical data model.

physical schema

SEE schema, database.

pie chart

SEE chart, pie.

pivot

Verb. To rotate the view of data. Used in multi-dimensional analysis with OLAP tools, but can also be performed in spreadsheet applications.

pivot table

A multi-dimensional modeling scheme (specifically found in Microsoft Excel and many Business Intelligence tools).

plan

1. *Verb.* In general, to define goals and objectives and to devise approaches and activities to realize or achieve these goals.
2. *Verb.* In information services, to define mission and purpose statements, goals, objectives, critical success factors, strategy, architecture, programs, and projects for an enterprise, and then to assess and analyze to guide decisions. Often considered the first phase in the software development lifecycle, although occurring before project initiation.
3. An organized set of goals, objectives and activities.

plan-do-check-act

A circular process for continuous improvement. Also called the Shewhart cycle after its developer, W. A. Shewhart.

planning activity

In the DAMA-DMBOK Functional Framework, an activity that sets the strategic and tactical course for other data management activities. Planning activities may be performed on a recurring basis. SEE ALSO activity group.

platform

Any base of technologies on which other technologies or processes are built and operated to provide interoperability, simplify implementation, streamline deployment and promote maintenance of solutions. The platform resource consists of hardware and system software.

Platform As A Service (PAAS)

A software package delivered as a service that allows third-party applications to "plug in". For example, facebook.com, twitter.com.

pointer

A data type that serves specifically only to refer to another data point's storage address.

Poisson distribution

A distribution curve where the tail on one side is longer and thinner than the other.

polar area pie chart

SEE chart, polar area.

policy

A statement of a selected course of action and high-level description of desired behavior to achieve a set of goals.

polymorphism

1. In object oriented design, the implementation of subclasses of a parent class so that identical requests sent to different child classes are handled differently without the caller knowing.
2. A collection of things (instances) which are considered part of the same set, called a type.

population

1. In general, a collection of things (instances) which are considered part of the same set, called a type.
2. The process of loading and replicating multiple rows of data into a relational database on a one-time or recurring basis. SEE ALSO data loading; data replication.

population cartogram

SEE chart, area cartogram.

portal

A website designed to be the "front door" through which a user accesses links to relevant sites. Typically, a portal site has a catalog of sites, a search engine or both. A portal site may also offer e-mail and other services to entice people to use that site as the main point of entry or portal to the web.

Porter's five forces diagram

SEE chart, Porter's five forces.

portfolio

A collection of assets, liabilities and/or issues to manage.

portfolio diagram

SEE chart, portfolio.

portfolio management

SEE IT portfolio management.

positional notation **Alternate form: place-value notation**

A notation where position affects the value of a character or digit. Binary, octal, decimal, and hexadecimal are all examples of positional notation.

practice

A repeatedly performed, customary way of doing something.

practices and techniques

One of the DAMA Functional Framework Environmental Elements. Common and popular methods and procedures used to perform the processes and product the deliverables. Practices and Techniques may also include common conventions, best practice recommendations, and alternative approaches without elaboration. (DAMA-DMBOK Guide, 1st edition, pg. 13.)

precision

The level of detail of a data attribute, usually expressed as the number of numeric places to the right of a decimal point. SEE ALSO scale.

predicate

1. Generally, a statement that can be evaluated as true or false. For example, WHERE clauses of SQL SELECT statements define predicate logic for qualifying rows. SEE ALSO arity.
2. In Object Role Models, a labeled relationship on one or more objects. Depending on the number of objects, a predicate may be unary, binary, ternary, etc.

prediction

The estimation of future results or other data set results based on existing data.

predictive analysis

Methods of directed and undirected knowledge discovery, relying on statistical algorithms, neural networks and optimization research to predict and recommend actions based on discovering, verifying and applying patterns in data to predict the behavior of customers, products, services, market dynamics and other critical business activity.

predictive analytics

An area of statistical analysis that deals with extracting information from data and using it to predict future trends and behavior patterns

predictive customer relationship management

The discipline of getting to know your customers (or citizens) by performing complex analysis (including data mining) on customer data.

predictive modeling

The process of estimating the probability of a specified outcome given an input data set.

preservation meta-data

SEE meta-data, preservation.

Pretty Good Privacy (PGP)

An encryption program.

primary deliverable

One of the DAMA Functional Framework Environmental Elements. The information and physical databases and documents created as interim and final outputs of each function. Some deliverables are essential, some are generally recommended, and others are optional depending on circumstances. (DAMA-DMBOK Guide, 1st edition, pg. 13.)

Primary Key (PK)

SEE Key, Primary.

prime word

A word used in the name of an attribute to identify its domain (logical datatype). SEE ALSO class word.

primitive

1. *Adjective.* In general, simple, unsophisticated, and/or uncomplicated.
2. In data modeling, an entity or class that has no supertypes. There is disagreement over whether there are just a few semantic primitives from which all other entities can be considered subtypes, or not.

principle

Formally, a fundamental law, doctrine, premise, or assumption. Informally, a rule or code of conduct.

Principle of Full Normalization (POFN)

1. Free the database of modification anomalies.
2. Minimize redesign when extending the database structure.
3. Make the data model more informative to users.
4. Avoid bias towards any particular pattern of querying.

(Codd, E.F. "Further Normalization of the Data Base Relational Model", p. 34)

Principle of Orthogonal Design (POOD)

No two relations in a relational database should be defined in such a way that they can represent the same facts. (Codd & McGoveran, "A New Database Design Principle", July 1994, Database Programming and Design)

privacy

In data security, the need for access control and usage monitoring. (DAMA-DMBOK 1st edition, pg. 296.)

private

Adjective. Unavailable for observation at all, or only to a limited set of observers. SEE ALSO confidentiality. Opposite of public.

private key encryption

SEE encryption, private key.

probabilistic matching

A type of matching that relies on statistical analysis of a sample data set to project results on the full data set. (DAMA-DMBOK Guide, 1st edition, pg. 310.)

procedural DBA

SEE DataBase Administrator, procedural.

procedure

1. Generally, a series of low-level steps or tasks in a process followed in a defined and repeatable order.
2. In data management, a set of instructions for human users of computer systems that augment the automated work flow.

process

Generally, an action (or set of related actions in a value chain) occurring to accomplish something. Functions, activities, procedures, steps and tasks are subtypes of process. The execution or carrying out of a process constitutes behavior. Not the same as a functionally similar grouping of actions; the actions have to have a logical progression or relationship.

process architecture

SEE architecture, process.

process class

SEE class, process.

Process Configuration

Zachman Framework cell name, intersection of How/Process Transformations and Component Assemblies/Technicians as Implementers.

process control

The systematic evaluation of the performance of a process, taking corrective action if performance is not acceptable.

Process Definition

Zachman Framework cell name, intersection of How/Process Transformations and Business Concepts/Executive Leaders as Owners.

process flow

SEE chart, process flow.

process framework

Specifies methods for business and systems planning, analysis, and design processes. (DAMA-DMBOK Guide, 1st edition, pg. 67.)

Process Identification

Zachman Framework cell name, intersection of How/Process Transformations and Scope Contexts/Strategists as Theorists.

Process Instantiation

Zachman Framework cell name, intersection of How/Process Transformations and Operations Instance Classes/Workers as Participants.

process management

The analysis, control, and improvement of a business process and its inter-related steps.

process owner

The person responsible for process definition, execution and control.

Process Representation

Zachman Framework cell name, intersection of How/Process Transformations and System Logic/Architects as Designers.

Process Specification

1. The definition or specification of how a process is to be carried out. A computer program is a process specification, to be carried out by the computer (the processor).
2. Zachman Framework cell name, intersection of How/Process Transformations and Technology Physics/Engineers as Builders.

Process Transformations

Zachman Framework column name, matches How.

product

Generally, something produced. The output or result of a process. Something tangible, as opposed to a service. Synonymous with an output, result or deliverable.

product architecture

SEE architecture, product.

Product Data Integration (PDI)

Solutions for capturing and maintaining accurate, up-to-date data about an organization's products, and delivering information in an actionable form "just in time" at product development or distribution points. A specialized form of Master Data Management, focusing on product master data.

Product Information Management (PIM)

Processes and tools used to predict and evaluate success of products through marketing and sales efforts.

product master data

SEE master data, product.

profession

1. An occupational calling (vocation) requiring specialized knowledge
2. The body of persons engaged in that vocation.

professional certification

A designation earned by a person verifying that the individual has the knowledge, skills or abilities that qualify him/her to perform a job. While licensing is required by law, certification is generally voluntary. Professional certifications are awarded by certification body, usually a professional organization. People become certified through training and/or passing an exam. Individuals often advertise their status by appending the abbreviation for the designation to their name. SEE ALSO profession.

professional development

Training, mentoring and continuing education in a professional field of study to attain, maintain and extend one's mastery of professional skills. SEE ALSO profession.

professional ethics

Principles of standards of conduct with which all members of that profession are expected to comply. SEE ALSO ethics; morals.

program

A set of projects that address a common set of goals and objectives; a long-term initiative made up of several parallel or incremental projects.

Program Evaluation and Review Technique (PERT) **Alternate form: pert chart**

A model for project or process management to evaluate tasks involved in the project or process in order to find the shortest duration possible.

program management

The planning, supervision and control of a program.

project

An effort with a defined purposes, start and finish.

project charter/program charter

A statement of objectives, scope, and stakeholders or participants in a project or program.

Project Join Normal Form (PJNF)

SEE Normal Form, fifth.

project management

The planning, supervision and control of a project.

Project Management Institute (PMI)

A non-profit organization of project management professionals. PMI is the sponsor of the PMBOK® Guide and the certifying body for Project Management Professional certification.

project specification

A detailed description of a proposed effort.

Proof-Of-Concept (POC)

A minimal implementation or execution of a process that serves as a sample sufficient to prove the success of the whole implementation or process.

propagated data

Data that is transferred from a data source to one or more target environments according to propagation rules normally based on transaction logic. SEE ALSO data replication.

property

An attribute or a relationship of an object.

protocol

A set of conventions that govern the communications between processes. Protocol specifies the format and content of messages to be exchanged.

prototype

1. An artifact in iterative development. A prototype may be disposable or the base for further incremental development.
2. *Verb.* To create a test artifact for the sole purpose of determining whether the design is feasible or will be successful given environmental restraints.

provenance

Originally from the French *provenir*, meaning to come from. It represents the origin or source of something, the history of ownership, the location of an object. The term is used mostly for art work, but is now used in a wide range of fields, including science and computing. (Brackett 2011)

psychographics

Used in Customer Relationship Management, a segment of a population delineated by certain shared preferences, activities, or attitudes.

public

Adjective. Available for observation by everyone and anyone. Opposite of private.

public disclosure

The act of making information or data readily accessible and available to all interested individuals and institutions.

public domain

Works that have no copyright restrictions on them, are freely available, and usable without restriction.

Public Key Infrastructure (PKI)

Encryption technologies and services designed to protect the security of communications and business transactions on the Internet.

publish/subscribe

SEE subscribe and publish.

publisher

1. The entity or organization that makes something available for common use.
2. DCMI element in element set Intellectual Property: an entity that provides accessibility to a resource. SEE ALSO Dublin Core Metadata Initiative.

purge

1. *Verb.* Generally, to remove, cleanse, or empty.
2. *Verb.* In data management, to permanently delete data. SEE ALSO archive.

push vs. pull

The types of movement of things or data between two systems or entities. The system or entity that produces may push; the system or entity that consumes may pull.

Q

qualitative

Adjective. Cannot be measured in terms of objective quantitative values according to generally accepted scales, and is instead measured using individual, subjective, scales. Contrast with quantitative.

quality

1. The degree to which a set of inherent characteristics fulfills requirements. Quality is a multi-faceted concept. The dimensions of quality that are considered most important depend on user perspectives, needs and priorities, which vary across groups of users.
2. *Adjective.* In common use, of or having superior or high quality, or being perceived as superior, without specific qualification.
3. A peculiar and essential character, the degree of some characteristic meeting expectations. Quality is defined through four virtues -- clarity, elegance, simplicity, and value.

Quality Assessment (QA)

The process of measuring the quality of something. Quality assessment focuses on defect measurement.

Quality Assurance (QA)

The process of ensuring that the development effort will result in the desired product. Quality assurance focuses on defect prevention. Typical quality assurance tools are check lists, project audits, and documented standards. QA activities typically occur up-front in a project.

Quality Control (QC)

The process of verifying that product deliverables are complete, correct, and meet expected outcomes. Quality control focuses on defect identification. Typical quality control tools include product inspection and testing processes, and peer reviews. QC activities typically occur at the end of a project.

Quality Function Deployment (QFD)

1. A method of defining and implementing customer requirements.
2. An organized approach to involving customers in requirements specification and product design.

quantitative

Adjective. Can be measured in physical terms according to generally accepted scales of quantity, amount, or range. Contrast with qualitative.

quantity

A class word, abbreviated usually to qty.

query

1. Generally, a request.
2. In data management, a statement written and issued against a database for decision support. It may be an ad hoc query or a reusable standard query that populates an existing report format. Colloquially, any SELECT SQL statement.
3. *Verb.* To request data from a database.

Query From Hell (QFH)

A query that takes a long time to return a result set to the user (or never concludes), and uses significant computing resources, causing a negative impact on the performance experienced by other users.

query governor

A facility that terminates a database query when it has exceeded a predefined threshold of elapsed time, used computing resources or estimated cost.

QUEry Language (QUEL)

QUEry Language, as developed in Ingres, similar in semantics with SQL but with a different syntax.

query tool

Software that allows a user to create and direct specific questions to a database. These tools provide the means for pulling the desired information from a database. They are typically SQL-based tools and allow a user to define data in end-user language.

R

radar chart

SEE chart, radar.

Radio Frequency IDentification (RFID)

Technology for tracking the location of goods. RFID tags are transponders, devices that upon receiving a radio signal transmit one of their own. Transponders were first used during World War II as a means of identifying friendly aircraft, but now RFID technology is becoming economical for widespread use. While their main function remains identification, they can also be used for detecting and locating objects as well as monitoring an object's condition and environment.

RAID 0

Block striping without parity or mirroring. A method of data storage configuration consisting of writing blocks of data across different data storage devices with no redundancy so that no two contiguous blocks of data are written to the same storage device. This method allows contiguous blocks to be accessed simultaneously, improving I/O performance. If one device fails, the data is lost. This method is best suited for volatile storage where speed is more important than failure prevention. SEE ALSO Redundant Array of Independent Disks.

RAID 0+1

Striped sets in a mirrored set. A second striped set is created to mirror the original striped set. If devices fail within one mirrored set, data can be recovered from the other mirror, but if devices fail within both mirrored sets, the data may be lost. SEE ALSO Redundant Array of Independent Disks.

RAID 1

Mirroring without parity or striping. A method of data storage configuration consisting of simultaneous writes over mirrored data storage devices. If one device fails, all data can be recovered from the other. SEE ALSO Redundant Array of Independent Disks.

RAID 10 **Alternate form: RAID 1+0**

Mirrored sets in a striped set. A method of data storage configuration consisting of stripes of blocks across a number of mirrored drives, combining RAID 0 and RAID 1 techniques. If any device fails, the data can be recovered from blocks on other drives as long as no mirror loses all disks. SEE ALSO Redundant Array of Independent Disks.

RAID 2

Bit-level striping with Hamming code parity disks. A method of data storage configuration where the disk rotation is synchronized and the bits and calculated parity are distributed across the disks such that all bits in a byte can be read at once with multiple spindles, resulting in very fast reads. If one device fails, it may be possible to reconstruct the data from the parity data written to other disks. SEE ALSO Redundant Array of Independent Disks.

RAID 3

Byte-level striping with parity disks. A method of data storage configuration where the disk rotation is synchronized and the bytes and parity are distributed across the disks such that sequential bytes can be read at once with multiple spindles, resulting in fast reads. If one device fails, it is possible to reconstruct the data from the parity data written to other disks. SEE ALSO Redundant Array of Independent Disks.

RAID 4

Block striping with a parity disk. A method of data storage configuration where sequential blocks are stored on different disks, and parity is calculated and stored on another disk. May have performance bottlenecks due to the parity being limited to one disk. If one device fails, it is possible to reconstruct the data from the parity data written to other disks. SEE ALSO Redundant Array of Independent Disks.

RAID 5

Block striping with striped parity. A method of data storage configuration where sequential blocks are stored on different disks, and parity values for those blocks are striped along with the data. If one device fails, the data can be reconstructed from the parity data written to other storage devices. SEE ALSO Redundant Array of Independent Disks.

RAID 6

Block striping with double distributed parity. A method of data storage configuration where sequential blocks are stored on different disks, and parity is calculated and stored twice on different disks. If up to two devices fail, the data can be reconstructed from the parity data written to other storage devices. SEE ALSO Redundant Array of Independent Disks.

Random Access Memory (RAM)

1. A form of data storage that uses integrated circuits that allow changes in the data contents. Originally called Read Alterable Memory, to distinguish from Read Only Memory (ROM), which is still used.
2. Memory in which the time to access any unit of information, is the same as the time to access any other unit of information. Also called uniform access memory.

range

A restricted set of attribute values, defined by a pair of minimum and maximum, or start and end, values.

range partitioning

SEE partitioning, range.

Rapid Application Development (RAD)

Methods, tools and techniques that dramatically accelerate application development time.

rate

A class word, abbreviated usually to rt.

readiness assessment

A process of reviewing environmental, resource and work effort measurements in order to predict success of an implementation.

Read-Only Memory (ROM)

A form of data storage that uses integrated circuits that is written to once, and then static afterwards. Usually mass-produced in a factory as a secure distribution method for code and/or data.

real number

A number that contains no imaginary components, of unspecified precision. Almost always displayed with decimal points. Contrast with integer.

real time **Alternate form: real-time**

1. *Adjective.* Refers to the utmost level of timeliness regarding the use of information. Commonly defined as instantly or instantaneous, although not strictly the same.
2. The condition in which the time to process and respond to a request for information (processing) is less than the time in which it is needed in the environment (the source of the request) to make a difference.

real time data **Alternate form: real-time data**

Up-to-the-second, detailed data used to run the business and accessed in read/write mode, usually through predefined transactions.

real time data warehousing **Alternate form: real-time data warehousing**

SEE Data Warehouse, active.

Real Time OLAP (RTOLAP) **Alternate form: Real-Time OLAP**

SEE OnLine Analytical Processing, Real Time.

reasonableness

Expectations within specific operational contexts. (DAMA-DMBOK Guide, 1st edition, pg. 297.)

record

1. Generally, evidence of an organization's activities. These activities can be events, transactions, contracts, correspondence, policies, decisions, procedures, operations, personnel files, and financial statements. Records can be physical documents, electronic files and messages, or database contents.
2. In data management, the physical representation of data about an instance. A collection of fields about an instance generally representing the information pertaining to an instance of a member of the type population.

record-based data modeling scheme

SEE data modeling scheme, record-based.

Records Management (RM)

The management of evidence of an organization's activities. SEE ALSO record, def 1.

recoverability

The ability to reestablish service after interruption, and correct errors caused by unforeseen events or component failures. (DAMA-DMBOK Guide, 1st edition, pg. 134.)

recovery

1. Generally, the restoration of something to its status before an event or at a point in time.
2. In data management, the restoration of a database to its state as of a different point in time, typically in the wake of a hardware or software failure.

Recovery Point Objective (RPO)

The intent to recover data up to a specific point in a transaction stream following a down-time event. Expresses the amount of data an organization may tolerate to lose.

Recovery Time Objective (RTO)

The intent to recover lost applications, within specific time limitations, to assure a certain level of operational continuity. Expresses the amount of time a business will tolerate the computing system (hardware, software, services) to be offline.

recovery, backward

Consists of restoring a snapshot backup copy of the database (a valid snapshot copy of the data as of a point in time), followed by the re-execution of logged change activity since the backup copy was made. This method essentially reverses (rolls back) all changes after the snapshot was taken, and re-executes from that point forward.

recovery, roll-forward

Consists of restoring a full backup copy of the database, followed by re-execution of logged change activity since the backup copy was made. This method essentially starts over from a full copy of the database, and re-executes from that point forward.

recursive

1. *Adjective.* A process that can be infinitely repeated using one instance of the execution of the process as the input of the next instance of execution. A process calling itself.
2. Sometimes used to refer to a relationship in a data structure. SEE ALSO relationship, reflexive.

recursive relationship

SEE relationship, recursive.

redundancy

The storage of multiple copies of logically identical data. Physically, the data may or may not be identical across systems, and it is not known which is most current or accurate.

redundancy control

Management of a distributed data environment to limit excessive copying, update, and transmission costs associated with multiple copies of the same data. Data replication is a strategy for redundancy control with the intention to improve performance. SEE ALSO managed replication.

Redundant Array of Independent Disks (RAID)

A technology for configuring a logical data storage device across multiple physical devices to improve performance, availability or both. The primary goal is fault tolerance as in most configurations data can be recovered after a device failure and in some cases, without interruption. SEE ALSO RAID 0; RAID 1; RAID 10; RAID 0+1; RAID 2; RAID 3; RAID 4; RAID 5; RAID 6.

reference & master data management

Ensuring consistency with a "golden version" of data values. Managing golden versions and replicas. One of ten data management functions identified in the DAMA-DMBOK Functional Framework. (DAMA-DMBOK Guide, 1st edition, pg. 6.)

reference data

1. Generally, any data used to organize or categorize other data, or for relating data to information both within and beyond the boundaries of the enterprise. Usually consists of codes and descriptions or definitions.
2. In financial services, refers to both reference and master data together.

Reference Data Management (RDM)

Processes that control vocabularies (defined domain values), including control over standardized terms, code values and other unique identifiers, business definitions for each value, business relationships within and across domain value lists, and the consistent, shared use of accurate, timely, and relevant reference data values to classify and categorize data. (DAMA-DMBOK Guide, 1st edition, pg. 171.)

reference data, location

Reference data that includes geopolitical data such as countries, states or provinces, counties, postal codes, sales territories, etc. (DAMA-DMBOK Guide, 1st edition, pg. 180.)

reference entity

SEE entity, reference.

referential integrity

1. In data management, constraints that govern the relationship of an occurrence of one entity to one or more occurrences of another entity. These constraints may be automatically enforced by the DBMS. For instance, every purchase order must have one and only one customer. If the relationship is represented using a foreign key, then the foreign key is said to reference a file or entity table where the identifier is from the same domain. Having referential integrity means that IF a value exists in the foreign key of the referencing file, then it must exist as a valid identifier in the referenced file or table.
2. The condition that exists when all intended references from data in one column of a table to data in another column in the same or a different table are valid. (DAMA-DMBOK 1st edition, pg. 297.)

reflexive relationship

SEE relationship, reflexive.

refresh

A process of taking a snapshot of data from one environment and moving it to another environment, overlaying old data with the new data each time.

registry

1. Generally, a permanent collection of data related to some topic or collected through some process.
2. In Meta-data Management, an application which stores meta-data for querying, and which can be used by any other application in the network with sufficient access privileges.

regression

Using one data set to predict the results of a second.

regression analysis

A statistical technique which seeks to find a line which best fits through a set of data as plotted on a graph, seeking to find the cleanest path which deviates the least from any instance within the set.

regulatory compliance

The act of meeting the requirements of government legislation or self-regulating industry organizational mandates. For instance, public companies are required to provide specific financial reporting and disclosure. Regulators in the U.S. include the securities authorities (the SEC), tax authorities (the IRS) and banking authorities (the FDIC).

relation

1. Generally, the manner in which two objects may be associated, ordered, connected, or otherwise grouped, using inherent attributes.
2. In data management, a physical structure (a flat file, inverted list, linked list, bitmap, hash table, b-tree, etc.) consisting of a set of one or more columns and zero or more rows. The relation is between the row category and column category.
3. DCMI element in element set Content: a relationship between any two resources or a resource and another instance of that same resource. SEE ALSO Dublin Core Metadata Initiative.

relational data modeling scheme

SEE data modeling scheme, relational.

relational database

SEE database, relational.

Relational DataBase Management System

SEE DataBase Management System, Relational.

Relational Definition Framework (RDF)

SEE Resource Description Framework.

Relational OLAP (ROLAP)

SEE OnLine Analytical Processing, Relational.

relationship

1. Generally, an instance of a connection between two or more things.
2. In data management, a link between two entities describing the business rules governing how the two entities interact in the real world, including their cardinality and dependency. Typically described using Verb parts of speech.

relationship cardinality

SEE cardinality.

relationship generalization

SEE generalization, relationship.

relationship notation

In data modeling, the particular graphical representation of a relationship and its characteristics. Most frequently, a relationship is represented by an arc drawn between two related things, with additional notations to reflect its characteristics. For example, the multiplicity characteristic of many (more than one) could be represented by a fork, an arrow, a double headed arrow, an asterisk, or the letter M.

relationship rule analysis **association rule analysis**

In data analysis, a method for finding relationships between variables that exceed a rate of frequency or some other measure to determine a minimum significance.

relationship, attributed

In data modeling, a relationship between two entity types which itself has attributes. If the relationship is M:M, then the attributes on the relationship cannot logically be stored in either of the related entities.

relationship, binary

In data modeling, a relationship that involves two entity types or object types. The relationship could be defined on a single entity type, in which case it is called a reflexive relationship. In such a relationship, the members play different roles in the relationship, for example, a boss-employee relationship where all bosses are employees. Some have called a reflexive relationship unary because it involves a single population, but that is incorrect. It is still binary, with the members playing two different roles in the relationship.

relationship, contingent

In data modeling, a relationship where an instance of one entity is required, but an instance of the other entity is not required. Example: A product may not have any orders, but each order must have at least one product.

relationship, hierarchical

In data modeling, a one-to-many relationship between two entity types (which could be the same entity type, SEE relationship, reflexive), in which the entity type on the many side of the relationship is dependent upon the entity type on the one side; sometimes called a parent-child relationship. An instance of the child must relate to one and only one instance of the parent entity type.

relationship, identifying

In data modeling, a relationship where the child instance cannot be uniquely identified without knowing the parent instance or the identifier (key) of the parent instance in that relationship.

relationship, mandatory

In data modeling, a relationship where the both instances are required to be present. Example: An account must have an account holder. Each account holder must have at least one account.

relationship, non-identifying

In data modeling, a relationship where the child instance can be uniquely identified without knowing the parent instance or the identifier (key) of the parent instance in that relationship.

relationship, optional

In data modeling, a relation instance where not all instances of either entity participate in the relationship. Example: A company location may not have assigned orders (a data center), and orders may not have assigned company locations (for a service done over the phone).

relationship, recursive

1. In data modeling, a relationship within processes in which a process calls itself during execution. Sometimes used to refer to a reflexive relationship in a data structure.
2. SEE relationship, recursive.

relationship, reflexive

In data modeling, a relationship in a data structure in which individual instances are related to other instances of the same type, i.e., in the same file or table. For example, in an employee table, an employee could be related to some other employee who is their boss. Sometimes (erroneously) called a recursive relationship, which instead applies to a process calling itself.

relationship, ternary

In data modeling, a relationship that involves three entity types or object types. If only two of the participating entity types are required to uniquely identify instances of the relationship, then it would also be an attributed, binary, many-to-many relationship. For example, Employee, Skill, and Proficiency Level. For each Employee-Skill combination (a M:N relationship), if there can only be at most one Proficiency Level, then it can be viewed as a binary relationship between Employee and Skill, and Proficiency Level would be an attribute of the binary relationship.

relative address pointer

A method of assigning pointer values based on a start point other than the root of the structure.

release management

The process responsible for planning, scheduling and controlling the movement of Releases to test and live environments. The primary objective of Release Management is to ensure that the integrity of the live environment is protected and that the correct components are released. SEE ALSO ITIL.

reliability

1. Generally, closeness of the initial estimated value to the subsequent estimated value.
2. In data management, the ability for a technology component (server, application, database, etc.) or group of components to consistently perform its functions within stated timeframes.

Remote Method Invocation (RMI)

A technique used to create, distribute and use Java objects.

Remote Procedure Call (RPC)

A mechanism for invoking a service on another platform, or the communication using that mechanism that invokes execution of a subroutine or process on a different system.

repeating group

A group of data items that together describe something; an attribute with multiple values within an instance of its parent entity. When related to some other entity in a "something-to-many" relationship, and stored in the related entity type, it becomes a "sub-entity" within that "parent" entity. (Everest 2010) Also called a nested relation.

replication

1. Generally, the process of making copies of something.
2. In data management, the copying of data from a data source to one or more target environments based on rules.

replication transparency

In data management, the state when data is replicated but users cannot see which one of the duplicated systems is fulfilling the data request.

reporting

An automated business process or related functionality that provides a detailed, formal account of relevant or requested information.

repository

1. SEE meta-data repository.
2. Loosely used, any database or file (not recommended for use).

repository environment

SEE meta-data repository; managed meta-data environment.

requirement

1. A customer expectation of a product or service. May be formal or informal, stated or unstated, needed or desired.
2. A formal statement of need for data, functionality or other characteristic.

requirement specification

The formal documentation of requirements, typically using standardized formats and templates, often stored in a requirements database for further analysis and validation/testing/verification.

requirement, business

Requirements stated in business terms or ordinary language what must be delivered or accomplished in order to return value.

requirement, functional

A description of expected behavior of a system given a defined set of inputs or events.

requirement, non-functional

A description of expected operation of a system separate independent of any specific tasks or functions, and may not be measureable in the same terms as other requirements. Includes reliability, efficiency, portability, etc.

requirements analysis

The elicitation, specification and modeling of requirements.

reserved word

A term that has meaning outside of a computer language, and therefore may not be used for other than its defined purpose.

Resource Description Framework (RDF) **Alternate form: Resource Description Format**

The basic technique for expressing knowledge on The Semantic Web.

responsibility

1. Accountability for performance of a function, activity or task by a role.
2. In object-oriented design, synonymous with a method.

Responsible Accountable Consulted Informed matrix (RACI matrix)

A matrix used to describe classes of involved parties and their impact on a situation by role.

retention

1. Generally, the process of keeping something in place.
2. In data management, the length of time that data is stored or archived before purging.

Return On Investment (ROI)

The calculated financial return on a business initiative, comparing costs and benefits for a period of time.

reverse engineering

The process of deriving a draft physical model representing an implemented system (application and/or database) from automated scanning of the implemented application and database objects, as a first step towards redesign.

reverse index

SEE index, reverse.

rich picture

SEE chart, rich picture.

right join

SEE join, right.

rights

1. Generally, the entitlements or freedoms that may or may not be acted upon by an entity.
2. In database management, the permissions to perform CRUD activities assigned to a user or role.
3. DCMI element in element set Intellectual Property: rules regarding access to and through a resource. SEE ALSO Dublin Core Metadata Initiative.

rights management meta-data

SEE meta-data, rights management.

risk assessment

A process to identify potential situations that could cause change to an effort from both internal and external forces, assign severity and priority ranks in order to determine overall risk, managing a situation or project to mitigate or minimize the occurrence of risk, and if the risk materializes, to minimize loss or damage.

risk management

Managing a situation or project so that minimum loss or damage will result if a risk identified by a risk assessment materializes.

roadmap

Defines the actions required to move from current to future (target) state. Similar to a high-level project plan.

role

1. Generally, a label assigned to a set of connected behaviors, rights and obligations.
2. In data modeling, the way in which entities of one type relate to entities of another type in a relationship. SEE ALSO Object Role Model.
3. In data security, a name used to refer to the logical set of related responsibilities assignable to a person or organization, and to parties with these assigned responsibilities.

role class

SEE class, role.

roles and responsibilities

One of the DAMA Functional Framework Environmental Elements. The business and IT roles involved in performing and supervising the function, and the specific responsibilities of each role in that function. Many roles will participate in multiple functions. (DAMA-DMBOK Guide, 1st edition, pg. 13.)

roll down **Alternate form: roll-down**

SEE Drill Down.

roll up **Alternate form: roll-up**

SEE Drill Up.

roll up query

Queries that summarize data at a level higher than the previous level of detail.

rollback

To undo the database statements performed prior to a commit of the transaction.

roll-forward recovery

SEE recovery, roll-forward.

rolling forecast

A forecasting method that shifts planning away from historic budgeting and forecasting and moves it toward a continuous predictive modeling method. It requires access to relevant information from multiple data sources as well as business processes throughout the enterprise. Rolling forecasts can be updated continuously throughout the year to improve accountability.

root cause

The underlying fundamental cause of a problem. Also known as the basic problem, as opposed to a symptom.

rooted

A graph in which one node is designated as the root node (starting point) for a search.

rose diagram

SEE chart, polar area.

row

A set of column values describing one logical instance in a relational database table. Technically called a tuple in relational calculus. Equivalent to a record in a flat file.

RSA encryption (RSA)

A public key encryption program, named for the authors (Rivest, Shamir, Adleman). SEE ALSO encryption.

rubber-banding

The movement of a line or object with one point held fixed and the rest of the object stretches or compresses around that point as other points are moved.

rule

A statement that applies logic or an algorithm to information values to determine a resulting output or action, or to constrain the data relation or its valid values.

rule, authorization

Criteria used to determine whether or not a person or software agent has permission to access data or perform a process.

rule, business

1. Generally, a formally stated constraint governing the characteristics or behavior of an object or entity, or the relationship between objects or entities, used to control the complexity of the activities of an enterprise.
2. In data quality, constraints that can be used to validate the contents of a database. The defined characteristics of a database actually constitute business rules, such characteristics as dependency/optionality, multiplicity/exclusivity, and value set constraints.

rule, duplicate identification match

In data analysis, a rule that focuses on a specific set of attributes that uniquely identify an entity and identify merge opportunities without taking automatic action. (DAMA-DMBOK Guide, 1st edition, pg. 186.)

rule, match-link

In data analysis, a rule that identifies and cross-references records that appear to relate to a master record, without updating the content of the cross-referenced record. (DAMA-DMBOK Guide, 1st edition, pg. 186.)

rule, match-merge

In data analysis, a rule that matches records and merges the data from these records into a single, unified, reconciled, and comprehensive record. (DAMA-DMBOK Guide, 1st edition, pg. 186.

S

Sales Intelligence (SI)

Technologies, applications, and practices for the collection, integration, analysis, and presentation of information to help salespeople keep up to date with clients, prospect data and drive business. In addition to providing metrics for win-loss and sales confidence , SI can present contextually relevant customer and product information.

sample

1. Generally, a limited part or subsection of something intended to represent the qualities of the whole.
2. In data analysis, a selected subset of data from a population, used to better understand the entire population. Samples should be representative of the entire population.
3. *Verb.* To select a subset of data to test in order to deduce patterns, which then can be compared to the whole for accuracy. Sampling typically has shorter processing windows, and therefore can be tested more often until a pattern is defined.

Sarbanes-Oxley Act (SOX)

A United States law enacted in 2002 establishing stringent financial reporting and auditing requirements for publicly traded companies doing business in the U.S. It was designed to make executives more responsible and accountable for oversight of their companies. The act covers issues such as auditor independence, corporate governance, internal control assessment, and enhanced financial disclosure. The act also covers security of, and access to, computer systems.

Other countries have also adopted the principles of Sarbanes Oxley. In Canada Bill C198, in the UK Companies (Audit, Investigations and Community Enterprise) Act of 2004.

satisficing

Verb. To choose the first sensible solution, rather than examining all alternate solutions before deciding. Combines the ideas of "satisfy" and "suffice".

scalability

The ability to scale to support larger or smaller volumes of data and more or less users. The ability to increase or decrease size or capability in cost-effective increments with minimal impact on the unit cost of business and the procurement of additional services.

scalar

A data attribute of zero dimensions; a constant value. SEE ALSO array; matrix.

scale

1. Generally, an expression of size, volume or scope; magnitude, expressed as a ratio of the representation to the actual size.
2. *Verb.* In architecture, to change in size or capability according with requirements with minimal effort or resource impact.
3. In a numeric figures, the number of places to the left of the decimal place. SEE ALSO precision.

Scaled Vector Graphics (SVG)

An XML-based file format for describing images in terms of two-dimensional shapes, usually for interactive or animated graphic applications.

scatter diagram

SEE chart, scatter plot.

scenario modeling

The design of a dynamic process or financial model to support "what if" analysis, predicting outcomes when variables are changed.

schema

1. Generally, a diagrammatic representation of the structure, framework, or population of instances of something.
2. In data management, a data structure.
3. In some database software, a synonym for an instance of a DBMS.
4. In XML, the set of allowable XML tags, usually expressed in DTD or XSD.

schema diagram

A data model diagram that expresses the structure of a data model in graphical terms, depicting types, but not including any actual or sample data values, i.e., instances. (Everest 2010)

schema, database

The stored physical database definition derived from a set of DDL statements. The database schema contains all the information that defines the logical database and its physical storage.

schema, snowflake

A variation of a star schema in which the dimension tables are normalized, to remove all transitive dependencies.

schema, star

A set of relational tables representing multi-dimensional data, comprised of a single, central fact table surrounded by a single level of de-normalized dimension tables. Star schemas implement dimensional data structures with de-normalized dimensions. Snowflake schemas are an alternative to star schemas, containing at least one dimension normalized at least one level. The star schema and processes for managing them were invented by Ralph Kimball and first implemented in Red Brick, since purchased by Informix, and then IBM.

schema, XML

A set of XML tag definitions used to define and document XML applications.

scope

1. Generally, the boundary within which something has control, power, or obligation.
2. In project management, the definition of the business or technology impacted by a project's intended work.

Scope Contexts

Zachman Framework row name, matches Strategists as Theorists.

scorecard

An Business Intelligence application that helps manage an organization's performance by reporting a standard set of performance measurements against objectives, internal targets and industry benchmarks. SEE ALSO Balanced ScoreCard.

scrap and rework

The activities and costs required to dispose of something, and recreate it from scratch, saving nothing from the prior effort.

scrum

An iterative, incremental methodology for project management often seen in agile software development, a type of software engineering.

search engine

An information retrieval system designed to search data sets and return results based on input criteria.

second Normal Form (2NF)

SEE normal form, second.

secondary key

SEE key, alternate.

secret key encryption

SEE encryption, private key.

securability

The ability to provide differing access to individuals according to the classification of data and the user's business function, regardless of the variations.

Secure Electronic Transactions (SET)

An encryption program.

Secure Sockets Layer (SSL)

A security technology commonly used to secure server-to-browser transactions.

security

The prevention of unauthorized access to a database and its data, and to applications that have authorized access to databases.

SELECT

A SQL statement (command) that specifies data retrieval operations for rows of data in a relational database.

selection criteria

1. Generally, the features and characteristics used to narrow choices within a larger field. For example, when evaluating product alternatives.
2. In data queries, the data values used to select records to form a subset of instances/records/rows of a file or table, expressed as a Boolean expression.

Self-Organizing Map (SOM)

A type of neural network that uses unsupervised learning to produce two-dimensional representations of an input space.

semantic

Adjective. Having to do with meaning, usually of words and/or symbols (the syntax). Part of semiotic theory.

semantic data integration

Data integration based on semantics as opposed to based on structure. SEE ALSO data integration.

Semantic Data Model (SDM)

SEE data model, semantic.

semantic equivalence

The degree to which data stored in multiple places is semantically equal in value. For example, one database might use the code value F to designate female gender, another might use the code value 1 to designate female gender; these code values are semantically equal, because they stand for the same thing. The measure of semantic equivalence is the percentage of records appearing in both databases whose values are semantically equal.

semantic layer

A representation of data using business terms to enable ease of understanding and use.

semantic mapping

An association of meaning to entities and attributes. SEE ALSO meta-data, business.

semantic network

SEE chart, semantic network.

Semantic Web, The

The next-generation Internet in which all content is tagged with semantic tags defined in published ontologies. Interlinking these ontologies will allow software agents to reason about information not directly connected by document creators. A project currently under the direction of the Web's original creator, Tim Berners-Lee of the World Wide Web Consortium (W3C).

semantics

The study of the meaning behind the syntax (signs and symbols) of a language or graphical expression of something. The semantics can only be understood through the syntax. The syntax is like the encoded representation of the semantics. SEE ALSO syntax.

semiotic theory

A theory describing the relation between signs and symbols, and their interpretation. It consists of syntax, semantics, and pragmatics. (Brackett 2011)

semiotics

The branch of linguistics concerned with signs, symbols, syntax, and semantics, and their use in communication.

sequence

1. Generally, the order of things, or an ordering of things, often numbered.
2. In data management, a database object that generates numbers in order.

sequence chart

SEE chart, sequence.

Sequential Access Method (SAM)

A method of retrieving or touching data in some linear order.

server

1. A software service that provides standard functions for clients in response to standard messages from clients.
2. The physical computer hardware from which services are provided.

service

A software component invoked via a message. The message may come from outside the service's environment, and the results returned by the service may be delivered outside the service's environment (to the requesting component on a different platform).

Service Integration Maturity Model (SIMM)

Developed by IBM, a model for evaluating an organization's security maturity in seven levels, from Silo to Dynamically Reconfigurable Services.

Service Level Agreement (SLA)

The part of a contract between two parties that outlines the delivery of services within defined timeframes.

serviceability

The ability to determine the existence of problems, diagnose their causes, and repair and/or solve the problems. (DAMA-DMBOK Guide, 1st edition, pg. 134.)

Service-Oriented Architecture (SOA)

An application architecture organized around the use of services, especially web services.

Service-Oriented Development Architecture (SODA)

SEE service-oriented architecture.

Service-Oriented Integration (SOI)

Performing enterprise application integration (EAI) using service-based technology.

set theory

The branch of mathematics that studies collections of objects, and the manipulation of those sets.

Shewhart cycle

The "plan-do-check-act" cycle of continuous improvement developed by Walter Shewhart and popularized by W. Edwards Deming. Also known as the Deming Cycle.

Short Message Service (SMS)

Text messaging.

shredding

The parsing of an XML document into constituent parts to be stored atomically in a relational database.

sigma

1. A Greek letter (∑) that stands for the sum of a group of numbers.
2. In statistics, a shorthand term for standard deviation. The Greek letter omicron (ό) is used to stand for the standard deviation of an entire population and the lower case English letter (s) is used to stand for the standard deviation of a sample set. SEE ALSO six sigma.

signal-to-noise ratio

The ratio of meaningful data to nonsense within a data stream.

similarity analysis

A process in which the degree of similarity between any two records are scored, most often based on weighted approximate matching between a set of attribute values in the two records. If the score is above a specified threshold, the two records are a match and most likely represent the same entity. (DAMA-DMBOK Guide, 1st edition, pg. 310.)

Simple API for XML (SAX)

An event-based interface for processing XML documents.

Simple HTML Ontology Extension (SHOE)

An early project to extend HTML with semantic tags, superseded by RDF.

Simple Object Access Protocol (SOAP)

A wrapper specification from the World Wide Web Consortium (W3C) for requests for web services that facilitates interoperability between a broad mixture of programs and platforms.

simplex

Adjective. Describes a system that allows communication between two endpoints in only one direction. SEE ALSO half duplex; full duplex.

simulation model

A model that shows the expected operation of a system based solely on the model.

simultaneous update

A process of automatically searching for other objects that may need updating based on the update of one object.

single key encryption

SEE encryption, private key.

single-variable model

A model showing evaluation based on one variable.

sink

In data flow diagrams, where data leaves the data flow, without any definition of the target. SEE ALSO source.

situational awareness

The perception of an environment's state and conditions at a point in time.

six sigma

1. Generally, a rigorous and disciplined statistical analysis methodology to measure and improve a company's operational performance, practices and systems.
2. In many organizations, simply a measure of quality near perfection.
3. In data quality, a level of quality in which six standard deviations of a population fall within the upper and lower control limits of quality, allowing no more than 3.4 defects per million parts or transactions.

sixth Normal Form (6NF)

SEE Normal Form, sixth.

slice

A subset of a multi-dimensional array corresponding to a single value for one or more members of the dimensions not in the subset. (DAMA-DMBOK Guide, 1st edition, pg. 236.) SEE ALSO dice.

slice and dice

A data analysis function provided by multi-dimensional tools. Typically refers to allowing a user to filter and sort data in multiple ways.

Slowly Changing Dimension (SCD)

SEE dimension, slowly changing.

Small Computer Storage Interface (SCSI)

An interface for attaching disk drives to a CPU, usually on a small computer, via an input/output bus.

snaky chart

SEE chart, snaky.

snapshot

The state of an object, a system, or a collection of attributes regarding a state at a particular point in time.

snapshot fact

SEE fact table, snapshot.

snowflake schema

SEE schema, snowflake.

snowflake table

SEE table, snowflake.

social Business Intelligence **Alternate form: Social BI**

SEE Business Intelligence, social.

software

Computer programs, including operating systems, utilities, tools, Database Management Systems and application programs. Software is intellectual property that imposes semantic meaning on input from humans and devices.

Software As A Service (SAAS)

A distribution method for software through a network interface.

Software Configuration Management (SCM)

The control of changes made to software and documentation of an information system in development and operational maintenance. Source code/component library management and source code version control are each part of software configuration management.

Software Development Kit (SDK)

A set of tools that enable development of system modifications or customizations that will be more likely to properly interface or interact with existing system processes.

software engineering

SEE Systems Development LifeCycle.

Software Engineering Body of Knowledge (SWEBOK®)

SEE Body of Knowledge, Software Engineering.

Software Engineering Institute (SEI)

An IT research organization at Carnegie-Mellon University in Pittsburgh, PA, funded by the US Department of Defense.

Solid State Drive (SSD)

A data storage device that uses memory to persist data. Also known as thumb drives, ram drives, or flash drives.

sound

A class word, abbreviated usually to snd.

soundex

An algorithm developed to index sounds in order to sort or search text with like sounds.

source

1. In data management, a specific data set, meta-data set, database, or meta-data repository from where data or meta-data are available.
2. In data flow diagrams, where data enters the data flow. SEE ALSO sink.
3. DCMI element in element set Content: the origination of a resource. SEE ALSO Dublin Core Metadata Initiative.

source code

Human-readable procedural or declarative programming statements that can be compiled into equivalent machine-readable code.

Source Code Management (SCM)

The management of change to software instruction sets over time.

source database

SEE database, source.

spark line chart

SEE chart, spark line.

SPARQL endpoint

A SPARQL endpoint enables users (human or other) to query a knowledge base via the SPARQL language. Results are typically returned in one or more machine-processable formats. Therefore, a SPARQL endpoint is mostly conceived as a machine-friendly interface towards a knowledge base. Both the formulation of the queries and the human-readable presentation of the results should typically be implemented by the calling software, and not be done manually by human users.

SPARQL Protocol and RDF Query Language (SPARQL)

An RDF query language standardized by the World Wide Web Consortium (W3C).

sparse index

SEE index, sparse.

Spatial OLAP (SOLAP)

SEE OnLine Analytical Processing, Spatial.

Special Interest Group (SIG)

A community with a shared purpose of promoting some specific subject of interest.

specialization

The process of dividing an entity or object class into subtypes based on differing attributes, relationships and behaviors. The resulting subtypes inherit the characteristics of their more generalized supertype. Contrast with generalization.

specification

The formal documentation of requirements, data definitions and design descriptions to direct further development.

spectrogram

SEE chart, spectrogram.

spider

SEE web crawler.

spider chart

SEE chart, radar.

sponsorship

To support or aid, but not lead, another in an effort.

spread

The extent of variation in a set of items. SEE ALSO standard deviation.

spreadmart

A concept describing the use of spreadsheets to approximate Business Intelligence applications. Due to the limitations of spreadsheet applications, multiple redundant applications are developed, and spread across an organization, making it difficult to impose standards and formal support.

spreadsheet

A two-dimensional format for representing and storing information having columns and rows. A spreadsheet can be used to store a relational table or flat file, assuming the columns have headings and the rows represent entity instances. NOTE: Every flat file or table can be represented in a spreadsheet, but not every spreadsheet is a relational table, even though it consists of columns and rows.

SQL compliant

Conformity to current ANSI or ISO standards for SQL specifications.

SQL query tool

An end-user tool that accepts SQL to be processed against one or more relational databases.

SQL set operator

Set operators are commands in SQL that allow result sets from SELECT statements to be combined. There are four set operators in SQL: UNION, UNION ALL, INTERSECT, and EXCEPT (also known as MINUS).

staging area

SEE data staging area.

stakeholder

An organization, person, process, or system that can be affected by a change to a system or process.

stakeholder map

SEE chart, stakeholder map.

stakeholder rating map

SEE chart, stakeholder rating map.

standard

A model or example established by authority, custom or general consent, used in measurement and comparison of quality, value, quantity or extent.

standard deviation

A widely used measure of variability that measures the spread in a set of items; the square root of the variance from the mean; a percent of items in a set fall within a range of the mean plus or minus a standard deviation. SEE ALSO sigma; six sigma.

Standard Generalized Markup Language (SGML)

An early document markup language, since superseded by HTML and XML.

Standard Industrial Code (SIC)

A widely used standard taxonomy for classifying businesses as defined by the U.S. Department of Labor, replaced by the new NAICS taxonomy.

standard query

A stored, reusable SQL query that can be issued with or without modification as dynamic SQL to the database. Frequently users provide different parameter values to variables in the standard query to deliver different result sets.

star schema

SEE schema, star.

state

1. Generally, the way something is at a point in time as described by its attributes. State is something that is, as opposed to something that happens. Opposite of behavior.
2. In modeling, a stage in the lifecycle of an entity or object class. Transition to a state is triggered by an event. A state is represented by a status code attribute value.
3. Part of a state transition diagram, which is data-centric, versus a data flow diagram, which is process-centric.

state diagram

SEE state transition diagram.

State Transition Diagram (STD)

A representation of the various valid states in the lifecycle of an entity or object class. State transition diagrams are valuable supplemental additions to a data model beyond entity-relationship diagrams. SEE ALSO Data Flow Diagram.

static query

A stored, precompiled SQL query, optimized for access against a particular database design.

statistical analysis

The examination of data to see patterns of probability or effects from causes.

Statistical Data and Metadata eXchange (SDMX)

A set of technical standards and content-oriented guidelines, together with an IT architecture and tools, to be used for the efficient exchange and sharing of statistical data and meta-data. SDMX is a committee sponsored by multiple global financial institutions.

Statistical Quality Control (SQC)

Procedures and methods for measuring process quality, identifying unacceptable performance, variance and taking corrective action.

steward

Originally from the old English term *sty ward*; a person who was the ward of the sty. These people watched over the stock and were responsible for the welfare of the stock, particularly at night when the risks to the welfare of the stock were high. (Brackett 2011)

stewardship

The careful, responsible management of something entrusted to one's care on behalf of others. SEE ALSO data stewardship.

stochastic

Adjective. Involving some chance, randomness, or uncertainty. For example, stochastic analysis.

stock and flow diagram

SEE chart, stock and flow.

Stock-Keeping Unit (SKU)

A detailed and specific product type used by inventory control systems.

stop-lighting

A technique using colored circles to identify the content of a data attribute. The colors are defined by a set of predefined thresholds. SEE ALSO scorecard.

Storage Area Network (SAN)

A network system that stores data within the network, but separate from exterior networks that allow attachment by application servers.

Storage Networking Industry Association (SNIA)

An alliance of institutions that focuses on promoting storage network industry standards.

stored procedure

A precompiled code routine stored within a Database Management System.

Strategic Business Intelligence **Alternate form: Strategic BI**

The application of BI tools to provide metrics to executives, often in conjunction with some formal method of business performance management, to help determine if a corporation is on target for meeting its goals and objectives. Used to support long-term corporate goals and objectives. (DAMA-DMBOK Guide, 1st edition, pg. 208.)

strategic data steward

A role accountable for data quality within a major subject area, resolution of business rule and data quality issues, and identification of coordinating and operational data stewards. A member of the Data Governance Council. SEE ALSO executive data steward.

Strategists as Theorists

Zachman Framework row name, matches Scope Contexts.

strategy

A set of decisions that set a direction and define an approach to solving a problem or achieving a goal.

strategy canvas

SEE chart, parallel coordinates.

strategy map

SEE chart, strategy map.

Strengths, Weaknesses, Opportunities, and Threats (SWOT)

A type of analysis that provides companies with both internal and external factors that could affect the long-term success of the company.

structural meta-data

SEE meta-data, structural.

structure

A hierarchical classification for identifying relationships between categories.

structure, hierarchical

A data structure made up of hierarchical relationships between entity types. A hierarchical structure is not a tree structure since the parent entity type and child entity type in any hierarchical relationship need not be from the same population (not homogeneous).

structure, tree **Alternate form: tree-based structure**

A hierarchy of things from the same population. The things could be

a) instances from a population represented by a single type icon representing the population of instances, and a reflexive relationship on that type, or
b) types from the set of types defined in a database represented by a tree structure where each node of the tree is a population of instances of the same type.

In the first case, it is the instances that form a tree structure, and in the second, it is the types that form a tree structure. The latter is called a hierarchical data structure.

structured

Adjective. Arranged in a definite pattern of organization; manner of construction; the arrangement of particles or parts in a substrate or body, arrangement or interrelation of parts as dominated by the general character of the whole; the aggregate of attributes of an entity in their relationships to each other, the composition of conscious experience with its attributes and their combination. (Brackett 2011)

structured data

SEE data, structured.

Structured Query Language (SQL)

A standard language for accessing relational, Open DataBase Connectivity, Distributed Relational Database Architecture, or non-relational compliant database systems. The dominant database language, used to define, control, manipulate and access relational data. Originally just an abbreviation for SEQUEL, but later acquired the acronym of "Structured Query Language" (when IBM could not trademark the name SEQUEL), explaining why is it still pronounced 'sequel' today.

style sheet

A set of structured hints to be applied to a family of documents to create a particular type of display.

subject

1. A topic or central idea.
2. DCMI element in element set Content: the area of focus of a resource. SEE ALSO Dublin Core Metadata Initiative.

subject area

1. Generally, a discipline or branch of knowledge.
2. In data modeling, a group of related entities or tables, logically grouped for presentation and analysis as a view to part of a data model.

Subject Matter Expert (SME)

A person with significant experience and knowledge of a given topic or function.

subject-oriented data resource

A data resource that is built from data subjects that represent business objects and events in the real world that are of interest to the organization. (Brackett 2011)

subquery

A query called within another query.

subscribe and publish

A style of system interaction and data distribution in which consumer applications or persons indicate their interest in certain kinds of data from certain sources when certain events occur. When the events occur, the consumers receive the data via a message. This approach is an alternative to continual polling or scheduled batch interfaces.

subtype

A specialized subset of occurrences of a more general entity type, having one or more additional attributes or relationships not inherent to other occurrences of the entity. SEE also supertype; generalization; specialization; primitive.

summarization table

Tables created along commonly used access dimensions to speed query performance, although the redundancies increase the amount of data in the warehouse. SEE ALSO aggregate data.

super

Adjective. Over and above, higher in quantity, quality, or degree; exceeding a norm, in excessive degree or intensity, surpassing all or most others of its kind; situated or placed above, on, or at the top of; having the ingredient present in a large or unusual large proportion; constituting a more inclusive category than that specified; superior in status, title, or position. (Brackett 2011)

superkey

See key, superkey.

supertype

A more generalized entity of which some occurrences belong to a more specialized subtype. SEE ALSO subtype; generalization; specialization; primitive.

supply chain

The optimal flow of product from site of production through intermediate locations to the site of final use.

supply chain analytics

The process of extracting and presenting supply chain information to provide measurement, monitoring, forecasting and management of the chain.

Supply Chain Management (SCM)

The process of ensuring optimal flow of inputs and outputs.

supply demand curve

SEE chart, supply demand curve.

Support Vector Machine (SVM)

A modeling technique that assigns points to classes based on the assignment of previous points, and then determines the gap dividing the classes where the gap is furthest from points in both classes. SEE ALSO predictive modeling.

surrogate key

SEE key, surrogate.

swim lane chart

SEE chart, swim lane.

symmetric encryption

SEE encryption, private key.

Symmetrical Multi-Processing (SMP)

In computer architecture, the "shared everything" approach to parallel computing. Describes a computer system where all resources are shared, including data storage, memory, and processors. Each task may be processed using any shared resource. Growth is achieved by adding more resources, up to the limits of the hardware. Possible bottlenecks include memory bus contention. Contrast with Massively Parallel Processing.

synchronous

Adjective. Describes a style of communication in which the requestor waits for a reply.

synonym

1. A term that has the same or nearly same value as another term, but has a different label. Contrast with homonym.
2. In a database, an object that serves to refer to another object, encapsulating rights or protecting ownership.

syntax

The rules governing the encoded representation of a set of semantics, using certain constructs, notations, and grammar. SEE ALSO semantics.

synthesis

Verb. To put together; the combination of parts or individual items to form a whole; the production of a substance by the union of components, or groups to form a whole. (Brackett 2011) SEE ALSO analysis.

system

An interacting and interdependent group of component items forming a unified whole to achieve a common purpose.

system dynamics simulation

A dynamic form of visualization that combines causal loop diagrams and stock and flow diagrams to create a simulation of the workings of a system from one point in time to another.

System Logic

Zachman Framework row name, matches Architects as Designers.

system of record

A system that stores the 'official' version of a data attribute.

system test

SEE test, system.

systems analyst

An IT or business professional responsible for identifying, understanding and specifying business information requirements and system functional requirements, defining business process models, participating in data modeling and information value chain analysis, defining test strategies and test plans to verify requirements. Systems analysts also serve as liaisons between IT and business units and as facilitators for organizational and cultural change. SEE ALSO business analyst; business systems analyst.

Systems Development LifeCycle (SDLC)

The phases and activities common to software development projects. Common phases include: Initiation, Concept Development, Planning, Requirements Analysis, Design, Development, Integration and Testing, Implementation, Operations and Maintenance, and Disposition.

Systems Modeling Language (SysML)

An extension of UML that adds notation for additional resources such as hardware, software, and facilities.

systems thinking

The 'fifth discipline" of a learning organization, which sees problems in the context of the whole system, applications in the context of the entire value chain, and data as a shared, reusable enterprise resource. SEE ALSO knowledge management.

T

table

In data management, a cluster of data attributes; a collection of data values associated with a population of entities, each of which is described by the same set of attributes. A cluster of one or more columns to represent information about the entities. Each attribute must be atomic (single valued). SEE ALSO flat file; relation.

table scan

The process of examining all rows of data in a table sequentially.

table think

When the data modeler thinks first of tables when developing a data model for a user domain. At the outset, everything must be represented in tables. As a consequence, they sometimes incorrectly include data items in a table such that it violates the rules of normalization. NOTE: fact oriented modeling schemes such as ORM do not model in terms of tables, rather just objects (encompassing both entities and attributes) and relationships, hence avoiding the need for normalization at all. (Everest 2010)

table, bridge

1. A term coined by Ralph Kimball to describe a Data Warehouse table with a multi-part key whose purpose is to capture a many-to-many relationship that cannot be accommodated by the natural grain of a single fact table or dimension table. Similar to an associative table, but specific to dimensional modeling.
2. A table that serves to link two dimension tables with a many-to-many relationship that cannot be resolved through a fact table. (DAMA-DMBOK Guide, 1st edition, pg. 215.) A table that captures parent-child relationships within a variable-depth or ragged hierarchy to enable more efficient traversal. (DAMA-DMBOK Guide, 1st edition, pg. 216.)

table, outrigger

In a snowflake schema data mart, a second-level dimension table linked to a primary level dimension table and not to any fact table.

table, snowflake

A table that is a de-normalized hierarchical component of another dimension table.

tabular data

SEE data, tabular.

tacit knowledge

The knowledge that a person retains in their mind. It is relatively hard to transfer to others and to disseminate widely. Also known as implicit knowledge. (Brackett 2011)

Tactical Business Intelligence **Alternate form: Tactical BI**

The application of BI tools to analyze business trends by comparing a metric to the same metric from a previous month or year, or to analyze historical data to discover trends that need attention. Used to support short-term business decisions. (DAMA-DMBOK Guide, 1st edition, pg. 208.)

tactical data steward

A person who acts as liaison between the strategic data stewards and the detail data stewards to ensure that all business and data concerns are addressed. (Brackett 2011)

tactical data warehouse development

The process of implementing a portion of an Enterprise Data Warehouse.

tag

Delimiters in a markup language than also contain information. Matched tags are used in pairs, preceding and following text.

Tagged Image File Format (TIFF)

A file format for storing images as electronic files.

tangible asset

SEE asset, tangible.

target database

SEE database, target.

taxonomy

1. Generally, a collection of controlled vocabulary terms organized into a structure of parent-child relationships. Each term is in at least one relationship with another term in the taxonomy. Each parent's relationship with all of its children are of only one type (whole-part, genus-species, or type-instance). The addition of associative relationships creates a thesaurus.
2. In content management, a vocabulary (the list of terms in a dialect of an organization or community) organized into a hierarchy, generally to find terms easily.
3. The hierarchical structure for outlining topics. The Dewey Decimal System is an example of a taxonomy. (DAMA-DMBOK Guide, 1st edition, pg. 80.)

taxonomy, facet

A taxonomy with a relationship between the center nodes and all other nodes. Facets are attributes of the object in the center. An example is meta-data, where each attribute (creator, title, access rights, key words, version, etc.) is a facet of a content object. (DAMA-DMBOK Guide, 1st edition, pg. 249.)

taxonomy, flat

A taxonomy with no relationship between equal categories. An example is a list of countries. (DAMA-DMBOK Guide, 1st edition, pg. 249.)

taxonomy, hierarchical

A taxonomy with a tree structure of at least two levels and with bi-directional relationships. An example is geography, from continent to address. (DAMA-DMBOK Guide, 1st edition, pg. 249.)

taxonomy, network

A taxonomy with both hierarchical and facet categories. Any two nodes in a network taxonomy link based on their associations. An example is a thesaurus. (DAMA-DMBOK Guide, 1st edition, pg. 249.)

technical architecture

SEE architecture, technology.

technical data resource data

The data that technicians need to build, manage, and maintain databases and make the data available to the business. (Brackett 2011)

technical meta-data

SEE meta-data, technical.

Technicians as Implementers

Zachman Framework row name, matches Component Assemblies.

technology

1. The application of knowledge to sustaining life, improving performance or productivity, conserving resources or increasing human comfort.
2. One of the DAMA Functional Framework Environmental Elements. Categories of supporting technology (primarily software tools), standards and protocols, product selection criteria and common learning curves. (DAMA-DMBOK Guide, 1st edition, pg. 13.)

technology architecture

SEE architecture, technology.

Technology Physics

Zachman Framework row name, matches Engineers as Builders.

technology roadmap

SEE chart, technology roadmap.

template

A pre-existing form or outline that serves as a pattern guideline for creating a document, specification or software object.

temple diagram

SEE chart, temple diagram.

Terabyte (Tb)

A trillion bytes of storage; a thousand Gigabytes.

terminology analysis

The process of gathering terms in common use which will become the basis of a conceptual model or vocabulary.

ternary

Adjective. Consisting of three components or values.

ternary relationship

SEE relationship, ternary.

test

Generally, a validation process that compares in an organized fashion the functionality or content of a thing or process against pre-established requirements for that thing or process.

test data

A data set that has been specifically created to enable testing of some process using the data set as a standard input.

test, beta

The process of testing a beta release.

test, integration

A validation process that evaluates functionality between individual components or modules.

test, performance

A validation process that evaluates the time of system performance during specific activities compared to expected performance parameters.

test, regression

Retesting existing code using passed test cases to verify that nothing changed.

test, system

A validation process that evaluates hardware and/or software on a complete integrated platform to evaluate compliance with requirements.

test, unit

A validation process that evaluates functionality of individual code sets or modules independent of any other code set or module, using a defined set of data.

Test, User Acceptance (UAT)

A validation process that evaluates functionality from a user's point of view, independent of any technical validation.

text

A class word, abbreviated usually to txt.

text mining

The process of evaluating unstructured text for patterns, extract actionable data and sentiment via semantic analysis, statistical methods, etc.

The Data Warehouse Institute (TDWI)

A leading provider of in-depth, high quality education and research in Business Intelligence and Data Warehousing. (www.tdwi.org)

The Open Group Architecture Framework (TOGAF)

A detailed method and set of supporting tools for developing an enterprise architecture, developed by The Open Group, www.opengorup.org/architecture/togaf.

thesaurus

A controlled vocabulary with both parent-child and associative relationships defined. SEE ALSO taxonomy.

Third Generation Language (3GL)

A high-level language for manipulating a database one-record-at-a-time, with non-essential, repetitive commands encapsulated in order to make programming more readable by a human. SEE ALSO Fourth Generation Language.

third Normal Form (3NF)

SEE normal form, third.

thrashing

A situation where a large amount of resources are involved in doing minimal amounts of work, mostly due to collisions or contention for resources in database access.

three-tier architecture

SEE architecture, three-tier.

tier

A level of separation of computing responsibility. Originally, computer architecture was monolithic with all processing occurring on the same machine. Over time, two-tier and three-tier systems separated processing for user interfaces, application logic and data persistence. Current architecture is n-tiered.

time

A class word, abbreviated usually to tm.

time series

A sequence of data points that can be related to points in time in some pattern of intervals.

time, transaction

The time period where a data value is stored in a database.

time, valid

The time period where a data value represents a true status in the real world.

time box

1. A period of time in which a task may be completed.
2. In project management, a technique for separating parts of a project schedule in order to distribute work as well as management of that work.

timeline chart

SEE chart, timeline.

timeliness

1. The degree to which available data meets the currency requirements of information consumers.
2. The length of time between data availability and the event or phenomenon they describe.

time-variant

A system that has a dependence on time for the content of output.

Timing Configuration

Zachman Framework cell name, intersection of When/Timing Periods and Component Assemblies/Technicians as Implementers.

Timing Definition

Zachman Framework cell name, intersection of When/Timing Periods and Business Concepts/Executive Leaders as Owners.

Timing Identification

Zachman Framework cell name, intersection of When/Timing Periods and Scope Contexts/Strategists as Theorists.

Timing Instantiation

Zachman Framework cell name, intersection of When/Timing Periods and Operations Instance Classes/Workers as Participants.

Timing Periods

Zachman Framework column name, matches When.

Timing Representation

Zachman Framework cell name, intersection of When/Timing Periods and System Logic/Architects as Designers.

Timing Specification

Zachman Framework cell name, intersection of When/Timing Periods and Technology Physics/Engineers as Builders.

tipping point

A term coined by Malcolm Gladwell describing the point at which a previously rare phenomenon begins to occur at an epidemic rate.

title

1. An identification assigned to an object.
2. DCMI element in element set Content: the name of a resource. SEE ALSO Dublin Core Metadata Initiative.

token

1. A discrete collection of identifying information.
2. In operating systems, a container for security information about a user.

topology

The spatial layout and interconnections of any network.

Total Cost of Ownership (TCO)

The cost to own, implement and maintain a product throughout its life.

Total Quality Management (TQM)

Techniques, methods and management principles for continuous improvement, based on the work of Deming, Juran, Crosby and others.

traceable

Adjective. Capable of being related to steps in a process.

traffic

In a networked system, the number of packets traversing a network segment.

training set

A collection of data whose purpose is to be analyzed to discover patterns that can then be applied to other data sets.

transaction

1. A business transaction is an event involving the exchange of products, money and/or data.
2. A system transaction is a unit of work including one or more actions performed together or not at all, usually in support of a business transaction.
3. A database transaction is a complete atomic unit of work; a set of statements to perform CRUD operations on data, in which the Database Management System must either complete performance of all the statements, or none of the statements. As the process continues, it requests locks on various database objects, according to the concurrent update protocols, deadlock handling scheme, and backup scheme. Any database updates performed are held in limbo until the END transaction statement is encountered. At that point, the system checks the integrity rules to ensure that the database remains in a valid state relative to its definition. If the check shows no errors, the updates are made permanent, and all locks on data are released. Otherwise, no changes are applied and the system is reset to the transaction starting point.

transaction fact

SEE fact table, transaction.

transaction time

SEE time, transaction.

transactional system

An information system designed to store and record day-to-day business information, often structured around events, business processes or business activities. These systems are optimized for storing large volumes of data and processing a high volume of requests for small amounts of data, but not for analyzing or aggregating data.

transformers

In data management, rules applied to change data.

transient data

Data that does not exist past the execution of a particular program.

transitive dependency

SEE dependency, transitive.

transitivity

In logic, a relationship where if A and B, and B and C, then A and C.

Transmission Control Protocol (TCP) and the Internet Protocol (IP) (TCP/IP)

A set of standard protocols used to organize data sent across a network.

tree

A graph in which child nodes do not have more than one parent. SEE ALSO chart; graph; structure, tree.

tree map chart

SEE chart, tree map.

tree structure

SEE structure, tree.

Tree, Classification And Regression (CART)

A predictive analytical technique that can use a combination of continuous and categorical data to produce a decision tree optimized for minimal complexity. CART is related to algorithms such as C4.5, and CHAID.

trend

A long-term movement in an ordered series, say a time series, which may be regarded (together with the oscillation and random component) as generating the observed values.

trigger

A software routine guaranteed to execute when an event occurs. Often a trigger will monitor changes to data values. A trigger includes a monitoring procedure, a set or range of values to check data integrity, and one or more procedures invoked in response, which may update other data or fulfill a data subscription.

true north

The direction from any location that points toward the geographic North Pole. Not the same as magnetic north.

Tukey box plot

SEE chart, box plot.

tuple

The formal mathematical term for a row in a relational table or record instance in a flat file.

two-key encryption

SEE encryption, public key.

two-phase commit

A transaction processing protocol that first ensures the transaction holds locks on all records involved before committing any updates.

two-stage sampling

A sampling method that combines samples from a set of common groups, then takes samples from the result.

type

1. Generally, a subdivision or category.
2. In data management, a population of instances defined by a common schema.
3. DCMI element in element set Content: the classification of a resource. SEE ALSO Dublin Core Metadata Initiative.

type 0

SEE dimension, type 0.

type 1

SEE data attribute, type 1; dimension, type 1.

type 2

SEE data attribute, type 2; dimension, type 2.

type 3

SEE data attribute, type 3; dimension, type 3.

type 4

SEE dimension, type 4.

type 6

SEE dimension, type 6.

U

unary

1. *Adjective.* Consisting of only one component or value.
2. In Object Role Models, describes a predicate consisting of a single object.

undo

Verb. To rollback or undo a transaction prior to any commit of that transaction.

Unicode

A character set rich enough to represent languages such as Chinese.

Unified Modeling Language (UML)

The dominant modeling language for object-oriented analysis and design, developed by Jacobsen, Booch, and Rumbaugh, by consolidating several earlier object-oriented modeling standards. Fundamentally, UML is a process-centric modeling scheme.

Uniform Product Code (UPC)

SEE universal product code.

Uniform Resource Identifier (URI)

The unambiguous location of a resource in RDF. SEE ALSO Semantic Web, The.

Uniform Resource Locator (URL)

A resolvable location for a document on the Internet. The path information in an HTML coded source file used to locate another document or image. The format for the URL is scheme://host-domain[:port]/path/filename.

UNION

A SQL set operator that concatenates two tabular SELECT answer sets with consistent column structures into one distinct answer set table.

UNION ALL

A SQL set operator that concatenates two tabular SELECT answer sets with consistent column structures into one answer set table, including all duplicates.

unique identifier

A redundant synonym of identifier. Identifiers are unique by definition. SEE identifier.

unique index

SEE index, unique.

uniqueness

The quality of having no entity existing more than once within a data set.

unit of recovery

An operation within a unit of work that might need to be undone.

unit of work

A set of operations performing a logical outcome in which either all changes are successfully performed, or none are performed.

unit test

SEE test, unit.

United States Postal Service (USPS)

US Government agency responsible for assigning two-character codes for US states and territories. Similar codes were adopted by Canada for its provinces and territories.

Universal Character Set (UCS)

A standard set of characters that may be encoded by different mechanisms.

Universal Description, Discovery, and Integration (UDDI)

A standard format for an XML registry, an online "yellow pages" directory that gives organizations a uniform way to describe their application services, discover other organizations' services and understand the methods required to conduct e-business with a specific company.

Universal Postal Union (UPU)

An agency of the United Nations, responsible for standards in address representation and naming within and for each country.

Universal Product Code (UPC)

A system of identifying things by using a sequence of vertical lines of variable thickness. UPCs are scannable representations of 12-digit numeric codes which represent products and their producers

Universal Standard Products and Services Classification (UNSPSC)

A standard coding system used for classifying products and services offered globally.

Universally Unique Identifier (UUID)

SEE globally unique identifier.

unstructured

Adjective. Not structured, having few formal requirements, or not having a patterned organization. (Brackett 2011)

unstructured data

SEE data, unstructured.

UPDATE

1. Generally, any change to a database, which may also include inserting and deleting data.
2. In SQL, the change of attribute values for one or more existing rows defined by predicate logic. A SQL statement (command) that specifies replacement of data in a relational database.

uplift modeling

A modeling technique that shows the change in probability of an outcome caused by events or actions. SEE ALSO predictive modeling.

upper control limit

SEE control limit, upper.

usage meta-data

SEE meta-data, usage.

use case

1. Generally, a description of behavior given specific input.
2. In Systems Development LifeCycle, the context for process or workflow scenarios.
3. In object-oriented analysis, a work flow scenario defined in order to identify objects, their data and their methods (process steps).

use case diagram

SEE chart, use case diagram.

user

A person or role recognized and authorized to access a particular application. The user's identity is what confers security authorization. The term has many inappropriate connotations and should be avoided in favor of role-based terms such as business professional, knowledge worker, data producer, or data consumer.

User Acceptance Test (UAT)

SEE test, user acceptance.

user hostile

Adjective. A colloquial way of describing a user interface that is non-intuitive and/or difficult to use.

utility analysis

A method of estimating monetary value of benefit realized by an improvement in worker productivity.

V

valid time

SEE time, valid.

validation

Determining and confirming that something satisfies or conforms to defined rules, business rules, integrity constraints, defined standards, etc. The system cannot perform any validating unless it first has a definition of the way things should be

validity

The degree to which data conforms to domain values and defined business rules. (Larry English, Information Quality, pg. 142)

value

1. Generally, the amount or extent of a measurement of space, time or quantity.
2. In data modeling, a data abstraction assigned to a single attribute representing a fact, which may be represented by an encoding of the value.
3. Commonly, the relative worth, usefulness, desirability, or importance of something, expressed numerically, sometimes using monetary values.

value by area map

SEE chart, area cartogram.

value chain

An end-to-end set of activities in support of customer needs, usually beginning with a customer request and ending with customer receipt of benefits. Also called value stream. SEE ALSO information value chain analysis; process.

variance

The amount of difference or distance between an expected result and an observed result.

vee diagram

SEE chart, vee diagram.

Venn diagram

SEE chart, Venn diagram.

veracity

The degree to which something is believed to be true.

verb

1. In language, a word describing a process or activity that occurs, has occurred, or will occur.
2. In data modeling, a predicate that implies a relationship between two (or more) objects or entities. It can be used to form an elementary fact sentence. (Everest 2010)

version

A specific modification of a basic object that shares the same identifier with other modified forms of the object. Supplementary version numbers or effective dates are often needed to uniquely identify an instance.

versioning

The unique identification and storage of multiple versions of an object.

vertical abstraction

SEE abstraction, vertical.

vertical partitioning

SEE partitioning, vertical.

Vertical retrace interval

The time it takes to redisplay updates to a screen - 1/60th of a second. Used in comparison to zero latency.

Very Large DataBase (VLDB)

Databases that pose unusual performance challenges due to their exceptional size.

Very Large Scale Integration (VLSI)

The process of combining transistor-based circuits to create integrated chips.

view

A presentation of a set of data from one or more physical tables as one logical table. A view can include some or all the rows and columns from each contributing table, and can be defined as the result table from a SELECT statement.

Virtual Reality Markup Language (VRML)

A tag language to describe a three-dimensional space in a tagged document.

Virtual Storage Access Method (VSAM)

A disk file storage management system invented by IBM.

visualization, compound

The use of multiple types of visualization formats in one display.

visualization, concept

Visual representation of qualitative concepts.

visualization, data

Visual representation of quantitative data in schematic form.

visualization, information

An interactive visual representation of data by transformation into an image that can be then manipulated.

visualization, metaphor

The positioning of information graphically using a secondary related framework to convey insight.

visualization, strategy

Use of complementary visual representations to enable development and communication of a strategy.

vocabulary

A collection of terms and concepts that have not necessarily been screened for duplication and ambiguity. SEE ALSO controlled vocabulary.

vocabulary management

A way to improve the effectiveness of information storage and retrieval systems, Web navigation systems, and other environments that seek to both identify and locate desired content via some sort of description using language. The primary purpose of vocabulary control is to achieve consistency in the description of content objects and to facilitate retrieval. (ANSI/NISO Z39.19-2005)

volatile

1. *Adjective.* Subject to sharp, frequent, or regular changes.
2. *Adjective.* Transient, not persistent.

wallet share

The percentage of a customer's requirements that are filled by a particular brand of product or service.

warehouse

SEE Data Warehouse.

warehouse business directory

SEE information directory.

waterfall chart

SEE chart, waterfall.

Web Content Management (WCM)

A system for creating and managing HTML content and other associated web materials.

web crawler **Alternate forms: ant, automatic indexer, bot, web spider, web robot, web scutter**

A program that browses the internet looking for publicly available resources that can be added to a database for future searching applications, for automation of simple monitoring and maintenance tasks, or for harvesting of specific types of data, such as email addresses.

Web Feature Service (WFS)

A standard interface for managing interactions with geographic data sets.

Web Map Service (WMS)

A standard protocol for delivering geographical images generated by a GIS database.

Web Ontology Language (OWL)

A markup language for showing terms and relationships in vocabularies.

web services

Platform-neutral, vendor-independent protocols that enable distributed processing to be performed using XML and Web-based technologies. Sometimes instantiated as remote procedure calls in which the request is an XML document.

Web Services Description Language (WSDL)

A specification of the XML needed to invoke a web service listed in a UDDI directory. WSDL provides interface/implementation details of available Web services and UDDI registrants. It leverages XML to describe data types, details, interface, location and protocols. Pronounced "whizdull."

Web Services for Remote Portlets (WSRP)

An OASIS specification for web services to deliver data to internet portals.

Web Services Interoperability Organization (WS-I)

An open industry effort chartered to promote web services interoperability across platforms, applications, and programming languages. A diverse community of web services leaders providing guidance, recommended practices, and supporting resources for developing interoperable Web services.

Web-based OLAP (WOLAP)

SEE OnLine Analytical Processing, Web-based.

What

Zachman Framework column name, matches Inventory Sets.

What-You-See-Is-What-You-Get (WYSIWYG)

A term describing the situation where a representation or recreation of a thing resembles the original to a close degree.

When

Zachman Framework column name, matches Timing Periods.

Where

Zachman Framework column name, matches Network Nodes.

Who

Zachman Framework column name, matches Organization Groups.

Why

Zachman Framework column name, matches Motivation Reasons.

Wide Area Network (WAN)

A network that connects multiple smaller networks (LANs) over a large geographic area.

wisdom

Knowledge in context; knowledge accumulated and applied in the course of actions. Deep understanding, keen discernment and a capacity for sound judgment.

Word of Mouth (WOM)

The process of passing information verbally between people.

WordNet

An open source semantic lexicon for the English language. It groups English words into sets of synonyms called synsets, provides short, general definitions, and records the various semantic relations between these synonym sets. The purpose is twofold: to produce a combination of dictionary and thesaurus that is more intuitively usable, and to support automatic text analysis and artificial intelligence applications. The database and software tools can be downloaded and used freely, and the database can also be browsed online. WordNet was created and is being maintained at Princeton University under the direction of psychology professor George A. Miller. Development began in 1985.

Workers as Participants

Zachman Framework row name, matches Operations Instance Classes.

workflow

A predefined sequence of activities that complete a process.

World Wide Web (WWW)

The layer on top of the Internet that most people now think of as the Internet. Includes all web servers reachable by URLs and DNSs, that accept HTTP requests on port 80, and that provide user interfaces in HTML.

World Wide Web Consortium (W3C)

The nonprofit organization responsible for creating and maintaining specifications for interoperable standards on which the World Wide Web is based.

Write Once, Read Many (WORM)

Data storage where once the data is written, it cannot be changed and is just used as-is.

XML for Analysis (XML/A)

A set of XML message interfaces using SOAP to define the data access interaction between a client application and an analytical data provider (OLAP and data mining) over the Internet. The jointly published XML/A specification allows developers, vendors and others to query analytical data providers in a standard way. The goal is to provide an open, standard access application program interface for OLAP providers and consumers

XML Meta-data Interchange (XMI)

A standard for interchanging meta-data.

XML schema

SEE schema, XML.

XPath

A shorthand term for XML Path Language, used to address parts of an XML document, with basic facilities for manipulation of strings and numbers.

XQuery

A query language for retrieving data from an XML document or XML database.

XSD

The schema language for XML, expressed in XML, equivalent to Document Type Definition in older SGML-family markup languages.

Y

Year 2000 (Y2K)

Used in reference to application maintenance projects enabling legacy systems to support processing in the new millennium by eliminating ambiguity about century years in dates. This ambiguity was due to hard coded expressions for the year in software and in databases as 2 digits (e.g. 1950 was expressed as 50). At the turn of the millennium, accurate calculations would not be possible without proper full 4 digit references.

Z

Zachman Framework for Enterprise Architecture

In 2003, John Zachman updated his Zachman Framework for Information Systems to classify descriptive representations contributing to an enterprise architecture. This framework is also represented by a matrix.

Each of the six columns contains a basic interrogative and what it represents in a functioning enterprise:

What - Data;
How - Function;
Where - Network;
Who - People;
When - Time;
Why - Motivation.

Each of the five rows represent a perspective:

Planner - Scope (Contextual);
Owner - Business Model (Conceptual);
Designer - System Model (Logical);
Builder - Technology Model (Physical);
Sub-Contractor - Detailed Representation (Out-of-Context).

The sixth row represents the Functioning Enterprise itself and the actual physical manifestation of the end product. In addition, each of the thirty cells within the matrix has a name.

Zachman Framework for Information Systems Architecture

A two-dimensional framework for classifying design artifacts contributing to an enterprise information systems architecture. A grid model based on 6 basic questions (What, How, Where, Who, When, Why) asked of 6 stakeholder groups (Planner, Owner, Designer, Builder, Subcontractor, System) to give an holistic view of the enterprise. Conceived by John Zachman in the 1980s.

zero-or-one-to-one (0..1:1)

The characteristic of a relationship in which a member of population A may be related to only one member of population B, and a member of population B may not be related to a member of population A. For example, a person (B) and a date of death (A). SEE ALSO cardinality.

zero-or-one-to-one-or-Many (0..1:1..M)

The characteristic of a relationship in which a member of population A may be related to one or more members of population B, and a member of population B may not be related to a member of population A, or may only be related to one member of population A. SEE ALSO cardinality.

zero-or-one-to-zero-or-Many (0..1:0..M)

The characteristic of a relationship in which a member of population A may be related to none, one, or multiple members of population B, and a member of population B may not be related to a member of population A, or may only be related to one member of population A. For example, a person (B) and a doctor (A). A person may not have a doctor, and a doctor may have zero, one or more people as patients. SEE ALSO cardinality.

zero-to-Many (0:M)

SEE zero-or-one-to-one-or-Many; zero-or-one-to-zero-or-Many.

16813646R00148

Printed in Poland
by Amazon Fulfillment
Poland Sp. z o.o., Wrocław